T0331950

PRODUCT DEVELOPMENT IN ISLAMIC BANKS

PRODUCT DEVELOPMENT IN ISLAMIC BANKS

Habib Ahmed

Edinburgh University Press

www.euppublishing.com

Typeset in Minion Pro by
Servis Filmsetting Ltd, Stockport, Cheshire, and
printed and bound in Great Britain by
CPI Antony Rowe, Chippenham and Eastbourne

A CIP record for this book is available from the British Library

ISBN 978 0 7486 3951 9 (hardback)
ISBN 978 0 7486 3952 6 (paperback)

CONTENTS

Acknowledgements   vi
List of tables and figures   ix
Note on Arabic terms and veneration   xi

1   Introduction   1
2   Islamic law and finance: concepts and principles   17
3   Islamic banking: institutional environment, organisational design and product features   53
4   Innovation and product development: strategy, structure and process   97
5   Product development practices in Islamic banks   131
6   Islamic financial products: categories and controversies   161
7   *Shari'ah*-based Islamic finance: the way forward   197
8   Conclusion   223

Glossary and abbreviations   227
Bibliography   237
Index   255

ACKNOWLEDGEMENTS

I have benefited from suggestions, input and support of many individuals at different stages of writing this book. The idea to write a book on product development came to me while I was working at the National Commercial Bank (NCB) in Jeddah, Saudi Arabia. During my brief one year experience at NCB, I was a part of the Islamic Banking Development Group that was created to help the bank to Islamise its products. During this short stint, I had opportunity to work and interact with professionals from various backgrounds. They provided useful insights on critical issues related to developing Islamic banking products. I would like to particularly thank the following in the Group who contributed profoundly to my understanding of the complex process of product development: Abdulrazak Elkhraijy, Mousa Adam Eisa, Khalid Ibrahim, Jamaluddeen Ismael, Ejaz Toor, Mohammed Malki, Adnan A. Basaleeb and Nabil Al Husseini. I am also thankful to Rodney Wilson of Durham University for his encouragement to undertake and complete the project.

I have also benefited from discussions with many senior product development professionals and managers of different Islamic banks in Malaysia and the United Arab Emirates. I thank the following individuals who shared their varied experience and patiently discussed various issues related to the product development processes with me:

Malaysia

Bank Islam:	Mahmood Jusoh
Kuwait Finance House:	Shahar Ashari
CIMB Islamic:	Shamsuddin Mazlan and Abd Hamid Ali
Asian Finance Bank:	Ismail Hj. Aminuddin
Bank Rakyat:	Mohd. Hazri Bin Idris, Jeffry Azrail, and Mahathir H. J. Mohammed
Bank Negara Malaysia:	Rustam Bin Mohd Idris

United Arab Emirates

Emirates Islamic Bank:	Mohamed Mustapha Khemira, Mabid AlJarhi
Noor Islamic Bank:	Amjad Naser, Taline Pamboukian, and Fariha Fatima
Al Hilal Bank:	Khairil Anuar Mohd. Noor and Mohamed Ismet Becic
Sharjah Islamic Bank:	Mustamir Ehtesham Siddiqui
Dal Al Sharia:	Sohail Zubairi

I further want to express my gratitude to Mohamad Akram Laldin and Asyraf Wajdi Dusuki of the International *Shari'ah* Research Academy, Malaysia and Mabid AlJarhi of Emirates Islamic Bank, Dubai for their assistance in organising interviews for me with different Islamic banks in Malaysia and the United Arab Emirates respectively. Some parts of this research were presented at a seminar at the Islamic Research and Training Institute of the Islamic Development Bank Group, Jeddah and the Durham Islamic Finance Summer School. I thank the participants of these events for their useful questions and feedback. My thanks are also due to Suzanne Dalgleish for her meticulous proof-reading of the manuscript and correcting the errors that escaped my eyes.

Last, but not least, I want to acknowledge the support and encouragement of my family in the writing of this book. I am grateful to my wife, Roohia, and my children (Saarah, Yousef, Zakariyya, Dawoud, Ishaaq and Ismail) who patiently endured my 'bringing work to home' for the last two years. I thank them for their understanding and support and making the completion of this book possible.

TABLES AND FIGURES

Tables

3.1	Balance sheet of the two-tier *mudarabah* model	74
3.2	Balance sheet of the one-tier *mudarabah* with multiple investment tools model	75
3.3	Balance sheet of the fixed-income liability with multiple investment tools model	76
3.4	Modes of financing in selected countries	77
3.5	Steps in the initiation of a financing product	81
3.6	Levels of product structure	82
5.1	Size of Islamic banks in the sample	133
5.2	Strategic positioning of Islamic banks	134
5.3	Strategic outlook and plans for product development	135
5.4	Drivers and authorisation of product development	136
5.5	Department responsibilities for product development and maintenance	137
5.6	Core teams and cross-functional teams	138
5.7	Formation of cross-functional teams	139
5.8	Coordination quality of cross-functional teams	139
5.9	Resource availability for product development	140
5.10	Staff members in relevant departments/bodies	141
5.11	Role of in-house *Shari'ah* organ in product development	141
5.12	Product development process	142
5.13	Status of idea generation and acceptance	143

5.14	Status of converting concept into product	144
5.15	Status of commercialisation	145
5.16	Sources of ideas for new products	147
5.17	Criteria used to identify new products for development	148
5.18	External barriers and risks to product development in Islamic banks	149
5.19	Internal barriers and risks to product development in Islamic banks	153
6.1	Social requirements and needs/segments matrix	165
6.2	*Shariʿah* requirements and product categories	169

Figures

4.1	Linking products to corporate mission and strategy	101
4.2	The product development cycle	108
6.1	*Murabahah-* and *salam*-based forward	180

NOTE ON ARABIC TERMS AND VENERATION

This book uses many Arabic words related to Islamic commercial law. The English meanings of the Arabic words are provided when used for the first time in the text and are also given in the Glossary. Plurals of Arabic words are presented in two ways. First, for words not commonly used in English literature, the plural form of Arabic is used (such as *hiyal* for plural of *hila*). Second, for words that are relatively well-known, the plural is derived by using an *s* after the Arabic word (such as *fatwa*s for plural of *fatwa*).

The word 'Prophet' throughout the book refers to the Prophet Muhammad (peace and blessings of God be upon him). It is common practice among Muslims to use the expression of veneration 'peace and blessings of God be upon him' after pronouncing the name of the Prophet. Following many other writers, however, I do not use the expressions of veneration either for the Prophet or other religious dignitaries in the text. I do so not out of disrespect, but for continuity and flow of reading.

In memory of my parents

CHAPTER 1
INTRODUCTION

In an interview conducted for this book, a senior official of an Islamic bank in Malaysia disclosed the following: 'Almost 70 percent of our customers are non-Muslims. In fact, we find it difficult to sell products to Muslims clients as they ask many questions about the authenticity of Islamic products'. This statement reveals the paradox facing Islamic banking practice today. On the one hand non-Muslims, who can use conventional financial services, are choosing Islamic financial products in large numbers. They do so, not due to religious reasons, but because they find the terms and conditions of the financing attractive. For Muslim clients, however, terms and conditions are not the only factors determining their business with Islamic financial institutions. For them, dealing with Islamic banks is a matter of faith. As such, compliance of banking practices with principles and rules of *Shari'ah* becomes vital for them.

The predicament contemporary Islamic finance practice faces is at two levels: the first is foundational and the second legal. At the foundational level, Islamic finance is considered to be a part of an Islamic economic system which has an inherent social orientation. The overall goal of this system is to realise the objectives of Islamic law (*maqasid al-Shari'ah*) which should manifest in the economy as enabling growth, justice and equity. This implies that other than fulfilling the legal requirements, an Islamic financial system should also cater to the social needs of a society. Other than Islamic economists and scholars, many other stakeholders of the industry expect the Islamic financial sector to play this social role. This is evident from a survey of 1,500 stakeholders conducted by Dusuki (2008) in Malaysia, who finds that the bulk of the local communities, customers and depositors identify alleviating poverty, contributing to social welfare and promoting sustainable development projects among the key goals of Islamic banking.

From the legal perspective, the contention is that the *Shari'ah* requirements are being diluted. The crux of the condemnation is focused on the products offered by the Islamic financial sector, which increasingly appear to be mimicking those of conventional finance. In doing so, the legalistic forms of contracts are fulfilled but the substance and spirit are not. For example, in a recent study Dusuki and Mokhtar (2010) find that only 11 out of a total of 560 *sukuk* (Islamic bond) issues (or around 2 per cent of the total) qualify to be asset-backed as these fulfil the legal *Shari'ah* requirements of an actual sale of the underlying asset to the investors. The remaining 98 per cent of the *sukuk* replicates conventional unsecured bonds with the sale of the underlying asset not being actual, from both accounting and legal perspectives.

The failure of Islamic finance to fulfil the legal requirements has generated criticism from both detractors and proponents of the industry. At the extreme end of the spectrum, the Islamic financial industry has been denounced as a 'deception' and 'charade' (Saleem 2006a,b). Seniawski (2001) and Holden (2007) identify the current practice in the Islamic financial industry as 'legal hypocrisy' and Hamoudi (2007) calls it 'semantic fantasy' and 'jurisprudential schizophrenia'. ElGamal (2007a, 2008) claims that Islamic financial institutions are 'rent-seeking Shari'a arbitrageurs' using 'ruses to circumvent prohibitions' of Islamic law at the product level. More recently, some *Shari'ah* scholars have joined the Islamic economists in pointing out problems with the legalistic approaches of approving Islamic financial transactions. Usmani (2007) points out the majority of the *sukuk* issues in the market replicate conventional bonds and are not in line with the spirit of Islamic law. Similarly, DeLorenzo (2007) is critical of total return swap and declares it to be unacceptable even though the form is *Shari'ah* compatible.

The dilution of Islamic financial practices both at the foundational and legal levels has disillusioned many proponents of the industry. Disappointment with the current practice of Islamic banking in their failure to fulfil the *Shari'ah* requirements (social and legal) is summed up by a comment by Dr Muhammed Obaidullah, a well-wisher and founder of the world's largest internet-based discussion group on Islamic banking and finance. Reacting to a news item about the Indian High Court's decision to halt Islamic banking plans in the country, he reacted in the following way:

> It is indeed a blessing in disguise for India's 150 million Muslims, a large majority of whom are poor and whose financial needs are certainly not going to be taken care of by the large banks practicing the 'spurious' variety of Islamic banking and investments. The so-called mainstream Islamic banking and finance is a sham, targeted at high net-worth individuals and corporations, against true Islamic ideals and spirits, a poor attempt to disguise conventional products in Islamic garb. (Obaidullah 2010)

To understand the context of the criticisms of the practice of Islamic finance, there is a need to reflect on the origins of the industry. Islamic finance was conceptualised under a broader movement of revitalisation of Islamic values, identity and institutions. After a long period of colonial rule, many Muslim countries gained independence in the twentieth century. Muslim scholars and communities in the newly independent nations aspired to revert to institutions and organisations reflecting Islamic values and principles. On the economic front this led to, among others, the study of issues under the banner of Islamic economics. From an urge to seek solutions to economic problems in the light of the injunctions of Islam, economists asserted that the value system of Islam would provide a better concept of economic development and a pragmatic approach to achieve it, not only for Muslims but humanity at large. The scholars envisaged the discipline to realise *maqasid al-Shari'ah*. In its broadest perspective, the *maqasid* would include growth and justice (Siddiqi 2004).

One of the first manifestations of Islamic economics was the initiation of Islamic finance. The first experiments of Islamic finance began in the countryside of Mit Ghamar in Lower Egypt in 1963. Under the leadership of Ahmed al-Najjar, savings/investment houses operated in small towns in Northern Egypt, providing financing on a profit-loss sharing basis to small entrepreneurs and poor farmers. In the same year, the Pilgrims' Management and Fund Board (Tabung Haji) was established in Malaysia to help people save money to go for *hajj* (pilgrimage). The funds were used to invest in industrial and agricultural projects.

After the formation of the Organization of Islamic Conference (OIC) in 1973, the Islamic Development Bank was established in 1975 in Jeddah, Saudi Arabia. The multilateral development bank was formed with an objective of fostering economic development and social progress of member countries in accordance with the principles of

Shari'ah. In the same year, the first Islamic commercial bank, Dubai Islamic Bank, was established in the United Arab Emirates (UAE) by a pious businessman named Saeed Ahmed Lootah. Initially, both banks did not have *Shari'ah* scholars or boards to guide their operations and operated according to their understandings of interest-free banking (Kahf 2004b).

As Islamic banking expanded, professionals from conventional banks and *Shari'ah* scholars got involved in its operations. While the former group managed the day-to-day activities of the banks, the latter group provided legitimacy to the operations. The role of *Shari'ah* scholars was to study individual transactions and approve their compatibility with *Shari'ah* principles. Initially, Islamic banks attempted to experiment with profit-loss sharing modes of financing. As bankers were not trained to manage the risks of equity-based instruments, they preferred to use debt-like sale-based modes of financing as these matched their background and skills. As Islamic finance grew, however, the main focus of the industry became providing 'Shari'ah-compliant structures for conventional products' (Dar 2007). In doing so, the practice of Islamic banking and finance gradually moved closer to conventional banking products and practices over the years.[1] Chapra (1985) and Siddiqi (1983) apprehend that using debt-based instruments not only represents the status quo but also may not conform to the true spirit of Islamic commercial law as they negate the basic principle of risk sharing.

The debate surrounding the practice of Islamic finance has led to the distinction between *Shari'ah*-compliant and *Shari'ah*-based Islamic products. Whereas some scholars insist that *Shari'ah*-compliant and *Shari'ah*-based products imply the same thing, there is a need to distinguish between different nuances of Islamic finance in terms of social and legal requirements discussed above. In legal terms, discussion about the form and substance of contracts is important. Many Islamic banking products are controversial as these use several contracts which may be separately legal, but when taken together may produce outcomes that are in substance similar to prohibited transactions. Fulfilling the spirit of Islamic law would embody the social dimensions in the practice of Islamic finance. Given the different shades of *Shari'ah* requirements, a *Shari'ah*-compliant product would be one fulfilling the legal requirements both in terms of form and substance. A *Shari'ah*-based product is one that fulfils both the legal and social requirements. Thus, a *Shari'ah*-based product is a *Shari'ah*-compliant one and realises the social goals. Finally, a pseudo-Islamic product is identified as one that fulfils the form but not the substance of Islamic law.

A firm, including a bank, is identified by the sum of its products and services. Evaluating the practice of the Islamic banking industry would, therefore, require examining its products. Products do not appear in a vacuum. There is a process through which products are developed within an organisational and institutional (regulatory/legal) framework. Development of Islamic financial products adds another layer of complexity in the process as an additional requirement of complying with *Shari'ah* principles and values has to be considered. To comprehend the practice of the Islamic financial sector in terms of its products would require an in-depth study of innovation and product development processes. The objective of this book is to do the same. By examining the product development system in Islamic banks, various factors affecting the decisions to identify and develop different products will be explored. In doing so, the book attempts to explain the circumstances under which products are developed and ascertain why

Islamic banks are unable to use products that satisfy the legal and social *Shari'ah* requirements.

Innovation and product development in finance

In a rapidly changing world, survival of businesses will depend partly on how evolving demands can be met by supplying innovative products and services. Innovation involves transformation of idea into 'product, process or service' (Popadiuk and Choo 2006: 303). Innovations take place in an institutional environment and are driven by many factors that include societal stock and growth of knowledge, market conditions and organisational capabilities. The ability of organisations to innovate and produce new products will, therefore, depend on what Merton (1992) calls the 'innovation infrastructure' and their ability to adjust to changing markets and environments.

Financial innovations surged in the 1970s and since then have shaped the dynamics of the industry. The factors driving innovation in the financial sector can be broadly classified as institutional and functional. Miller (1992) identifies different institutional factors that initiated the rapid growth in innovations during the 1970s. After a long period of stagnation that started during the Great Depression and continued until the 1950s, the stream of innovations picked up as a result of continuous global economic growth thereafter. The breakdown of the Bretton Woods fixed exchange rate system in the early 1970s increased the foreign currency risks and encouraged development of many risk-mitigating instruments. An important input in the innovation surge was the information and computer technology revolution that enabled fast and efficient transfer of information and capital within and across borders.

Another institutional determinant of innovations was the

legal and regulatory regime. While a stringent regulatory environment created incentives for regulatory arbitrage whereby financial institutions innovated to by-pass prohibitions or costly regulations and/or tax regimes, deregulation induced them to produce new products to satisfy increasingly sophisticated market needs and demands. The Bank of International Settlements (BIS 1986) also identifies market competition and historical dynamics of innovation as supply-side factors affecting advancement in product development.

Tufano (1995, 2003) and Macey (1995–1996), however, point out that the traditional institutional explanations are unable to explain aspects of financial sector innovations. They suggest that the functional approach can explain these changes much better. A financial system performs certain core functions that are stable across time and place (Merton 1992). Even though financial structures may differ, these basic functions are common to all of them. BIS (1986) recognises functions of the financial sector as transfer of risks (price and credit), enhancement of liquidity and generation of funds to support enterprises (through credit and equity). Merton and Bodie (1995) identify six functions of the financial system as managing risks, transferring economic resources, dealing with incentive problems, pooling of resources, clearing and settling payments (to facilitate trade) and providing price information. Similarly, Levine (1997: 689) identifies the functions of a financial system as 'the trading of risk, allocating capital, monitoring managers, mobilizing savings, and easing the trading of goods'.

The functional perspective views innovations as fulfilling one or more of these functions. Tufano (2003) summarises the role of innovation in the functional perspective by identifying six factors: complete incomplete markets, address agency concerns and information, minimise (transaction, search and marketing) costs, respond to taxes and regulation, react to increased globalisation and risk, and respond to technological shocks. If financial institutions do not innovate, existing products offered may become outdated and unable to perform the required functions efficiently and adequately.

Levine (1997) asserts that the functions a financial system performs can enhance growth by increasing saving and promoting capital accumulation and technological innovation. Experience, however, shows that certain new financial instruments can create risks that are not well understood and induce instability in the system.[2] While unrestrained product development can lead to undesirable events and cause harm to economies, there is a general belief that financial innovations can improve efficiency and enhance economic benefits at firm level and drive financial and economic growth at macro level.[3]

Factors determining innovation in Islamic finance will be similar to the ones discussed above. As Islamic products must comply with the principles and rules of *Shari'ah*, the nature of innovation will be more complex. From an institutional perspective, Islamic financial products would not only adjust to national laws and regulations, but also to Islamic commercial law. The functional perspective would imply that the Islamic financial products must be able to satisfy various functions. As the Islamic finance industry is relatively young, innovation in functional terms would take two forms. The first will be the inert type in which the industry has to provide various products that fulfil financial functions such as mobilising resources, allocating capital, managing risks, etc. These products already exist in conventional finance and inert innovation enables Islamic finance to catch up with the existing services offered by their conventional counterparts. The second from is creative innovation whereby the industry would come up with new innovative products that have no precedence.

Product development: fundamental issues

A financial product entails a fusion of characteristics that include size, yield, various risks, duration, liquidity, marketability, pricing rules, etc. (BIS 1986). Innovations create new products with varying combinations of these features. Comprehending various aspects of product development in financial institutions would require answering three fundamental questions of *why*, *what* and *how*.[4] 'What' relates to the nature of product development and the kind of new innovative activities that need to be undertaken. The second question of 'why' attempts to understand the rationale of developing new products from a financial firm's perspective. Answering 'how' details the processes and people involved in implementing product development. Issues in each of these questions are addressed next.

Why develop new products?

Fuller (2005) identifies several reasons why new products need to be continuously developed. First, products have life cycles. The stages of the life cycle can be identified as introduction, growth, maturity and stagnation, and decline (Fuller 2005; Lovelock 1984). If firms do not develop products to meet the new needs and demand, it will also follow the cycle of its existing products. Furthermore, life cycles of different elements of a society (individuals, firms, industries and nations) also create new demands and needs (Tufano 1995). New products attempt to fulfil these new requirements. Second, new products create opportunities for growth in the future thereby fulfilling long-term business goals. Third, developing new products enables the firm to penetrate new markets and retain the existing ones that change continuously. Fourth, new knowledge and technologies can enable development of new products that were not feasible before and existing ones at lower costs so that profitability can be increased. Finally, changes in legal and regulatory regimes may allow new profitable products that were previously not permitted.

BIS (1986) identifies demand factors driving innovation in financial institutions as mitigating risks, enhancing liquidity, generating debt and creating equity. Within each of these broader classifications, sub-classes can be identified. For example, risk-mitigating innovations can include those alleviating market risks, credit risks, liquidity risks, etc. Market conditions and legal/regulatory regimes will determine the demand for a particular function that needs to be satisfied. For instance, countries with legal systems protecting creditors' rights more rigorously than equity-holders' rights will produce more debt-based instruments than equity-based ones. Similarly, if there is more uncertainty in markets, instruments that mitigate market risks would appear to reduce the vulnerabilities. Note that some instruments may perform multiple functions.

What is product development?

Product development is understood and defined in different ways. Ulrich and Eppinger (2008: 2) take a market perspective and define it as 'the set of activities beginning with the perception of a market opportunity and ending in the production, sale, and delivery of the product'. Smith and Reinertsen (1998: 167) view product development as an information problem and define it as 'a process of gradually building up a body of information until it eventually provides a complete formula for manufacturing a new product'.

Output of financial firms differs from physical products as they produce intangible services that are essentially processes (Shostack 1982). Given the intangibility, a service requires a structured blueprint that outlines all the features, steps and functions needed for the service to be provided. Cooper *et al.* (1994: 296) assert that the performance of intangible products like financial services is 'intimately tied to the customer contact people and their skills: these people almost become the product!' Thus, developing financial products requires diligent planning not only of the product features, but also of the delivery infrastructure.

The scope of product development in a financial firm is wide and can be viewed in different ways. Lovelock (1984) identifies six types of innovations in developing products. In descending order of the extent of change required, these are major innovations, start-up business, new products for currently served markets, product line extensions, product improvements, and style changes. Avlonitis *et al.* (2001) identify four general types of innovations in firms providing services: new-to-the-market service, new-to-the-company service, changes in the operating or delivery process, modification of service. Similarly, Kelly and Storey (2000: 48) define new products as those that are new-to-the-world, new-to-the-company, improvements over existing ones, and supplementary and value-added services. Note that the more innovative a product is, the riskier and more costly it will be to produce.

How are new products developed?

Product development is a complex process involving various stages and sequencing several steps within each stage. The product development cycle usually includes idea generation, converting the idea into product, and launching of the product. There is no unique product development system that fits all organisations. To succeed would require a good strategy and plan that can be implemented efficiently.

As product development is a multifaceted process involving several steps, it involves coordinating input from different departments of the organisation. Baxter (1995) asserts that successful product development is closely tied to mitigating risks. Risks of failure can be minimised by choosing to develop products that are in demand, provide value to customers and produced at reasonable costs. New products also have to comply with internal organisational requirements/policies and external laws/regulations.

Overview of the chapters

Being a relatively new industry and due to the uniqueness of the Islamic banking products, no in-depth study has been done on the processes of product development for Islamic banks. Most of the publications on Islamic banking and finance discuss the basic principles, *Shari'ah*-related matters and specific topics such as risk management, corporate governance, regulation, etc. While a few publications touch on some aspects of product development-related themes (such as *Shari'ah* foundations, financial engineering, etc.), none has studied the product development process in its entirety. The aim of this book is to provide a comprehensive coverage of issues related to product development in Islamic banks. In doing so, the types of products being developed and the associated legal and social features will be explored.

The initial chapters of the book provide the concepts and principles that will serve as foundations for the latter chapters on product development. The groundwork material includes presentation of principles of Islamic commercial law and an overview of the Islamic banking industry. The focus then turns to products and the product development system. By using theoretical analysis and empirical results from surveys on product development, issues related to alternatives available and choices made by Islamic banks are critically evaluated.

Chapter 2 introduces concepts and principles of Islamic law related to finance and outlines the features of traditional Islamic nominate contracts. Among others, the concepts of *riba* and *gharar* will be discussed and traditional Islamic nominate contracts related to transactions will be presented under three main categories – exchange, accessory and gratuitous. The chapter concludes by presenting *Shari'ah* principles related to financial transactions in general and product development in particular.

Chapter 3 provides the background material related to Islamic banking at three levels: institutional, organisational and product.[5] The chapter starts by presenting the legal and regulatory regimes under which Islamic banks operate and then presents various Islamic banking models. The banking models affect the structure of the balance sheet and have implications regarding the products offered by banks. As financial products are different from physical products, their nature and features are evaluated. The chapter then examines the nature of a financial product and identifies different levels of its structure. Finally, risks in a sample of Islamic financial modes are presented.

Product development is a complex process and requires involvement of the whole organisation. Chapter 4 discusses various aspects of the product development system under the headings of strategy and plans, structure and resources, and product development process. A product has to go through different phases of development before it is ready for use by the clients. In order to incorporate product development at different levels of any financial institution, it has to be a component of the strategic goal that is implemented through annual operating plans. As product development is costly, it would require commitment and support in terms of resources. The chapter explains various steps in three main phases of the product development process: idea generation and acceptance, converting concept to product and commercialisation.

Chapter 5 presents findings from a survey on product development in Islamic banks. Results from a questionnaire-based survey for a sample of 20 Islamic banks from different parts of the world show the strategic approaches, resource availability and the various features of the product development cycle. These results are supplemented by information gathered from interviews with senior officials responsible for product development in a few Islamic banks based in Malaysia and the UAE.

Chapter 6 discusses some critical issues related to the types of products developed and used by Islamic banks. Using different features of product structure, the chapter provides definitions of *Shari'ah*-based, *Shari'ah*-compliant and pseudo-Islamic products. The concepts of potential product space and feasible product set are also introduced. While the potential product space includes all possible alternative modes that can be used for a particular product, the feasible product represents the modes that Islamic banks can use under the institutional and organisational constraints. The chapter distinguishes between cases in which Islamic banks may be forced to forgo *Shari'ah* compliance due to unavailability of products in the feasible set and cases where banks choose pseudo-Islamic products even when *Shari'ah*-compliant products are available.

The concluding chapter discusses some concerns raised on the types of products used by Islamic banks and suggests ways to resolve these. To minimise the external constraints, accommodating and amenable legal and regulatory environments for Islamic banks are needed. Other than investing in research and development to produce new knowledge that can be the basis of new products, the chapter proposes to go beyond the product level to seek solutions for a *Shariʿah*-based financial system. The chapter suggests using different organisational models that can satisfy the legal and social *Shariʿah* requirements. The future credibility of the Islamic financial industry would depend partly on moving towards *Shariʿah*-based products and systems. One way of doing this is by strengthening the *Shariʿah* governance regimes.

Notes

1. For a review of the current state of Islamic finance, see Siddiqi (2006b).
2. For example, some new instruments such as interest-only loans, collateralised debt obligations and credit default swaps are partly blamed for the current financial crisis.
3. For a discussion on the impact of innovation on economic performance, see Merton (1992).
4. Avlonitis *et al.* (2001) identify three issue in product development as 'what', 'how' and 'who'. We discuss the 'who' under 'how'.
5. 'Institutions' are used in a broader sense and refer to the legal and regulatory environment under which Islamic banks operate.

CHAPTER 2
ISLAMIC LAW AND FINANCE: CONCEPTS AND PRINCIPLES

The essence of Islam is *tawhid* which means unity of God (Allah) and creation. Though the word signifies oneness and sovereignty of God, it has implications related to all aspects of life including economics and finance.[1] Among others, the concept of *tawhid* implies that Allah is the owner of resources which are given to mankind in trust. In fulfilling the role of trustee, humans act as vicegerents (*khalifah*) of God on earth. These notions have implications for property rights and the nature of economic transactions that can be undertaken. All humans are created equal and given freewill by the Creator. An important inference of equality is the concept of justice, which forms one of the hallmarks of Islamic teachings. *Tawhid* also implies that Allah is the source of knowledge and value. As such, all discussions on law and morality ensue from this concept (Kamali 2008: 17). A Muslim is one who accepts the sovereignty of God and freely submits to His will. The will of God is expressed to humans through different Prophets and revelation.

The teachings and commandments of Islam can be broadly categorised into three types: faith and belief (*aqidah*), ethics and morality (*akhlaq*), and rules and laws (*fiqh*) (Laldin 2006: 3). *Fiqh* consists of laws and principles related to dealings with other humans and the environment and include rules related to economic activities and transactions. *Fiqh al muamalat* constitutes rules and laws related to economic transactions and can be termed Islamic commercial law.[2]

The overall aim of Islamic law is to promote the welfare or benefit (*maslahah*, pl. *masalih*) of mankind and prevent harm (*mafsadah*). According to Shatibi, *maslahah* is achieved by promoting the essentials (*dururiyyat*), the complementary requirements (*hajiyyat*) and the beautifications or embellishments (*tahsiniyat*) (Hallaq 2004: 168). Essentials entail the basic elements of a good life and protecting them constitutes the goals of *Shari'ah* (*maqasid al Shari'ah*). Al-Ghazali identifies the *maqasid* as safeguarding the faith, self, intellect, posterity, and wealth (Chapra 2008a). Two preventive principles of *Shari'ah* namely removal of hardship (*raf al haraj*) and prevention of harm (*daf al darar*) complement realisation of essentials and enhance welfare (Kamali 2008: 35). The objective of Islamic commercial law would be to protect and enhance one or several of the *maqasid*. Contractual and commercial transactions are sanctified and encouraged as these preserve, enhance and support property and progeny (Hallaq 2004).

As Islamic finance involves incorporating Islamic law and values in financial transactions, the basic principles of *fiqh* related to economics in general and financial transactions in particular are presented in this chapter. After providing a brief historical overview of Islamic law and its methodology, the concepts of *riba* and *gharar* are discussed. The basic features of traditional Islamic nominate contracts are then presented. The chapter concludes by discussing some of the *Shari'ah* principles relevant to financial transactions and product development.

Islamic law: sources and methodology

The sources of knowledge in Islam can be broadly classified into two: revealed and derived. The revealed knowledge or *Shari'ah* can be further divided into the recited revelation (the *Quran*) and the non-recited revelation (the *Sunnah*; Al-Alwani 1990).[3] The Quran and *Sunnah*, together forming the *nas*, constitute the primary source of Islamic principles and rulings. The Quran, revealed to Prophet Muhammad over 23 years, provides general guidelines on almost every major topic of Islamic law. The *Sunnah* is the Prophetic traditions and constitutes Prophet Muhammad's sayings (*hadith* pl. *ahadith*), doings and tacit approvals. While much of the law in the Quran is revealed in general form, the *Sunnah* clarifies and interprets the laws of the Quran as practical applications (Dien 2004: 39).

The second source of Islamic law is the derived knowledge developed by human intellect through the process of *ijtihad* (exertion). *Ijtihad* is the use of independent reasoning by qualified scholars to obtain legal rules from *Shari'ah* and the injunctions (*fatwas*) of the preceding jurists. The knowledge resulting from *ijtihad* is referred to as *fiqh* (Hassan 1992). While *fiqh* can evolve over time, *Shari'ah* being divine cannot change. Thus, when a ruling on a certain issue exists in *Shari'ah*, it becomes binding and there is no need of *ijtihad*. *Ijtihad* is used to come up with appropriate judgment only when there is no explicit rule on a subject matter in *Shari'ah* (Weiss 1978).

The formation of Islamic law was initiated by individual jurists in the later part of the seventh century. By the early eighth century scholarship on legal issues was centered on two geographical regions of Iraq (Basra and Kufa) and Hijaz (Makkah and Madinah; Kamali 2008: 69). These regions adopted different approaches to derive laws. In Hijaz the focus was on the Prophetic traditions due to the availability of *hadith* in the region. The Iraqi scholars, however, had limited access to the sources of *hadith* and used personal opinion to come up with legal injunctions. The introduction of *fiqh* led to diversity of the legal opinions that crystallised into four major schools of thought in the Sunni tradition: Hanafi, Maliki, Shafi'i and the Hanbali.[4] Of the four Sunni schools, the Hanafis adopted a rationalist (*ra'y*) approach and the Hanbali and Maliki schools opted for a more traditionalist line. The Shafi'i school combined elements of both, with more inclination towards the rationalist (Owsia 1994).

The fundamental matters (*usul*) in Islamic law can be classified as Islamic legal theory (*usul al-fiqh*) and legal maxims (*quwaid al-fiqh*) (Laldin 2006: 129). Muslim jurists attempt to formulate rules which are concealed in the revealed sources by using various methods in order to expand the body of Islamic law through *ijtihad*. Shafi'i organised a set of rational principles (*usul al aqliyyah*) which laid down the rules of application of reason in developing laws from *Shari'ah*. These principles later evolved into the methodological discipline of Islamic legal theory or *usul al-fiqh* (Owsia 1995: 20). *Usul al-fiqh* is the formal science in which Muslim jurists deal with legal theories, the principles of interpretations of the legal texts, methods of reasoning and deduction of rules and other such matters (Masud 1995: 20).

The legal maxims or *quwaid* form an important source of Islamic law. Though maxims originated in the Hanafi tradition, they are widely accepted as an additional tool from which to derive legal rulings. The maxims evolved over a period of time and entail the essence of Islamic law. Legal maxims play an important role in the development of Islamic law as they reflect the spirit of Islamic law and can be linked to the overall goals or *maqasid* (Kamali 2006). Most of the *quwaid* are based on recognised legal references in the Quran or *Sunnah* (Dien 2004: 113). When legal injunctions are difficult to deduce from text and other methods, the legal maxims are used for guidance and inspiration. Other than depending on the rules in the primary sources and the essence of laws (*quwaid*), various methods of *usul al-fiqh* are used to derive new law. Brief introductions of the important methods are given below.[5]

- *Ijma* (**consensus**). *Ijma* means to determine, to agree or unanimous agreement. After the Quran and *Sunnah*, *ijma* is considered the third source of Islamic law. *Ijma* is considered to be unanimous agreement of scholars of the Muslim community on a particular matter. While *ijma* was practised during the time following the Prophet's death, it became difficult to practice with the spread of the scholars across geographical regions (Laldin 2006).

- *Qiyas* (**analogy**). Literally, *qiyas* means measurement (measuring the length, weight or quality of something) but is used as a source of Islamic law for analogical deduction. In *qiyas*, the *Shari'ah* concept is identified in the original case (*asl*) and extended to a new case if the latter has the same effective cause (*illah*) as the original. If the original case in the Quran/*Sunnah* and the new case have shared or similar *illah*, then the ruling from the former case can be applied to the latter situation. This method requires identifying and discovering the goals and objectives of the law-giver and involves using human intellect and evaluating new cases in light of preceding ones.

- *Istihsan* (**juristic preference**). *Istihsan*, a verbal noun derived from *hasan* (good), is a process of designating 'preference of one object or idea over another' (Dien 2004: 57). Abu Hasan al-Karkhi, a Hanafi jurist defines it as 'a legal principle which authorizes departure from an established precedent in favor of a different ruling for a reason stronger than the one which is obtained in that precedent' (Laldin 2006: 104). *Istihsan* is using personal opinion in order to avoid rigidity and unfairness that might result from a literal understanding of law. In using *istihsan* a former *fiqh* ruling arrived at by *qiyas* can be repealed by using a better proof from *Shari'ah*, using new *qiyas* or due to necessity (*darurah*).

- *Masalih mursalah* **(unrestricted interests).** *Maslahah* (pl. *masalih*) means benefit or interest, *mursalah* implies 'unregulated'. Thus, *maslahah mursalah* is the benefit or interest that is not regulated in *Shari'ah*. *Maslahah mursalah* are those interests or acts for which there is no expressed legal provision of validity or invalidity (Kharoufa 2000b: 54). While there is no textual validation, rulings based on *maslahah* bring benefit to people and prevent harm.[6]

- *Sadd al-Dhara'i* **(blocking the means).** *Sadd* means blocking and *dhara'i* (plural of *dhari'ah*) translates as means of obtaining a certain goal. Thus *sadd al-dhara'i* is used to block the means that lead to unlawful activities. Saleem (2008) argues that *sadd al-dhara'i* can be used to block the means to public harm (*mafsadah*) or to open the means to public welfare (*maslahah*).

- *Urf* **(custom).** *Urf* is social custom or practice that does not contradict *Shari'ah* (Dien 2004). *Urf* can constitute a basis for legal decision if it is a prevailing and consistent practice of a group of people. It should be distinguished from the practice of individual habits which cannot form the basis of law. To have legal effect, *urf* has to be common and recurrent and a custom that is normally practised during the time period under consideration. To be acceptable, however, *urf* should not contradict principles of *Shari'ah* directly or indirectly.

- *Istishab* (**presumption of continuity**). The literal meaning of *istishab* is companionship or maintaining a status.
It is used as a legal doctrine to reflect that past facts, rules
and reasoning are presumed to continue in the same
state unless there is evidence to the contrary.

Property rights and contracts

The concepts of property and ownership rights are clearly
defined in Islamic law. Property is referred to as *mal* and
the Majallah (2001, Article 126) defines it as 'a thing which
is naturally desired by man, and can be stored for times of
necessity'. Messick (2003: 721) defines *mal* as a commodity
or thing of economic value that is exchanged in contracts.
Anything considered *mal* must be legal, desirable, storable,
usable and have material value for people (Ali 2003; Ayub
2007).

Property is classified in different ways under Islamic law.
Properties can be moveable or immovable. Another distinction is between fungibles (*mithliyyat*) and non-fungibles
(*qimiyyat*). Fungibles are commodities that are usually sold
by weight or capacity (e.g. gold, grain, oil, etc.) and non-
fungibles are unique things sold individually or by numbers (such as land, houses, furniture, automobiles, etc.).
Property can be in the form of assets (*ayn*), debt (*dayn*), and
usufruct (*manfa'ah*). A determinate, specific and existent
object is *ayn* while a nonspecific, generic or abstract object
defined as an obligation is *dayn* (Vogel and Hayes 1998:
114–15). Examples of *ayn* would be 'this house' or 'this radio'
and *dayn* would be 'payment of £100 in two months time' or
'deliver 1000 barrels of palm oil today'.

Ownership, termed *milk*, is defined as 'a legal relationship between a person and a thing which allows that person
to dispose of it to the exclusion of everyone else' (Delcambre

1993: 61). Gulaid (2001) provides definitions of ownership from the perspective of different schools. While the Hanafi and Hanbali view ownership as a legal authority that begins with or justifies the right of disposal, the Maliki school defines it as 'a legal authority that allows a person or his delegate to process the use or ownership rights, and also to accept compensation in case of transfer of owned properties or use rights to others' (Gulaid 2001: 12). Owners of assets (*ayn*) also own the usufructs rights to asset (Ayub 2007: 102). While the ownership of *ayn* exists until the property is destroyed or sold, the ownership of usufructs is time bound and can be held or sold for a limited time period.

In Islam, property rights are deemed sacred and gainful exchange by mutual consent is encouraged. Kahf (1998) also identifies some rules related to acquiring and using one's property. Private property is rightfully attained by lawful work, growth of an already owned property, exchange through contractual relationships, tort liability and inheritance. There should be balance in the use and waste must be avoided, property should be used without harming others, inheritance laws as prescribed by *Shari'ah* must be followed and exchanges of property must conform to the principles of *Shari'ah*. Furthermore, ownership of properties beyond a threshold level obligates payment of alms (*zakah*).

Contracts

A contract (*'aqd*) is 'an engagement and agreement between two persons in a legally impactful and binding manner' (Kharofa 2000a: 4). The *Shari'ah* validates contracts as a cause which creates a legal effect (Kamali 2000: 66). To be valid from a legal perspective, a contract must fulfil certain fundamental requirements and subsidiary conditions.[7] The fundamental conditions or pillars of a valid contract are as follows:

1. **Consent.** Consent of the contracting parties is the main pillar of a contract. Majallah (2001, Article 103) defines contract as 'two parties taking upon themselves and undertaking to do something. It is composed of the combination of an offer and an acceptance.' The consent takes the form of an offer or positive proposal (*ijab*). The acceptance (*qabul*) from the contracting parties must be free of errors, misrepresentation, coercion or duress, deceit and fraud.

2. **Legal competence and capacity of the contracting parties.** Parties to the contract must be able to 'possess and exercise legal rights' (Mahmasani 1955: 196). Incapacity to sign contracts arises for cases that include physical conditions like being minor, imbecile and ill and behavioural conditions like being prodigal, a debtor, drunk and lunatic.

3. **Subject matter.** The object of the contract must fulfil certain conditions. Messick (2003) identifies the features of a permissible sale object as purity, usefulness, capacity to deliver, ownership and specific knowledge. Furthermore, the object of the contract must exist, be legal or permissible and known to the parties. For example, prohibited items such as pork are not considered legitimate property and cannot be objects of sale. Public goods such as air, rivers, and so on cannot be treated as private property and be sold.

4. **Purpose and consideration.** Mahmasani (1955) asserts that all contracts must have purpose or consideration. Some contracts may not have consideration, but the purpose is benevolence or to do good (such as a gift). The purpose or consideration must be permissible and valid. Due to this reason, selling fruits to breweries is not valid as the object of sale can be used to make alcoholic drink which is a prohibited item under Islamic law.[8]

The purpose of the contract should also continue. If the purpose ceases to exist, the contract gets cancelled. For example, if a consultant is hired for a specific project, then the cancellation of the project will annul the hire contract.

Usually contracts are classified as valid (*sahih*) and invalid (*batil*).[9] A valid sale is one that satisfies both the main pillars and the subsidiary conditions of the contract. If one of the pillars and/or conditions is not fulfilled then the contract will be invalid. For instance, a sale may fulfil some pillars of the contract (such as offer and acceptance, existence of the object, etc.) but if the object of the sale is illegal, then it will invalidate the contract.

Major nominate contracts

While Islamic law gives freedom of wording in different contracts, in certain cases jurists have provided certain forms. The Majallah (2001, Article 105) identifies contracts such as sale hire, gift, loan, deposit, guarantee, pledge, agency and partnerships. The types of contracts vary depending on the status of the object of sale, ownership, possession, use and consideration. Though the scope of contracts is wide in Islam, some relevant ones related to financial transactions are presented next.[10]

1. Contracts of exchange or mutually onerous contracts

Contracts of exchange involve those in which parties exchange goods/services for a payment or consideration. The types of contracts used include the following:

1.1. *Sale contracts* (bay'). Sale involves the exchange in which the ownership of some lawful, specific, known asset/good/property is transferred for a fixed price. The price can be paid either as money or other known asset/ good/property. While in most cases sale is immediate and delivery and payment occur on the spot, there are special cases in which either the delivery or the payment can be delayed. For example, in *bay' al-muajjal* the good is delivered on the spot and the payment is delayed to a future date. Similarly, in a *salam* contract the price is paid on the spot and the delivery of the good is postponed, and in *istisna* both payment and delivery can be postponed to a future date.

1.2. *Hire contract (*ijarah*).* *Ijarah* involves a transaction of selling services of labour or benefits/usufruct of an asset for rent. In case of financial intermediation the latter kind of *ijarah* is of interest. Note that *ijarah* is similar to a sale contract, the difference being in the object of sale. While in a sale contract the asset/good itself is traded, in *ijarah* the usufruct or the right of use of the asset is sold.

1.3. *Work done for reward (*jualah*).* In this transaction, a reward is given to complete a work that is uncertain. Examples include 'I'll pay anyone who finds my lost camel SAR 1000' or 'We'll pay USD 100,000 to anyone who can invent a cure for cancer'. While this contract is not binding on either party until the work is completed, the Malikis make it binding on the promisor.

2. Accessory contracts

Accessory contracts are ones in which one party assigns work/capital/obligation to another party (or parties). Different types of accessory contracts are given below.

2.1. *Agency (*wakalah*).* An agency contract creates a principal–agent relationship whereby the agent represents the principal to perform certain duties. The agent can do the work for the principal free (gratuitous) or be paid a compensation. The compensation structures can be varied. One of the differences between *ijarah* (in labour contracts) and *wakalah* is that the job description in the case of the former is expressed in general terms and in the case of *wakalah* it is specific.

2.2. *Partnerships (*sharikah*).* In a partnership, the partners agree to create an association of mutual agency by contributing labour/capital/credit and sharing the profit among the partners in agreed upon ratios. Losses are borne in proportion to the share of capital in the venture. Different kinds of partnerships can exist. Two common partnership contracts are *mudarabah* and *musharakah*. *Mudarabah* is a silent partnership whereby some partners contribute capital and others manage the business or the project. Profit is shared according to a predetermined ratio, but loss is borne by the providers of capital only. In *musharakah* partners contribute both capital and labour in different proportions and profit is distributed according to agreed upon ratios among the partners.

2.3. *Assignment (*hawalah*).* The obligation of a debt can be assigned to third parties through the *hawalah* agreement. Under the arrangement, the debt is transferred to the assignee and the creditor cannot ask for repayment of the dues from the debtor (Al-Zuhayli 2003b: 51).

2.4. *Pledge or mortgage (*rahn*).* *Rahn* is the use of a valuable non-fungible asset/good as security to secure debt obligations for creditors. *Rahn* is binding only upon delivery of the asset and used to recover dues in case of default.

3. *Gratuitous contracts*

These contracts transfer ownership or possession (rights of use) without consideration (payment) or compensation.

Gratuitous contracts are those involving flow from one party to the other. These are usually benevolence acts and considered contracts of gratuities under *Shari'ah*. The main contracts under this category are:

3.1. *Loan (*ariyah *and* qard*).* In these gratuitous contracts, either the ownership or possession is transferred for a limited period of time without consideration. In a loan (*qard*) contract, a fungible item such as money is transferred to the loanee for a certain time period. Note that in loan transactions, repayment should be in exact quantities as excesses charged would constitute *riba*. Actual administrative costs incurred, however, can be charged by the creditor in *qard* transactions. In an *ariyah* contract an asset is given for use for a certain time period. In these contracts, usufructs of the asset are used by the loanee for the period of the contract.

3.2. *Deposit (*wadi'ah*).* This is a contract in which gratuitous safekeeping of property takes place. The use of deposited funds without the depositors' permission is not allowed. A deposit contract can be terminated by either party at any time.

3.3. *Gift (*hibah*).* A gift is the gratuitous transfer of something with any consideration. It requires an offer and acceptance or its implied substitute. Before a gift is actually transferred, a gift can be cancelled or revoked.

3.4. *Guarantee and personal security (*daman *or* kafalah*).* A guarantee contract adjoins the liability of a debt to the guarantor whereby she becomes liable to pay the debt when the debtor defaults. Being gratuitous, guarantees have to be offered free or the actual costs of providing the guarantee can be charged by the guarantor.

Basic approach to Islamic commercial law, *riba* and *gharar*

The injunctions of *Shari'ah* classify acts into five categories: obligatory (*wajib*), recommended (*mandub*), permissible (*mubah*), abominable or reprehensible (*makruh*), and prohibited (*haram*) (Laldin 2006). Kamali (1993) asserts that only the obligatory and forbidden acts are determined by *Shari'ah* and carry legal weight. The other three categories do not carry legal obligations but are meant to enhance morality and good conduct. Kamali (2008: 33) further adds that the obligatory and recommended acts are meant to increase welfare, and the reprehensible and forbidden to reduce evil and corruption.

The basic norm for commercial transactions is permissibility which signifies that all acts/contracts are permissible unless there is a clear injunction of prohibition (Kamali 2000: 66).[11] Summarising the views of the majority of the jurists, Ibn Qayyim confirms freedom and permissibility in contracts and points out that illegality should be on the basis of clear provision from law (Mahmasani 1955). The two broad categories of prohibitions related to economic transactions recognised in *Shari'ah* are *riba* and *gharar*. At the contract level, these prohibitions are intended to bring about fairness and good measure and, as such, these get more consideration over complete freedom of contracts (Saleh 1992: 146). The concepts of *riba* and *gharar* are discussed next.

Riba

Riba (literally meaning increase or growth) is prohibited by both the Quran and *Sunnah*. Although it is common to associate *riba* with interest, it has much wider implications and can take different forms. The common premise of *riba*, however, is that it arises from unequal trade of values in exchange (Siddiqi 2004). Fadel (2008) distinguishes between *ex-ante* and *ex-post riba*. The *ex-post riba* (*riba jahiliyyah*) was practised during the pre-Islamic period and was prohibited by the following verse of the Quran:

> Those you devour *riba* will not stand except as stands one whom the evil one by his touch hath driven to madness. That is because they say: 'Trade is like *riba*', but Allah hath permitted trade and forbidden *riba*. (Quran 2:275)

The *riba* of the Quran is closely linked to insolvent or bankrupt debtors. In a debt created by a credit sale, if the debtor was unable to pay the due amount on the maturity date, then the repayment date was postponed in return for an increase in the amount owed. The prohibition forbids the settlement of a current debt with a larger future debt. The *ex-ante* forms of *riba* are derived from the following *hadith* reported by Ubadah bin As-Samit as follows:

> Gold for gold, silver for silver, wheat for wheat, barley for barley, dates for dates, salt for salt, like for like, same for same, hand to hand. But if these commodities differ, then sell as you like, as long as it is hand to hand. (Muslim 2007: 306)

The six goods mentioned in the above *hadith* are called *ribawi* goods.[12] A number of important rules related to transactions arise from the above saying. Violation of 'same for same' can lead to *riba* of excess (*riba al fadl*) and not fulfilling 'hand to hand' (i.e. spot transaction) would constitute *riba* of delay (*riba al nasi'ah*, root word *nasaa* means to postpone). Furthermore, 'gold for gold' and 'silver for silver' provides the rules of monetary exchange (*sarf*) as these were used as currency during that time.

If there is exchange among the same specie of *ribawi* goods, it has to be done on the spot and should be of equal quantities. If the quantities exchanged differ, even in spot transactions, then it will constitute *riba al fadl*. Rules of *riba* of excess also prohibit exchange of dissimilar quantities of a genus with different qualities (such as exchanging one unit of high quality dates with two units of low quality dates) (Fadel 2008: 622). To avoid *riba*, the commodity has to be exchanged with some other genus and then traded with the desired commodity (high quality dates with wheat or silver and then wheat or silver with low quality dates). *Riba* of delay prohibits sale of commodities in the future even if the counter-values are equal.

To avoid *riba* of delay, the *ribawi* goods must be exchanged on the spot. While there are differences of opinion regarding commodities that can be included in the *riba* of delay, all schools allow deferred sale if one of the counter-values is gold, silver, copper coins or non-fungible goods (Fadel 2008). Furthermore, the price in deferred sales can deviate from the market price. For instance, the price paid on the spot in a transaction in which the delivery of good takes place in the future can be lower than the market rate. Similarly, the deferred price for commodities sold on credit can be higher than the spot value (Vogel and Hayes 1998: 76–7).

The majority of jurists have expanded the Quranic prohibition of *riba al jahiliyyah* and *riba* of delay (*riba al nasi'ah*) to cover all forms of interest-bearing loans. Note that while exchange of the same specie over a period of time is prohibited (as it would constitute *riba* of delay), a loan (*qard*) in which an equal amount is repaid in the future is allowed. *Qard* falls under a charitable contract and as such no benefit can be derived by the creditor. It is excluded from the rules of *riba* due to its charitable nature (Fadel 2008: 666).

An implication of *riba* is the prohibition of sale of debt. As monetary debt takes the form of receivables, sale of debt at a discount would involve exchange of unequal amounts of money. An extension of the ruling on sale of debt relates to sale of debt for debt (*bai al-kali bil-kali*). Sale of debt for debt can take various forms and the majority of scholars prohibit these sales (Obaidullah 1999). As both counter-values of contemporary derivatives (forwards, futures, swaps, etc.) are postponed in the future, they would fall under the sale of debt for debt, and as such, are not allowed.

Sarf or monetary exchange is defined as 'the exchange of one monetary form for another in the same or different genera, i.e., gold for gold coins, silver for silver, gold for silver, silver for gold, etc.' (Al-Zuhayli 2003a: 281). Following the *hadith* on *riba*, Al-Zuhayli (2003a) confirms that *sarf* or currency transactions must be done on on the spot (hand in hand), be of equal amounts if monies are of the same genus or with different quantities for dissimilar genera. Note that while one counter-value in a sale of a commodity can be deferred to a future date, postponing a part of the currency transaction is not allowed. The rules for spot currency exchanges (*sarf*) are applied to avoid introducing interest rates in disguise in these transactions (ElGamal 2006: 51).

Gharar

Gharar literally means 'danger' and also signifies deception (Al-Zuhayli 2003a: 82; ElGamal 2001: 32). The word, however, has connotations of uncertainty, risk or hazard and also implies ignorance, gambling and fraud. Mustafa al Zarqa defines a forbidden transaction involving *gharar* as the 'sale of probable items whose existence or characteristics are not certain, due to the risky nature that makes it similar to gambling' (Al-Zuhayli 2003a: 83). While the Quran condemns gambling (*maysir*), the prohibition of *gharar* comes from Prophetic traditions. *Gharar* will have legal consequences if the following four conditions are fulfilled (Al-Dhareer 1997; Kamali 2000):

1. *Gharar* has to be excessive, not trivial. All transactions have some elements of uncertainty. Uncertainty can be classified as excessive, moderate and minor. While the existence of the major *gharar* makes contracts invalid, minor or trivial *gharar* is tolerated. Whereas minor *gharar* and excessive *gharar* can be identified, categorising transactions having moderate *gharar* as permissible/ prohibited involves subjectivity. Difference of opinion exists among various schools regarding treatment of moderate cases of *gharar*.
2. *Gharar* has to occur in commutative (or exchange) contracts. Thus, gratuitous contracts like a gift would not involve *gharar*. For instance, while sale of a catch of a diver from the sea is forbidden due to uncertainty (*gharar*) of the object of sale, saying the catch will be given as a gift is valid.
3. *Gharar* should concern the principle subject matter of the contract itself (object or price), not linked to something that is attached to it. For example, if a car is sold with added accessories, uncertainty about the quality of the latter would not constitute *gharar*.
4. Finally, the transaction should not involve something that falls under the public need category. In case of public needs, the transaction may be valid even with excessive *gharar*. An example of this is the *salam* sale contract, which is permissible even though the product does not exist thereby introducing *gharar*.

The interpretations of *gharar* differ among the schools. The restrictive interpretations consider *gharar* as transactions having elements of ignorance (*jahalah*) and nonexistence (Vogel and Hayes 1998). The Shafi'is and Hanafis take a restrictive view and prohibit sales of absent objects altogether.[13] Both schools forbid sale of objects that are present but invisible (such as carrots under the ground). The broader perspective considers forbidden *gharar* as transactions with gambling-like features. The Hanbalis and Malikis take a broader view and allow sales of objects by description as long as the description is complete. Ibn Taymiyyah, a Hanbali jurist, has a broad perspective and maintains that restricting sales by strictly applying the rules of ignorance and existence can undermine contractual freedom. He equates *gharar* to unjustified devouring of people's wealth and leading to evils as happens in case of gambling (Vogel and Hayes 1998). A contemporary interpretation of *gharar* in line with the broader standpoint is provided by Al-Suwailem (2006). Focusing on the outcome of transactions, he equates *gharar* to a zero-sum game in which one party gains at the expense of the other. Contrary to the positive-sum game, in zero-sum games there is a transfer of wealth in one direction with no corresponding transfer of counter-value in the other. In this sense, gambling forms the purest type of *gharar*.

Gharar can exist in the essence or terms of a contract or in the object of a contract. Some specific factors that may make a contract invalid due to *gharar* under these two cases are presented next.[14]

Gharar in the essence of the contract

Gharar in the essence of the contract arises when there is uncertainty about whether a transaction will take place and when the consequences of a transaction are not clear. Some cases in which this type of *gharar* may arise are given below:

1. **Two sales in one.** This is a contract that entails two sales either in the form of having two prices for a good being sold or selling and buying two items in the same contract. An example of the former would be 'I'll sell you this item for $10 paid today or $15 paid in three months time'. An example of the latter kind of sale would be one such as 'I will sell you my car at such and such price if you sell me your house at such and such price'. These contracts involve *gharar* as there is doubt whether the sale will take place and hence they are forbidden.

2. **Pebble, touch and toss sale.** Sales that depend on the outcome of some other unrelated event like throwing a pebble, of the item being touched, or the thing being tossed by one of the parties.

3. **Suspended sale.** The sale is realised based on the outcome of some other uncertain event. In these contracts a condition or clause is attached that triggers the outcome of the transaction. For example, a contract that says 'I will sell you my car at such and such price if someone else sells me his at such and such price'. *Gharar* exists as the outcome of the sale is uncertain.

4. **Future sale.** While it is allowed to postpone the execution of one side of a transaction, a contract in which both the payment and delivery of items are postponed to a future date are not allowed. These future sales would fall under sale of debt for debt (*bai al-kali bil kali*) and entail risks of completion. An exception to this general rule is the *istisna* contract.

Gharar in the object of the contract

Gharar in the object arises when the subject matter of sale does not exist or the seller and/or buyer do not have the knowledge of various aspects of the transaction. The specific cases when *gharar* in these sources will make the contract void are discussed below:

1. **Attributes and quantity of the object.** There are several uncertainties related to the good itself that can make the contract void. These can be broadly discussed under the following headings:

   a) *Ignorance of the attributes/properties of the object.* This would constitute ignorance about the entity, type and attributes of the object being transacted. To avoid *gharar*, the object of sale should be clearly identified (the sheep among the herd or a piece of cloth in a bunch).

   b) *Ignorance of the quantity sold.* For objects that are in sight and known, there is no need to point out the specific quantity of the object for the contract to be valid. If, however, the good is not in sight, knowledge of the quantity is a condition to make the transaction valid.

2. **Existence of the object and the ability to deliver.** Selling an object that is not existent at the time of the contract is not valid. Examples include selling calves of cattle before their birth and selling fruits from a tree before they are formed or matured. Jurists conclude that the non-existent thing whose future existence is uncertain must not be sold, but the non-existent thing that has high probability of existence may be sold. Due to this condition, sale of debt is not allowed as the object of the debt is not in the possession of the person selling it.[15] Another implication of *gharar* of the object of sale relates to risks in transactions. Risk is not a commodity in itself and cannot be sold separately. Only risks inherent in sale transactions can be priced and sold along with the real asset. In this sense, ElGamal (2001) views

gharar as a prohibition of unbundled and unnecessary sale of risk.

3. **Price and delivery time.** To avoid *gharar,* the price of the good has to be known at the conclusion of a contract. In case of a deferred transaction, the time of the conclusion of the contract has to be clearly specified. For example, in a sale with deferred payment, the time when the price will be paid needs to be clearly mentioned in the contract.

Legal concepts and principles for contemporary finance

The traditional nominate contracts in their pure forms involve real transactions and may not directly cater to the needs of the contemporary financial markets and institutions. The challenge for Islamic finance was to adapt the traditional contracts to the new financial structure. This required creating a new set of contractual arrangements that could cope with transactions of the contemporary financial system. These new contracts would have to fulfil the financial needs of various sections of society without violating the principles and spirit of *Shari'ah*. The underlying principles and concepts of Islamic law relevant to contemporary financial transactions are presented next.

Maqasid al Shari'ah

As discussed, *maqasid al-Shari'ah* forms an essential element of the ends of Islamic law and becomes an important goal in framing new rules through *ijtihad* (Masud 1995: 120). The objective of *Shari'ah* is to promote the welfare or benefit of mankind which can be achieved by protecting and promoting the essentials (*dururiyyat*), the complementary requirements (*hajiyyat*) and the beautifications or embellishments (*tahsiniyat*). Compliance with the spirit of Islamic law would require fulfilling the *maqasid al Shari'ah*, which are broadly defined by Siddiqi (2004) as growth and justice. Kahf (2006) discusses *maqasid* at the product level as fulfilling the objectives in transactions. These include upholding property rights, respecting consistency of entitlements with the rights of ownership, linking transaction to real life activity, transfer of property rights in sales, prohibiting debt sale, and so on. Furthermore, as the legal maxims are linked to achieving the *maqasid*, they provide guiding principles for developing rulings related to Islamic finance.

Permissibility

The principle of permissibility maintains that in economic transactions everything is permitted unless explicitly forbidden by divine guidance. Kamali (2000: 69–70) presents three conclusions arising from the principle of permissibility that relate to economic transactions. First, a transaction can be valid without affirmative evidence from the sources. What is needed is a clear prohibition and if there isn't any found then the transaction is presumed to be valid. Second, the types of transactions explicitly validated by *Shari'ah* are not exhaustive. Thus, new transactions on which *Shari'ah* is silent can be introduced. Finally, for new transactions there is no need to seek evidence from previous *fiqh*.

Substance and form

The legal maxim 'in contracts, attention is given to the objects and meaning, and not to the words and form' (Majallah 2001, Article 3) provides the guiding principle of devising contracts in financial transactions. While the form is the contractual construct of the transaction, the substance relates to the outcome. For example, the outcome of a sale contract is the transfer of ownership of an asset in exchange for the price. Based on the maxim, Al-Suwailem (2006: 102) proposes the principle of consistency which states that 'form should serve substance, and means should conform to the ends'. Whereas both form and substance are necessary to satisfy the *Shari'ah* requirements, consistency principle would ensure that form does not overshadow substance. Fulfilling the form, but not the substance, would create inconsistency and will not be harmonious with the spirit of Islamic law. To achieve consistency, Al-Suwailem (2006) suggests starting with the substance of the transactions and then moving to the appropriate contractual form.

*Necessity (*darurah*) and concession (*rukhsah*)*

The legal maxim 'hardship causes the giving of facility' (Majallah 2001, Article 17) implies that leniency can be used in cases that cause hardship or injury. A related maxim 'harm must be eliminated' leads to the maxim of necessity (*darurah*) stating 'necessities make forbidden things canonically harmless' (Majallah 2001, Article 21). The implication is that during hardship concessions (*rukhsah*) can be used to dilute the force of established law as an exception. However, it must be noted that exceptions made due to certain hardship become void once the difficulty ceases to exist. This is deduced from the maxim 'a thing permitted on account of an excuse becomes unlawful on the cessation of the excuse' (Majallah 2001, Article 23). Thus, necessities are assessed according to their intensities and permitted accordingly. Once the excuse ceases to exist, the concession related to the necessity becomes unlawful (Laldin 2006: 144).

*Ruses (*hiyal*) and exits (*makharij*)*

Hiyal (sg. *Hila*) are 'legal devices or skills to achieve a certain objective, lawful or not, through lawful means' (Horii 2002:

312). *Hiyal* are closely linked to *makraj* (pl. *makharij*) which means exit or a 'way out of any circumstances that places a constraint upon the people' (Horii 2002: 321). Scholars agree that *hiyal* and *makharij* used to attain lawful ends are allowed and those used to obtain unlawful results are not. The lawful goals include exit or defence against oppression, achieving the principle necessities of human life, easing hardship, and so on. While Hanafis and Shafiʻi consider these as legal but immoral, the Malikis and Hanbalis declare them illegal. Even though the Hanafis support using *makharij*, they agree that lawful *hila* are 'solutions that are in full accord with the purpose of law' or in accordance with the 'spirit of law' (Horii 2002: 322).

Risk and returns

Two key principles governing Islamic financial transactions link return to risks. The first is the legal maxim of 'the detriment is as a return for the benefit (a*l-ghurm bi al-ghunm*) (Majallah 2001, Article 87). This maxim links 'entitlement of gain' to the 'responsibility of loss' (Kahf and Khan 1988: 30). It is usually used to propose the preference for profit-loss sharing instruments. The second principle arises from the Prophetic saying *al-kharaj bi al-daman* which developed into a legal maxim 'the benefit of a thing is a return for the liability for loss from that thing' (Majallah 2001, Article 85). The Prophetic saying means that the party enjoying the full benefit of an asset or object should bear the risks of ownership (Vogel and Hayes 1998). In other words, returns of an asset should be associated with the risks of its possession (Kahf and Khan 1988). Note that association of returns to risks of ownership does not necessarily relate to profit-loss sharing contracts. The principle is linked to risks associated with ownership and is relevant in the case of sale and leasing transactions. For instance, the implication of the maxim for a leasing contract is that the lessor should be responsible for the asset leased out.

Trust and guarantee

Liability of loss or damage related to possession of property depends on whether the relationship is based on trust or guarantee (ElGamal 2006). Trust is a fiduciary contract in which the trustee (*amin*) holds property and is not liable for injury to object, unless negligence, misconduct or breach of contract can be established. In contracts like agency and deposit the party holding the object does not benefit from the property and as such does not bear the risk of the loss as long has he acts in accordance with the trust placed in him (Vogel and Hayes 1998: 113). One implication is that a trustee (such as a *mudarib*) cannot be a guarantor (*damin*) of the capital of financiers.

A guarantor (*damin*), however, bears the risk of loss of a property similar to an owner (even if the property is damaged by force majeure; Vogel and Hayes 1998). As mentioned in the Prophetic saying linking gain to liability for loss (*al-kharaj bi al-daman*), the party enjoying the benefit of an object should bear risks of the ownership. Thus, while the owner is responsible for the upkeep of the property in the case of *ijarah* as she benefits from the asset in the form of rental income, the borrower bears the risk of the loaned asset in an *ariyah* contract as she enjoys the benefit during the contract period. Note that the liability of loss in different contractual relationships is determined inherently by law and cannot be altered by agreement.

Sale and actual/constructive possession

The consequence of a valid sale is exchange of ownership of an object and consideration (price) (Al-Zuhayli 2003a). The concept of ownership and possession (*qabd*) in sale contracts signifies complete transfer of the object of the sale from the seller to the buyer. While ownership gives the owner the right to benefit from the property or its usufruct, the actual use of the benefits is possible with possession (Mahmasani 1955). There is, however, a distinction between actual and constructive possession. The former is the case when moveable objects of sale are physically transferred to the buyer. In the latter case, physical transfer does not take place but possession is implied by having the right to control and use the object/asset. This would be the case for immovable objects (such as land) or financial transactions such as bank account transfers. The Islamic *Fiqh* Academy has ruled that constructive possession without physical possession is legally valid in financial transactions.[16]

Combination of contracts

Contracts are combined when parties 'put together two or more contracts of different features and legal consequences to achieve a desired viable transaction' (Arbouna 2006: 527). All obligations and legal consequences arising from the combined contracts are realised as one as though they were a single obligation. However, some *ahadith* forbid combining some specific contracts. For example, a loan and sale contract cannot be combined or a sale that is restricted with a condition is explicitly prohibited by the Prophet. The main reasons of forbidding combining contracts is that these may lead to a result that is illegal. Specifically combining two or more valid contracts that can lead to *riba*, *gharar*, or injustice and exploitation (favouring one party of the contract the other) is not allowed.

There are certain combinations of contracts that may not lead to illegal results and, as such, are allowed. Arbouna (2006) indentifies cases in which contracts can be combined without violating *Shari'ah* principles. First, the combination of contracts cannot contradict explicit text. An example of this would be the combination of sale and loan contracts which is prohibited in Prophetic saying. Second, the combination of contracts should not create impermissible transactions like *riba* or *gharar*. For example, *bay' al'inah*, which combines two sale contracts to create an outcome that resembles an interest-based loan transaction, would fall under this category. Finally, combination must not contain contradictory contracts in terms and objectives. Contracts that play a complimentary role can in principle be combined with key contracts. An example of these would be a loan and a collateral contract or a sale contract with a guarantee. While two binding contracts can be combined, a binding and non-binding may not be combined as it can create legal conflicts. Note that contracts can be dissimilar but not contradictory. For example, sale and *ijarah* or sale and currency exchange can be combined but structured separately.

Promise (wa'd)

Promise (*wa'd*) is a unilateral promise. Under Islamic law, it is similar to social promise making it morally binding but not legally binding (Kharoufa 2000a). While promises are unilateral and not legally binding, the Islamic *Fiqh* Academy issued a resolution making the promise of the buyer in a *murabahah* sale binding to the extent that the promisor (the buyer) has to pay for losses incurred by the promisee (the bank) as a result of the undertaking.[17] According to the resolution the 'binding nature of the promise means that it should be either fulfilled or a compensation be paid for damages caused due to the unjustifiable non-fulfilling of the promise' (IRTI and IFA 2000: 86). Based on this resolution, the binding principle of a unilateral promise has been expanded to other financial transactions. Al-Masri

(2002), however, cautions that a binding unilateral promise should not be used to replace contracts that are prohibited by Islamic law.

Rebate

The concept of rebate is derived from *ibra'* which means to surrender one's right to a claim on debt. Based on Prophetic sayings, scholars have allowed rebates in cases of early settlement of loans. This is confirmed by the Islamic *Fiqh* Academy (Resolution no. 64/2/7) which states:

> To reduce a deferred debt with the aim of accelerating its repayment, whether at the request of the creditor or the debtor (pay less but ahead of time), is permissible in Shari'a and does not fall within the province of *riba* (which is forbidden) if it is not based on the advance agreement and as long as the relationship between the creditor and the debtor is bilateral. If there is a third party between them, the reduction is not permissible as it will then be subject to the ruling of discount of commercial papers. (IRTI and IFA 2000: 135–6)

Rebates are widely used by Islamic banks in debt-based products to adjust the payment of dues by the debtor to reflect the actual usage of funds and/or tenor of financing.

Options and stipulations

The contracting parties are free to stipulate options or terms and conditions in contracts that are beneficial to the parties and satisfy their needs. These conditions and stipulations, however, should not contradict the principles of *Shari'ah* (Kamali 2000). While stipulations are allowed, they cannot contradict the essence and lawful purpose of the contract in question. The legal status of stipulation puts the burden on the writer of the option and she is obligated to fulfil the option if it is exercised. Note that dealings in independent options that are detached from real transactions are prohibited.[18] Khan (1999/2000) indicates that options that are embedded in real transactions are not covered by this ruling and can be included in these contracts.

Kamali (2000: 76–7) classifies stipulations into three types: valid (*sahih*), irregular or defective (*fasid*) and void (*batel*). A valid stipulation does not change either the substance of the contract or its requirements. An irregular or defective stipulation is one that benefits one party but is not validated by law. An example of this would be selling a house on condition that the seller continues living in it. A void condition may be one that is neither valid not irregular. For instance, selling a book on condition that it cannot be read would be an invalid contract as the ownership and control of the object is curtailed. The contract itself may be valid and upheld, but these options are null and void.

Approaches of Islamic law related to finance

With the spread of Islamic banking and finance, *Shari'ah* advisory committees/boards constituting groups of scholars/jurists were established at organisational, national and international levels. These bodies pronounced various rules or resolutions (*fatwas*) related to economics and financial transactions. These rulings form the essence of Islamic commercial law during contemporary times. Approaches to Islamic law related to finance can be discussed under the methodological and contractual perspectives.

Methodological approaches

Vogel and Hayes (1998: 34–41) identify the four methods used by scholars to come up with contemporary legal injunctions in Islamic finance. The first is *ijtihad* in which scholars refer to principles of the Quran and *Sunnah* and use the different methods of *usul al-fiqh* and the legal maxims to come up with rulings. However, they assert that *ijtihad* is not used to come up with new inventions, but to modify existing conventional financial practices. For example, after studying the contemporary option the scholars ruled that it is not an acceptable contract. On the other hand, a corporation has been accepted and insurance has been modified to *takaful*.

The second approach used is that of choice (*iktiyar*) or selection (*takhayyur*) of views of past scholars from different schools. Sometimes *talfiq* (amalgamation or patching) is used to derive rulings by combining views from different sources. This technique 'combines opinions from different schools to reach an outcome that is otherwise impermissible under any one school if each were exclusively consulted on the validity of the entire transaction' (Hegazy 2007: 601). An example of this approach would be to consider scholar A's permissibility in one case and scholar B's prohibition on the same case and choose the ruling of permissibility. If done in extremes, rulings from different sources can be patched to come up with structures that have properties of conventional contracts.

A third method is to use the concept of necessity (*darurah*) and make lawful a traditionally unlawful injunction. Examples of this include placing funds in conventional interest-bearing accounts when no Islamic alternatives are available on the condition that the resulting income is used in charitable activities. Allowance of taking interest-bearing mortgages when Islamic alternatives are not available can also be rationalised under necessity.

Finally, the fourth method is to use legal artifice (*hiyal*). All classical schools accepted that *hiyal* should not be used and discouraged it if it is used to attain illegitimate ends.

Examples of unacceptable *hiyal* that can lead to unlawful results are *bay' al-'inah* and *bay' al-wafa*.[19]

Contractual approaches

Iqbal and Mirakhor (2007) identify two broad approaches used in developing Islamic financial products: 'reverse engineering' and 'innovative engineering'. While in the former approach an Islamic replication of a conventional product is engineered, in the latter approach new products are developed from an established menu of Islamic instruments entailing both the form and substance of Islamic law. Most of the products developed in Islamic finance, however, appear to be using reverse engineering whereby the industry is imitating products from conventional banks or other Islamic banks. Ahmed (2006) identifies the following specific ways in which Islamic products are being structured.

Adapting traditional contracts to contemporary concepts/transactions

Traditional nominate contracts are being adapted by redefining the concepts and applying these to contemporary transactions by the process of analogy. For example, the concept of copyright and patent is novel and important as it may drive inventions and innovations. Even though these concepts do not fulfil the condition of 'materiality', the Islamic *Fiqh* Academy has recognised their status as property that can be bought/sold in the market.[20] Another example of using a traditional concept for contemporary settings is the use of sale of *arboon* (advance payment) as a call option. In the case of traditional sale of *arboon*, a buyer is paid a fraction of the price of a good on the understanding that she will buy the good at some future date and the seller will fulfil his obligation to sell. If the buyer did not acquire the good by paying the full price within the stipulated time, the advance paid was forfeited to the seller. ElGari (1993) shows how *arboon* can be used in stock markets as a 'call option'. The buyer of the call option, by paying the option price, buys the right to purchase a specific number of shares of a certain company at fixed price during a particular period. The seller of the call option is equally obliged to sell these shares when the buyer decides to do so. In case the buyer does not exercise the option, the seller keeps the amount paid in advance as *arboon*.

Adapting conventional financial products

Another method of creating new contracts in the Islamic financial sector is to adopt and adapt conventional products/contracts that meet the *Shari'ah* criteria. The conventional contracts or products can be modified by removing the undesirable components to make them comply with the *Shari'ah* principles. This approach conforms to the principle of permissibility as conventional products void of prohibited elements can be considered *Shari'ah* compliant.[21] For example, equity based mutual funds have been adopted by Islamic financial institutions by adapting the stocks that can be included in these funds. Investments in stocks are allowed if they fulfil certain business and financial criteria derived from *Shari'ah* and *fiqh*. Accordingly, investment in companies that deal with forbidden goods/services like alcohol and tobacco, gambling, pornography, interest-based financing institutions, and so on are not allowed. The financial filter is used to weed out firms that have unwarranted dealings with interest-based transactions.[22]

Using multiple traditional contracts to create new financial contracts

The most common method of creating financial contracts by far has been the combination of traditional nominate contracts to create new contracts.[23] Examples of these include the contemporary financial *murabahah* (or *murabahah* to the purchase orderer) a widely used instrument in Islamic financial institutions. The original sale contract (*murabahah*) is used with several other concepts (promise, agency, guarantee, etc.) to produce a financing tool. Similarly, a traditional *ijarah* contract is used with a sale or gift contract to form the *ijarah wa iqtina* or *ijarah muntahiyyah bittamleek* financing instrument. Diminishing *musharakah* associates a *musharakah* contract with that of a sale for financing purposes. Similarly, contemporary *sukuk* is a composite of multiple transactions/contracts.

Some products resulting from combining different contracts can be controversial. An example of a contentious product is organised *tawarruq* which is being used both on the asset and liability sides. On the asset side, the bank first buys a certain quantity of commodity and then sells it to the client at a mark-up. The bank then acts as an agent of the client and sells her commodity to a broker and deposits the proceeds of the sale into the client's account. The result of these multiple sales and agency contracts is that the client has the cash and owes the bank the amount financed plus a return. While some Islamic banks practice *tawarruq*, the Islamic *Fiqh* Academy recently issued a ruling declaring organised *tawarruq* illegal as it entails elements of *riba*.[24]

Notes

1. For a discussion on the implications of Islamic principles and values on economic aspects, see Chapra (1992) and Haneef (1997).

2. As *fiqh al-muamalat* means jurisprudence related to transactions, Islamic commercial law can be considered the equivalent of and not the exact translation of the term.

3. Sometimes the word *Shari'ah* is used to mean the whole body

of Islamic law. In this paper, it is defined more narrowly as laws entailed in the Quran and *Sunnah*. The bulk of the jurisprudence derived by *ijtihad* is referred to as *fiqh*.

4. The other major division in Islam being the *Shia* tradition. For a discussion on the evolution of *Fiqh* schools see Owsia (1994) and Phillips (2006).

5. See Laldin (2006) and Kharoufa (2000b) for a discussion on these methods.

6. Some writers discuss *istislah* as another source of Islamic law which derives new rules based on public interest.

7. A sale contract must satisfy certain subsidiary conditions to avoid disagreement and protect rights of the parties. Al Zuhayli (2003a: 36–9) discusses various conditions identified by different schools. For example, the Hanafis point out additional stipulations of valid sale to include conditions of conclusion, validity, execution and bindingness.

8. The Hanbali, Maliki and Zahiri schools forbid such sales (Mahmasani 1955: 195).

9. The Hanafis classify them as valid (*sahih*), voidable/defective (*fasid*) and void (*batil*).

10. This material is based on Vogel and Hayes (1998, ch. 5) and Rayner (1991).

11. Also see Fatwa No. 1 of the First Albaraka Seminar 1981 (Dallah Albaraka 1994: 75–6).

12. There is difference of opinion among various schools as to what constitutes *ribawi* goods. The Hanafis have the broadest interpretation and include any item sold by weight or volume as *ribawi* goods. The Shafi'is apply *riba* of excess to food only (and exclude metals other than gold and silver). The Malikis have the narrowest understanding as they limit the commodities to non-perishable staple foods and exclude all metal other than gold and silver (Fadel 2008: 661; Vogel and Hayes 1998: 76).

13. The Hanafis permit sale of an absent object by description with provision that the buyer can reject it upon inspection.

14. For a detailed discussion on *gharar* see Al-Dhareer (1997) and Kamali (2000).

15. Note that sale of debt is also forbidden due to *riba*.

16. See Resolution no. 53/4/6 in IRTI and IFA (2000: 107–8).

17. See Resolution no. 40–41 (2/5 and 3/5) in IRTI and IFA (2000: 86–7).

18. Resolution no. 63/1/7 (IRTI and IFA 2000: 131).

19. *Bay' al 'inah* is sale and buy-back of an object at different prices between two individuals so that the result mimics a loan transaction. *Bay' al-wafa* is sale with a promise to buy back an asset with similar results.

20. See Resolution no. 43 (5/5) in IRTI and IFA (2000: 89).

21. Zarqa (2002: 261) maintains that contracts and social institutions from non-Muslim societies can be accepted with little or no modifications if they meet the *Shari'ah* criteria.

22. According to the Shari'ah Board of the Dow Jones Islamic Index, a company must meet three specific financial constraints. First, its debt ratio must not exceed 33 per cent; second, cash- and interest-based securities as a percentage of capital should represent less than 33 per cent; and finally accounts receivables to total assets must remain below 45 per cent (Dow Jones Indexes 2004).

23. For a discussion on combining contracts from a *Shari'ah* perspective, see Arbouna (2006).

24. The ruling was issued by the International Council of *Fiqh* Academy in its nineteenth session which was held in Sharjah, United Arab Emirates, 26–30 April 2009.

CHAPTER 3
ISLAMIC BANKING: INSTITUTIONAL ENVIRONMENT, ORGANISATIONAL DESIGN AND PRODUCT FEATURES

A financial system entails markets and intermediaries providing products and services that satisfy various needs of different stakeholders in an economy. The key difference between Islamic finance and its conventional counterpart is that the former abides by the principles of *Shari'ah*. Grais and Pellegrini (2006a: 13) identify three aspects of *Shari'ah* requirements for the Islamic financial industry. First, conduct financial transactions in accordance to the laws of *Shari'ah* primarily by avoiding *riba* and *gharar*. Second, promote social benevolence by undertaking activities that foster societal objectives. Finally, develop an integrated Islamic financial system based on the principles and goals of *Shari'ah* (*maqasid al-Shari'ah*). While the first requirement relates to the legal requirement of Islamic finance, the latter two deal with the social requirements of Islamic law, discussed in Chapter 1. A key factor that determines the legal and social *Shari'ah* requirements is the type of products marketed by Islamic banks. The nature of the products offered will have implications for the current practices and future direction of the industry in the long run.

Any financial system, including the Islamic one, does not exist in a vacuum. The ability of Islamic finance to develop products and services that can fulfil the *Shari'ah* requirements will depend on various factors at different levels. At the macro level, the institutional environment in the form of legal and regulatory regimes determines type of organisations and their overall role and functions. The introduction of Islamic banks initiated the use of Islamic commercial law in financial contracts. By sanctioning products used in transactions, scholars in the *Shari'ah* Supervisory Boards (SSB) in Islamic financial institutions create law in the private domain. Given the external institutional settings, the organisational structure and capabilities will determine the types of products that banks can offer. To have a holistic understanding of product development in Islamic banks would, therefore, require comprehension of the institutional infrastructure along with the relevant organisational and product-related issues. This chapter discusses the issues related to Islamic banking practices and products at these three levels and identifies the key risks facing the sector.

The institutional environment

The word institution is used in a broader sense and constitutes the nature of polity, state, constitution, judiciary, and so on. The institutional environment specifies the formal constraints and enforcement rules in an economy.[1] Following Pistor and Xu (2003), three types of infrastructure institutions relevant to the Islamic banking industry can be identified. First, statutes and laws specify formal rules that define the nature of property rights and their exchange through contracts. Second, a proactive enabling regulatory and supervision framework ensures the application of rules and laws and protection of property rights. In a well-functioning financial system, the supervisors and regulators act on behalf of the society at large and protect the interests of the different stakeholders and ensure stability in the financial system as a whole. Third, courts and other dispute settlement institutions ensure *ex post* implementation of contracts and enforcement of property rights in case of any breach of contracts or exercise of rights. As Islamic banking uses Islamic law in financial transactions, an institutional *Shari'ah* governance mechanism may also be required. Given the above, the institutional environment relevant to Islamic banking can be discussed under four headings: laws and legal environment, regulatory and supervisory regimes, *Shari'ah* governance systems and dispute resolution institutions.

Legal regimes and laws

With the exception of a few countries, most Muslim countries have adopted some variant of Western legal systems either due to colonisation or imitation. Countries that were ex-British colonies have adopted the English common law framework and the ex-European colonies the civil law regime. Many countries in the Arab world adapted variants of the Egyptian legal system, which has a legal code based on French civil law. Each legal family shapes the legal rules that affect the financial markets and their development (La Porta *et al.* 1999). Laws relevant to financial transactions relate to organisation, banking, tax and contracts. Organisational law determines the types of organisations that can be formed. Banking law specifies the legal requirements to establish and operate banks. Tax laws relevant to banking are related to income (profit), transactions (capital gains and stamp duties) and goods and services (value-added tax). Contract law provides the principles and basis of conducting transactions. While the former three laws are determined by the state, contract law in the case of Islamic banking is principally determined by *Shariʿah* scholars in SSB. The legal dichotomy between the Islamic law generated in the private domain and non-Islamic state laws in the public sphere can create legal risks for products offered by Islamic banks.[2]

The legal regimes under which Islamic banking operates can be broadly divided into three types. The first group of countries is ones with Islamic legal systems. These countries include Iran, Saudi Arabia and Sudan. Iran adopted an Islamic legal system after the revolution of 1979. The Islamic Banking Law was enacted in 1983 to cover all banking operations. Saudi Arabia has a traditional Islamic system whereby the legal authority and control of the judiciary lies with the clergy. Though contemporary laws in the form of royal edicts exist, the country does not have any specific Islamic banking law. Sudan transformed its banking sector into an Islamic system during the 1980s and enacted Islamic Transactions Law in 1984.

The second group of countries has a predominantly Western legal system, but introduced Islamic banking law to provide the legal basis for Islamic financial practices and dealings.[3] The countries in this group can be further divided into ones with common law and those with civil law systems. Examples of common law countries with Islamic banking laws are Malaysia and Pakistan. Malaysia enacted the Islamic Banking Act (IBA 1983) and Bank and Financial Institutions Act (BAFIA 1993, amended) to cater to Islamic banking practices. Pakistan amended laws to accommodate Islamic finance including the enactment of the Banking and Financial Services Ordinance 1984. There are some other common law countries, such as Bangladesh, in which

Islamic banking is covered under a section of the existing banking law.

Among civil law countries, Indonesia introduced the Islamic Banking Act No. 10 in 1992 and amended it in 1998. The country also introduced the Central Banking Act in 1999 to support creation of instruments of liquidity management for Islamic banks. In countries of the Gulf Cooperation Council (GCC) region that have variants of the civil law system, specific Islamic banking laws do not exist. However, there are provisions for Islamic banking in other laws and/ or in regulatory rules. For example, the Central Bank of Kuwait Law of 1968 has some stipulations about Islamic banking practice. Similarly, the Financial Institutions Law 2006 gives the Central Bank of Bahrain (CBB) authority to regulate all banks including Islamic ones. The CBB issued a Rulebook for Islamic Banks which governs various issues related to the operations of Islamic banks.

The third group of countries are ones in which Islamic financial institutions operate under Western legal systems with no supporting Islamic banking law. The conventional banking laws may not be appropriate for Islamic banking practices due to the different conceptual nature of the latter. For example, whereas Islamic banks' main activity is trading (*murabahah*) and investing in equities (*musharakah* and *mudarabah*), conventional banking law may forbid commercial banks to undertake such activities. Similarly, contrary to the practice in Islamic banks, these jurisdictions do not allow the return on deposits to be linked to the asset side to protect depositors. Under these legal systems, Islamic finance would use organisational formats and offer products that comply with the existing laws and regulations. Islamic financial products will tend to replicate the economic substance of the products sanctioned by the laws of the country.

The form of practice of Islamic finance under Western legal regimes, however, depends on the approach of the regulatory authorities and their perspectives on the substance of transactions. In countries where the regulatory authorities are accommodating to Islamic banking, Islamic banks and other financial institutions can be established under the existing legal framework. The United Kingdom has successfully introduced Islamic banking without introducing any specific Islamic banking law. However, to place Islamic banking on par with their conventional counterparts, some tax laws were altered so that Islamic finance is not unduly penalised for using sale-based contracts. For instance, the tax law was amended in 2003 to eliminate double real estate transfer tax (stamp duty) for Islamic mortgages. More recently the tax framework was altered in 2008 and 2009 to enable issuance of *sukuk*.

In countries where the regulatory authority does not pro-actively support Islamic banking, Islamic financial products can be provided by some other appropriate organisational format. This is particularly feasible in countries that emphasise substance over form in accounting standards.[4] For example, in Canada and the US several financial institutions are providing Islamic products. Among others, finance companies such as American Finance House Lariba (California) and Guidance Residential (Virginia) are providing mortgage financing in the US and Ansar Cooperative Housing Corporation Ltd is doing the same in Canada as a cooperative. In the US, a couple of Islamic products can be used by the finance companies as they resemble their conventional counterparts in substance. For example, citing the Generally Accepted Accounting Principles recognition of the substance over form, the Office of the Comptroller of the Currency (OCC) in the US permitted the use of the proposed Islamic lease programme as it was functionally equivalent to that of financing with secured lending. Similarly, OCC ruled in 1999 that *murabahah* financing was permissible as it is 'functionally equivalent to either a real estate mortgage transaction or an inventory or equipment loan agreement'.[5]

Regulatory regimes

The banking industry is one of the most regulated sectors in the economy. This is because the industry is highly leveraged and does business with other people's funds. The banking sector is also interlinked with other sectors of the economy creating potential systemic risks. Furthermore, the financial sector supplies 'prudence' products and their quality is difficult to ascertain without incurring significant transaction costs (Llewellyn 1999). These products require regulatory oversight as their value is spread over a long period of time and can change to the detriment of the consumer. Given the above, Llewellyn (1999) identifies three core objectives of regulation as sustaining systemic stability, maintaining soundness and safety of financial institutions, and protecting the consumer. Issues related to the practice of Islamic banking under these headings are discussed below.

Systemic stability

One of the major roles of regulators is to ensure stability and soundness of the financial system. One key objective of regulators is to minimise information and market failures that can lead to financial instability. Other than the regulatory roles applicable for the conventional banking sector, there are some additional issues related to Islamic banks. Relevant risks for the Islamic financial system from the regulators' perspectives can be identified as macro-prudential or systemic risks, liquidity risks, and *Shari'ah*-compliant and reputation risks.

To avoid systemic risks, practices and rules that create incentives of taking the responsibilities of bearing risks and limit the transfer of these to others are required. As Chapra (2008b) suggests, using equity modes of financing can induce stringent due diligence and monitoring of assets by financial institutions. Another system-wide risk for Islamic banking is the liquidity risk. Liquidity risks arise from difficulties in obtaining cash at reasonable cost in times of need. Islamic banks are prone to face liquidity risks due to various reasons. First, there are no organised Islamic money-markets in most jurisdictions from which funds can be sought in times of need.[6] Second, as most assets of Islamic banks are predominantly debt-based, these become illiquid due to restrictions on sale of debt.

The Islamic financial system can become susceptible to instability from a unique and vital source. Qattan (2006) points out that *Shari'ah* non-compliance can be a reason for reputation risk that can trigger bank failure and cause systemic risk. The Islamic financial system can become susceptible to instability if the perception of stakeholders about the Islamic products becomes negative causing a serious loss of trust and credibility.[7] Additionally, as *Shari'ah* boards produce *fatwas* by interpreting different legal sources, the possibility of coming up with conflicting opinions increases the legal risks. With the expansion of the industry, the likelihood of conflicting *fatwas* will increase undermining customer confidence in the industry (Grais and Pellegrini 2006c). The *Shari'ah* compliance, reputation and legal risks arising in Islamic finance can be mitigated to some extent by establishing a *Shari'ah* governance regime that can oversee the *Shari'ah*-related issues of the Islamic financial sector in general and products in particular.[8]

Soundness of financial institutions

The second role of a financial regulator is to ensure the safety and soundness of financial institutions. Noyer (2008) suggests three levels of regulatory requirements applied to financial institutions. At the first level, institutions would be required to register and commit to comply with a code of best practice. At the second level, institutions would be required to disclose activities and accounts. At the final level, there will be an overview of the transactions and risks involved.

Supervisors and regulators develop substantive standards of good governance and risk management procedures for financial institutions to minimise the overall economic and operational risks faced by banks. The regulators may induce governance processes in financial institutions that exert sufficient pressure on managers to avoid excessive risk-taking. Regulators can minimise risks by requiring higher levels of regulatory capital.

As many of the risks arising in Islamic financial institutions are unique, there is a need to understand the nature of these risks before devising the regulatory standards. The Islamic Financial Services Board (IFSB) standards provide some guidelines for regulators regarding prudent capital adequacy and risk management standards for Islamic financial institutions.[9] Excessive profiteering and risk-taking can be controlled by setting appropriate rules and standards for all financial institutions, including Islamic ones. Some rules that can mitigate risks are setting up investment criteria to prevent excessive risk-taking, imposing restrictions on excessive leveraging, requiring stringent capital requirements, ensuring more transparency and accountability. Furthermore, if Islamic banking can be offered by conventional banks through Islamic windows, care has to be taken to separate the two kinds of operations. There is a need to have firewalls between the Islamic window and the parent conventional bank so as to ensure the *Shari'ah* compliance of the operations of the former. There may be a requirement to allocate a minimum capital for the Islamic banking window.

Davies (2002) points out that one of the roles of regulatory authorities is to work to maintain confidence in the financial markets. While this can be done by ensuring maintenance of accounting and auditing standards and truthful financial reporting, there is an important factor that needs to be addressed in Islamic finance. To reduce information-related risks the regulators should have power to intervene when there is a lack of or misleading information about products and institutions. Davies (2002) maintains that regulators should promote public understanding of the financial system. Given the newness and complexity of Islamic financial products, this role of regulator of enhancing financial literacy among the public is very relevant for the Islamic financial industry.

Protecting the consumer and investors

The regulators consider the interests of stakeholders who may not always be protected at the organisational level. While consumers should be aware of the risks involved in different financial transactions and take responsibility for their financial decisions, they are not in a position to fully assess the soundness of financial institutions. The regulators can improve the operations of these institutions by ensuring that the contracts used are fair and understood by the consumers, banks are financially sound, and there are ombudsmen and compensation schemes to support the market when it is adversely affected.

Chapra and Khan (2000) outline elements of the regulatory framework related to protection of both the demand

and investment depositors in Islamic banks. The demand deposits in Islamic banks take the form of loans (*qard hasan*). The regulators must have some guidelines to protect these depositors by requiring banks to minimise risks in using these funds. The use of profit-sharing investment accounts (PSIA) to reward depositors introduces some additional risks in Islamic banks.[10] As PSIA depositors share the profit/loss of the bank, it may lead to withdrawal risks. If a bank fails to pay depositors comparable market rates of return then there is a risk that the depositors will move their funds to other banks.[11] This can cause systemic risks and affect the whole financial sector. Furthermore, as many of the depositors use Islamic banks for religious reasons, the regulators have to ensure that the banks perform their fiduciary duty by complying with the principles of *Shari'ah*. This requires greater transparency regarding the operations of banks and products offered. It may also require having a regulatory framework for *Shari'ah* governance.

Shari'ah *governance regimes*

A *Shari'ah* governance framework is an important determinant of Islamic banking practices and the types of products offered. The IFSB (2008) proposes four aspects that a *Shari'ah* governance system should entail at the level of Islamic financial institutions. These are issuance of *Shari'ah* pronouncements, ensuring day to day compliance with the *Shari'ah* pronouncements, internal *Shari'ah* compliance review and audit, and an annual *Shari'ah* compliance audit to ensure that the internal *Shari'ah* compliance review has been properly carried out. To undertake these functions, the IFSB identifies different *Shari'ah* organs which include an in-house *Shari'ah* compliance unit/department, internal *Shari'ah* review/audit unit and SSB.

The IFSB (2008) leaves the responsibility of *Shari'ah*

governance at the level of organisations without any firm commitment for regulatory overview. However, to reduce *Shari'ah* compliance risks and ensure that the Islamic banks fulfil their fiduciary duties of conducting business according to *Shari'ah* principles, there may be a need for the regulatory bodies to provide a *Shari'ah* governance framework and guidelines. Two broad criteria can be used to classify *Shari'ah* governance regimes. The first is the existence of a national framework for *Shari'ah* governance in the form of law/regulations supported by a complementary national *Shari'ah* supervision mechanism at the regulatory level. The goal of the national *Shari'ah* governance framework will be to accomplish the broader *Shari'ah* requirements of the industry and protect the interests of stakeholders not served at the organisational level. An active National *Shari'ah* Authority (NSA) will address the *Shari'ah/fiqh*-related issues, harmonise the *Shari'ah* interpretations and ensure compliance with *Shari'ah* principles. Another important area that would help reduce legal risks is a product clearance role whereby the NSA would identify the permissible modes of financing/investment and clear all new products coming into the market.

A second aspect of the *Shari'ah* regulatory framework would set up requirements to strengthen the organisational *Shari'ah* governance structures and processes. Other than requiring Islamic banks to have a *Shari'ah* unit/department, elements can include requirements related to various aspects of *Shari'ah* governance at the organisational level. The issues under regulatory purview can include the terms of reference of the SSB, defining the duties and role of SSB members, approving appointment of SSB members, specifying the qualifications and minimum number of members in the SSB, and identifying the position of the SSB in the governance structure. The code of conduct of SSB members can limit the number of banks they can serve in, maintain independence, avoid conflict of interest, and so on. The banks may also be required to have a *Shari'ah* compliance manual and external *Shari'ah* audit. The operational issues related to *Shari'ah* governance would be to ensure information disclosure related to products, proper use of charity funds and separation of funds and risks if Islamic windows exist.

Given the two-criteria framework above, the *Shari'ah* regulatory regimes can be identified as the following four types.

Legally constructed

This system is similar to the conventional financial system whereby the banking law broadly determines the operations of banks. Under this structure, the *Shari'ah* framework is determined by law with no supporting *Shari'ah* bodies at the national or organisational levels. An example of this system is the governance regime in Iran where the products that can be offered by banks are identified by the Usury Free Banking Act 1983. While the central bank is responsible for implementing the law, there is neither any *Shari'ah* body at the national level nor any requirement to have an SSB at the organisational level. If a new product is introduced, the central bank seeks advice and endorsement on the *Shari'ah*-related issues from well-respected *Shari'ah* scholars.[12]

Robust *Shari'ah* governance

This regime has an active *Shari'ah* governance system both at national and organisational levels. The NSA also plays an active role in *Shari'ah* issues in the industry and regulators provide detailed guidelines to strengthen the *Shari'ah* supervision at organisational level. Examples of robust *Shari'ah* governance regimes include Indonesia, Pakistan and Malaysia. In Indonesia, the National *Shari'ah* Board

(*Dewan Sharia Nasional* or DSN) is an independent body under the Ministry of Religion. All new products coming to the market must be approved by this national body. The State Bank of Pakistan (SBP) established a central *Shari'ah* Board (SB) to guide the Islamic financial sector and the SBP in matters related to Islamic finance. Other than *Shari'ah* scholars, the central SB has members from various fields such as banking, accounting and law. The roles of the SB include reviewing and approving *Shari'ah*-compliant products developed by the SBP. The SB provides the broad guidelines of the model agreements of various permissible products which all Islamic financial institutions must abide by. The rulings of the SB are binding on all Islamic banks.

The central bank of Malaysia (Bank Negara Malaysia or BNM) established a national *Shari'ah* Advisory Council (SAC) in 1997 as the highest authority for *Shari'ah*-related issues in Islamic banking and *takaful* industry. Among others, the SAC advises BNM on Islamic banking and *takaful* issues, coordinates *Shari'ah* issues and evaluates *Shari'ah* aspects of new products submitted by the Islamic banks. Each Islamic bank has its own *Shari'ah* Committee guided by the *Guidelines of the Governance of Shari'ah Committee for the Islamic Financial Institutions* provided by the BNM. All new products developed must be submitted to the BNM for scrutiny which includes review approval by the SAC. A current law has made the SAC the sole authority to interpret Islamic contractual laws related to the operations of Islamic banks in Malaysia.

Passive *Shari'ah* governance

The third category of countries has a passive framework of *Shari'ah* governance at national level and active *Shari'ah* governance at organisational level. Countries in this category may have a NSA, but its role is limited and does not include approval of new products. Examples of countries falling under passive *Shari'ah* governance regimes are the UAE and Kuwait. The UAE Federal Law No. 6 of 1985 calls for the creation of a Higher *Shari'ah* Authority comprising people with backgrounds in *Shari'ah*, legal and banking backgrounds to ensure the legitimacy of the transactions according to the provisions of *Shari'ah*. The law also requires the creation of an SSB with at least three members in Islamic banks to ensure that the transactions are in accordance with the principle of Islamic law. Similarly, the Central Bank of Kuwait Law of 1968 stipulates that Islamic banks should have an SSB of at least three members appointed by the General Assembly. A higher level *Fatwa* Board of the Ministry of *Awqaf* is consulted only in case of conflict of opinions among the members of the SSB. In both cases, there are no specific provisions in the law for the higher national *Shari'ah* body to either clear the products approved by the SSB at the organisational level or issue directives to strengthen the structure and processes of *Shari'ah* supervision at the organisational level.

Market driven

Under the market-driven regime, *Shari'ah* compliance is left to the banks and there is no central NSA to oversee the products being marketed.[13] Furthermore, there is no regulatory oversight or guidelines for the SSB at the organisational level. The system is market driven whereby new Islamic products are cleared by the SSBs at organisational level. A market-driven practice of Islamic banking is found in Bangladesh, the Kingdom of Saudi Arabia, and the UK.

Dispute settlement/conflict resolution institutions

As the contracts used in Islamic banking products are derived from *Shari'ah* and the Islamic financial contracts' legitimacy should be judged by the principles of Islamic law, the ideal situation would be to use *Shariʿah* as the governing law to settle disputes. However, the dispute resolution issue becomes complicated due to the duality of laws in play in Islamic finance transactions. While the contracts use Islamic law, the courts in most jurisdictions use some variant of Western commercial law to adjudicate. To resolve these issues, Islamic financial contracts include choice-of-law and dispute settlement clauses to reduce legal risks (Vogel and Hayes 1998).

If Islamic law is chosen as the law of choice to settle disputes, the contracts can opt for commercial arbitration and be shielded from the national legal environment. While some Islamic arbitration centres exist, parties are reluctant to take disputes to these institutions due to lack of precedence. Furthermore, there is uncertainty regarding the outcome due to the differences of opinion among different scholars and schools and absence of a standardised codified Islamic law. As such, partners in transactions avoid using Islamic law as they want to avoid the 'impracticalities or the uncertainty of applying classical Islamic law' (Vogel and Hayes 1998: 51).

The alternative approach is to use the law of the country to settle disputes. This would mean using a non-Islamic legal system to resolve disputes involving Islamic financial contracts. The outcome of these disputes will partly depend on the legal system and whether supporting Islamic banking law exists or not. Djojosugito (2003) discusses the scope of operations of Islamic banks and difficulties that may arise under the common and civil legal systems.

As the laws and their implementation are codified under the civil law regime, it would be difficult to resolve disputes involving Islamic finance in these countries if Islamic banking law does not exist. Even if Islamic banking law is enacted, it has to be comprehensive and include the details of Islamic financial transactions and the administrative procedures for carrying out these activities. Islamic banking laws worded in general terms and lacking details of the different Islamic modes of financing can create risks in dispute settlement. For example, if the banking law excludes important aspects of Islamic financial transactions, such as the profit-sharing principles, then using the *mudarabah* and *musharakah* contracts can entail risks. While some issues can be covered by the freedom of contract principle, other features of the contract such as dual or multiple ownership (in diminishing *musharakah*) and implications in the case of insolvency may not be governed by the civil law doctrine.

While in the civil law system, the courts will interpret the contracts on the basis of codes, reasonableness and fairness, the common law system will give the provisions in a legal document more weight irrespective of other considerations like materiality or fairness. Common law regimes, therefore, provide more predictable results in legal documents relative to the civil law system. As the sanctity of the contract is greater in the common law system, there may be lower legal risk involved for Islamic banking instruments under this regime. Islamic contracts and transactions under the common law regime may have problems of interpretation as no precedents on these activities may exist.

To reduce legal risks arising from the absence of Islamic courts and arbitration centres, the dispute resolution clause in most international transactions usually choose English law as the preferred governing law. Doing so, however, makes the English common law dominant over the principles of *Shari'ah* with the rules of English law determining the outcome (Hamid 1998; Vogel and Hayes 1998). To avoid the problem of interpretation and enforcement of Islamic contracts, the documentation of contracts used in different products must conform to *Shariʿah* and also be prepared to enforce them under English law. A contract that elaborates all main elements of the transactions that make it Islamic will most likely be honoured in an English common law court. However, the problem in this case may be enforcement of judgments from an English court in jurisdictions where the respective national laws apply.

Organisational design and operations

Organisational and banking laws determine the type of financial institutions that can be established and the kinds of activities that can be undertaken. Conventional banking laws typically require a commercial bank to take a corporate structure and define it as a debt-based financing organisation. Accordingly, a bank is traditionally defined as 'an institution whose current operations consist in granting loans and receiving deposits from the public' (Freixas and Rochet 1999: 1). Defining banks narrowly, however, can be problematic as it omits many other functions that commercial banks perform. Furthermore, other non-bank financial institutions carry out functions performed by banks and the roles of different financial institutions evolve over time (Rose 1999).

The objective of a bank is to generate income by achieving 'an optimum combination and level of assets, liabilities, and financial risk' (Van Greuning and Bratanovic 1999). On the liability side, banks raise their funds by offering transaction (demand) and non-transaction (saving, fixed) deposits and non-deposit investment products (mutual funds, stocks, pension fund reserves, etc.).[14] Individuals, businesses, governmental bodies and institutions deposit their funds with banks for safekeeping, liquidity, access to a safe and efficient payment system and earning returns. Similarly, on the asset side, banks provide financing to households, businesses and public bodies. The household may require financing for consumption of nondurable goods and/or purchase of durable assets and businesses may need funds for working capital and/or fixed assets. When products are structured, the needs of the customer and the bank are kept in mind. For example, while an appropriate product for financing nondurable consumption may be a credit card, financing a durable asset like real estate may be structured as a mortgage-based loan.

Organisational aspects of Islamic banks will cater to both the economic aspects and compliance with the principles and objectives of *Shariʿah*. To understand the organisational and operational issues related to Islamic banking, the business operating model and assets/liabilities structure has to be examined. Whereas the former defines the diverse operational functions of different departments and units within the organisation, the latter outlines the nature of products offered by Islamic banks.

Organisational operating model

An organisation is a complex entity composed of different parts that interact to produce value (Reinertsen 1997). Being a corporation, the aim of a bank would be to ensure reasonable returns to shareholders. In case of Islamic banks, the objective of corporate governance is to fulfil the goals of shareholders by complying with the principles of *Shariʿah*. An organisational operating model shows how the operations of an organisation are organised to achieve these goals. WEF (2008) indentifies the business operating model for a financial service provider as consisting of distribution, customer and product hub, manufacturing, and enterprise functions. An organisational operating model of an Islamic bank can be presented as consisting of five main functional divisions.[15]

The first component of the business operating model is the enterprise-wide supporting functions such as finance, human resources, information technology, legal, operational risk, compliance, and so on. These diverse functions fulfil various aspects of operations and are vital to the smooth functioning of the organisation and to it fulfilling its goals.

The second constituent is the manufacturing segment that produces and delivers various products. Different departments in the bank will be involved with the initiation, delivery and maintenance of products. The operational infrastructure includes not only the delivery outlets and systems visible to the customers, but also the behind-the-scenes systems and processes that clients cannot observe (Lovelock 1984). The quality of the service depends on what the customer sees and also is affected by things they do not see.

The third aspect of the business operating model is the distribution element dealing with market access and service delivery systems. The objective of this functional division is to enhance the marketing capabilities in order to increase sales and revenues. This is done by, among other things, branding, packaging and selling products to meet the expectations of the customers.

The fourth functional unit is the customer and products hub which gathers and uses information and data to manage the customers and portfolio of products offered. The objective of the hub is to enhance customers' satisfaction by improving the efficiency of production and the efficacy of product delivery. It can also help improve business processes such as risk management practices and facilitate compliance with organisational and regulatory policies.

Islamic banks have the additional organisational function of *Shari'ah* governance. By providing *Shari'ah*-compliant products, Islamic banks are able to introduce financial services to a new segment of the population who did not deal with interest-based banks due to religious reasons (Kahf 2004b). *Shariʻah* governance plays a key role in ensuring the 'Islamic' character of Islamic finance. While the status of organisational *Shariʻah* governance will depend partly on the regulatory regimes and requirements, it's effectiveness in facilitating *Shariʻah*-compliant products will depend primarily on the SSB and Board of Directors at bank level.

Islamic banking models

Islamic banking models have implications related to the structure of the balance sheet and products offered. The models of Islamic banking have evolved over time. When Islamic banking was mooted in the 1970s, it was envisaged to be a 'two-tier *mudarabah* model', whereby profit-loss sharing modes of financing would be used on both the asset and liability sides. The Islamic bank was expected to invest in productive projects on a profit-loss sharing basis on the asset side using *mudarabah* and *musharakah* contracts. On the liability side, the demand deposits would take the format of interest-free loans (*qard-hasan*) and savings and investment deposits would take the form of profit-sharing investment accounts (PSIA) using the *mudarabah* concept. The balance sheet of the ideal two-tier *mudarabah* Islamic banking model is shown in Table 3.1.

Proponents of Islamic banking pointed out that a system based on a two-tier *mudarabah* banking model would fulfil the overall objectives of *Shariʻah* and achieve growth, equity and stability. They asserted that using profit-loss sharing modes of financing would result in increased investment, allocative efficiency, equity and reduction of poverty.[16] Furthermore, risk-sharing investment deposits on the liability side would make the Islamic banks more stable as these would absorb the negative shocks of the asset side protecting the net worth of the bank.[17]

Table 3.1 *Balance sheet of the two-tier* mudarabah *model*

Assets	Liabilities and equity
Mudarabah/musharakah financing	Profit-sharing investment accounts (PSIA; *Mudarabah* based) Demand deposits (*qard hasan*) Capital

When Islamic banks were established, they used the organisational models of conventional commercial banks. As pointed out in Chapter 1, professionals from conventional banks and *Shari'ah* scholars played dominant roles in the operations of Islamic banks. While Islamic banks initially attempted to implement the two-tier *mudarabah* model, they gradually moved towards debt-like sale-based modes of financing like *murabahah* and *ijarah* on the asset side. Various other reasons such as the moral hazard problem, minimising risks, ensuring a certain return, and so on are given to explain the use of fixed-income instruments instead of profit-loss sharing modes.[18]

On the liability side, Islamic banks created two reserves to smooth returns of PSIA in order to avoid withdrawal risks. The first is the Profit Equalising Reserve (PER) created by deducting an amount from gross income to smooth the returns of shareholders and investment account holders. Another amount was appropriated from the income of PSIA depositors only to create the Investment Risk Reserve (IRR) to meet future losses on investments financed by the investment deposits (IFSB 2005b). These changes in practice of Islamic banking, sometimes referred to as *murabahah* syndrome, resulted in the second-best model in the form of the 'one-tier *mudarabah* with multiple investment tools'. The structure of the balance sheet of this model is shown in Table 3.2.

Table 3.2 *Balance sheet of the one-tier* mudarabah *with multiple investment tools model*

Assets	Liabilities and equity
Murabahah	*PSIA-Mudarabah* based
Ijarah	Demand deposits (*Qard hasan*)
Istisna	Reserves
Mudarabah/Musharakah, etc.	Capital

As Islamic finance expanded over time, the main focus of the Islamic financial industry became providing *Shari'ah*-compliant versions of conventional products. While financial engineers and lawyers devised the products, the role of *Shari'ah* scholars became dealing with the technicalities of individual transactions and approving their compatibility with *Shari'ah* and *fiqh*. In so doing, the practice of Islamic banking and finance gradually moved towards conventional banking products and practices over the years.[19] One product introduced by Islamic banks in the GCC region is organised *tawarruq*, whereby synthetic loans resembling interest-based debt are created by buying/selling commodities.[20] *Tawarruq* was also used on the liabilities side, thereby giving investment depositors a fixed return that had no links to returns on the assets side. Delinking the liability side returns from the asset side has compromised the stability feature of Islamic banks and brought the practice of Islamic banking closer to their conventional counterparts. The result is the third-best Islamic banking model of 'fixed-income liability with multiple investment tools' dominated by *tawarruq*. The balance sheet of the third-best '*tawarruq* syndrome' model is shown in Table 3.3.

Table 3.4 shows the diversity of the banking practices on the asset side in different countries. The numbers show the

Table 3.3 *Balance sheet of the fixed-income liability with multiple investment tools model*

Assets	Liabilities and equity
Tawarruq	Fixed-income investment
Murabahah	accounts (*tawarruq*)
Ijarah	Demand deposits (*Qard hasan*)
Istisna	Reserves
Mudarabah/Musharakah, etc.	Capital

dominance of *murabahah* in all countries, except Jordan and Saudi Arabia. In all countries, except Sudan, equity-based modes constitute a small percentage of the total financing. 'Others' indicates non-traditional modes used for financing. While the General Council for Islamic Banks and Financial Institutions (CIBAFI) takes 'Others' to include 'RE, bai-muajjal, etc.,' one significant component of it is *tawarruq* in some countries. For example, a large percentage of 'Others' financing in Saudi Arabia is *tawarruq*-based products. One of the key factors that can explain the diversity of modes in different countries is the overall institutional regime in general and the *Shari'ah* governance regime in particular.

Products

The primary function of a financial system is to 'facilitate the allocation and deployment of economic resources, both spatially and across time, in an uncertain environment' (Merton 1992: 12). Financial institutions perform these functions by providing various products and services. To understand the intricacy of product development in financial institutions, the nature of the products offered need to be scrutinised. Easingwood (1986), Cooper and de Brentani (1991) and Vermeulen and Raab (2007) identify the following features of the products provided by financial institutions.

Table 3.4 Modes of financing in selected countries

Modes	Sudan	Pakistan	Bahrain	UAE	Malaysia	Jordan	Saudi Arabia
Murabahah	42.45	50.96	51.73	49.29	41.04	15.41	15.81
Musharakah	17.77	2.52	0.89	2.59	0.24	2.99	0.65
Mudarabah	3.10	–	1.96	4.36	0.27	11.36	0.05
Ijarah	0.87	20.41	5.56	18.90	9.40	13.8	0.04
Istisna	0.95	–	0.63	3.22	1.72	1.2	3.74
Salam	0.55	0.23	–	–	–	–	–
Others	34.31	25.88	39.23	21.65	47.33	55.25	79.71

Source: CIBAFI (2007) Islamic Finance Directory.

- *Intangibility*. Unlike physical products, services are intangible. Due to their intangibility, defining new service sector products becomes vague (de Brentani 1993). This is because customers cannot observe, touch or feel a service before buying it and can experience it only after being exposed to it. In introducing new products, marketing plans of banks need to help clients comprehend the distinguishing features. Cooper and Edgett (1999: 19) and de Brentani (1991) identify various difficulties and risks that can result due to the intangibility feature of services. Difficulties include conducting research, having a prototype for market-testing, determining the actual cost of the service and measuring success. Risks that can arise are disorganised development, ease of duplication by competitors, confusing the customer with information overload and excessive new services.

- *Simultaneity*. Services have the feature of simultaneity of production and consumption and may involve interaction with the client. Simultaneous production and consumption has implications regarding development of the product. Shostack (1982) indicates that this feature may require more input from various functional specialities in developing services compared to that of physical products. Cooper and Edgett (1999: 19) identify the requirement of a higher level of customer input in developing new products. The delivery system of the product becomes very important as it ultimately would determine the quality of the product. Service processes need to be clearly delineated. Thus marketing of the product is not only towards the client, but also towards personnel in the bank who directly deal with the clients (de Brentani 1991, 1993; Easingwood 1986).

- *Heterogeneity*. Services are not just processes, but also human interactions (Lovelock 1984). As products sold by financial institutions depend on the individuals serving the clients along with the supporting delivery infrastructure, there will be variability of services for different clients. In terms of product development, heterogeneity makes it difficult to test concepts while developing products (Cooper and Edgett 1999). Whereas service variability may have some advantages of customising products according to the needs of the clients, it can also introduce lack of consistency and risks of degrading the services (de Brentani 1991). This would require careful monitoring of the delivery structure and system so that the quality of service remains within tolerable limits. Easingwood and Mahajan (1989) suggest training the contact personnel, packing the services and industrialising the service production system to improve the quality of the product.

- *Perishability.* Services cannot be stored and are perishable as they are produced while consumed. This can cause difficulty in managing supply to meet the demand over the business cycle (de Brentani 1991). When demand for a service is less than the supply potential, the resources used in the delivery system remain unutilised. Similarly, when the demand is higher than the capacity of the delivery system, it not only becomes difficult to serve many clients but also to retain the quality of service. The feature of perishability requires planning on making the delivery and marketing system more flexible to meet the various demand needs.

Anatomy of a product

Financial products create intricate and sometimes long relationships between a bank and its clients. Due to the nature of these relationships, a product requires initiation, maintenance and termination. Though the client deals with an official of the bank, many other departments of the bank may be involved at different stages of the product tenure (such as IT systems, risk, legal, accounts, etc.). An example of initiation of a simple financing with front-end and back-end activities is shown in Table 3.5.

To understand how *Shari'ah* requirements fit at the product level, in-depth features of products need to be examined. Islamic banking products can be classified at different levels based on the balance sheet entries, functions or purpose, modes of financing, market segment served and responsible business segment. The different levels of product structure are identified in Table 3.6 and discussed below.

At the first level, products can be broadly identified as assets, liabilities and off-balance-sheet items. While liabilities represent sources of funds, assets show the use of funds and off-balance-sheet items indicate the activities that generate fee-based income.

Within these broad categories, the second level of different product classes can be identified according to the functions they perform. The functions that the financial sector performs are many. Merton and Bodie (1995) identify the functions provided by a financial system as clearing and settling payments (to facilitate trade), pooling of resources, transfer of economic resources, managing risk, proving price information, and dealing with incentive problems. Levine (1997: 689) identifies the functions of a financial system that relate to economic growth as 'the trading of risk, allocating capital, monitoring managers, mobilizing savings, and easing the trading of goods'. Similarly, BIS (1986) recognise functions of the financial sector as transfer of risks (price and credit), enhancement of liquidity, and generation of funds to support enterprises (through credit and equity). From the above discussions, the main functions that a bank performs would be mobilising savings,

Table 3.5 *Steps in the initiation of a financing product*

Front end (experienced by client)	Back end (not seen by client)
1. Customer fills form with staff at branch.	
	2. Relevant department (operations) checks the status of client and creates a file.
	3. File sent to processing centre and identity and documents cross-checked.
	4. Approving committee makes a decision (depending on the amount may need different levels of approval).
	5. Approval and letter of offer sent to the branch.
6. Acceptance of letter of offer by client.	
7. Client asked to sign documents with relevant people (lawyer, valuer, developer, etc.).	7a. Legal department of the bank deals with the contracts and legal documents.
8. Upon acceptance, an account created for disbursement.	
	9. Relevant department (Credit Administration) handles the disbursement, collection and documentation.
	IT System maintains the records of the transactions during the transaction period

Table 3.6 *Levels of product structure*

Levels	Type	Examples
1	Balance sheet entry	Assets, liability, off-balance-sheet items
2	Function	Mobilising savings, allocating capital, mitigating and trading risks, clearing and settling payments (to facilitate trade), etc.
3	Market segment	Affluent, middle-class, poor
4	Purpose/need	Essential (demand deposits, savings deposit, real estate financing, working capital financing), complementary (cash reserve and risk management needs) and embellishments (risk and tax protection, etc.)
5	Legal mode	*Murabahah, ijarah, salam, istisna, mudarabah, musharakah*, etc.
6	Brand/ programme	A specific brand name or programme name, such as Amana Mutual Fund, Taysir account, etc.
7	Business department	Retail, consumer, corporate, etc.

allocating capital, clearing and settling payments (to facilitate trade) and providing price information. For example, products under capital allocation would be financing real estate, transport, working capital, trade, credit cards, and so on. Similarly, under liabilities mobilising savings will include products such as demand deposits (for liquidity and safe keeping), short-term savings (saving deposits) or long-term savings (time deposits).

The third level of identifying product type is the target market segment. There are two aspects to market segments relevant to Islamic financial institutions. The first is the sector-based screening that will weed out involvement in prohibited products and activities such as alcohol, interest-based financial institutions, gambling, pornography, and so on. The second aspect of market segmentation relates to classification of the clients. One way to do this would be to classify clients according to their net worth or income. Accordingly, the relevant market segments for the household sector can be identified as the affluent, the middle-class and the poor, and for the business sector as large, medium and small/micro. Note that the risk features of the product targeted to the poor and micro-enterprises will not be similar to those targeted for the affluent and large corporations. As a result, products targeted to different market segments will require different risk mitigating approaches.

The fourth feature would be the purpose or need that the product satisfies. Closely linked to the market segment, the product structure has to suit the financial needs of the target population. The hierarchy of financial needs indicates the purpose served by different products. There are different ways in which financial needs can be categorised. Maslow (1954) distinguishes between lower-level and higher-level needs, with people seeking to fulfil the higher needs only after the former are satisfied.[21] Similarly, Xiao and Anderson (1997) identify three levels of need, survival, security and growth. As income increases, the demand for security- and growth-related needs increases. Harrison (1994) and Kamakura *et al.* (1991) put forward the five levels of a financial needs hierarchy as foundation products, emergency cash reserves, risk management, growth to offset inflation, and risk and tax protection.

From an Islamic perspective, the hierarchy of needs can be discussed in terms of different levels of *maqasid al Shari'ah* discussed in Chapter 2. Social welfare can be enhanced by promoting the essentials (*dururiyyat*), the complementary requirements (*hajiyyat*) and the beautifications or embellishments (*tahsiniyat*). The classical classification of needs can be converted into three types of financial products and services in line with the classification provided by Xiao and Anderson (1997). First, the necessities would be the *survival* products that satisfy basic needs. The products included would be different kinds of deposits (checking and savings), mortgage and financing required for essential activities/items, and so on. Second, *security* or complementary products would satisfy additional needs beyond the necessity level. These products would satisfy cash reserve and risk management needs and include insurance, pension plans, endowments and time deposits. Finally, *growth* or higher level needs will be satisfied with ameliorable products that can offset inflation and protect against risk and taxes. The products under this category would include investment in stocks, mutual funds, tax-protected bonds, real estate, and so on.

Once the product function and purpose are established, the next level would be to identify an appropriate Islamic contract or mode. Different Islamic contracts can be used for a single transaction. For example, real estate financing can be done using *murabahah, ijarah*, diminishing *musharakah* and *istisna* modes. The choice of the appropriate mode will depend on a variety of factors including the risks involved. After the mode of financing is determined, the final level will be to identify the appropriate programme or brand name under which the product is sold.

The relevant business department that will sell the product also needs to be identified. Business departments can be categorised in different ways such as retail, corporate, trade, wealth management, treasury, and so on. The nature of products will also depend on which business department uses the product. For example, a retail product cannot be customised to satisfy the preferences of each customer as it will be too costly and time consuming (Machauer and

Morgner 2001). Thus, while the retail department usually uses standardised products for all clients, the corporate sector will use standardised products with the flexibility to change features to meet the needs of specific clients. For treasury department and project financing, each transaction can be unique and structured without delay for quick implementation. The focus of this book will be mainly on standardised products that can be used by the retail and corporate departments.

Risks in Islamic banking

As pointed out above, a key function of all financial institutions including banks is to manage the risks associated with financing (Allen and Santomero 1997; Heffernan 1996; Scholtens and van Wensveen 2000). Risks are classified in different ways. One broad classification is that of business and financial risks. While business risk arises from the nature of a firm's operations and is mainly affected by the product market variables, financial risk occurs due to movements in the financial market variables. The latter risk is usually associated with leverage and the danger that obligations and liabilities cannot be met with current assets.[22] Specific risks that financial institutions face are, among others, credit risk, liquidity risk, operational risk, market risk and legal risk.[23] Note that while the former three risks are endogenous in the sense that they arise from within the organisation and depend, to a large extent, on how the business of the institution is managed, the latter two risks are exogenous as they originate externally.

Other than the risks found in conventional banks, there are some unique risks arising from the nature of assets and liabilities of Islamic banks. A variable rate of return on saving/investment deposits introduces uncertainty regarding the real value of deposits. Asset preservation in terms of mini-mising the risk of loss due to a lower rate of return may be an important factor in depositors' withdrawal decisions. From the bank's perspective, this introduces a 'withdrawal risk' that is linked to the lower rate of return relative to other financial institutions. A lower rate of return than the market can also introduce fiduciary risk, when depositors/investors interpret a low rate of return as breaching of investment contract or mismanagement of funds by the bank (AAOIFI 1999). Fiduciary risk can be caused by breach of contract by the Islamic bank. For example, the bank may not be able to fully comply with the *Shari'ah* requirements of various contracts. As the *raison d'être* of the Islamic banks' busi-ness is compliance with the *Shari'ah*, an inability to do so or not doing so wilfully can cause a serious confidence prob-lem and deposit withdrawal. Displaced commercial risk is the transfer of the risk associated with deposits to equity holders. This arises when under commercial pressure banks forgo a part of the profit to pay the depositors to prevent withdrawals due to a lower return (AAOIFI 1999).

Risks in financial products

A successful product is one that minimises the risks associ-ated with the product and operational risks arising in its delivery. Some of the risks involved with Islamic modes of financing are presented here. While the main concern in interest-based loans is credit risk, risks in Islamic financial products are more complex. As these instruments are either equity- or sale-based, they involve market risks along with credit risks. Furthermore, risks in different products evolve and change from one to another at different stages of the transaction. In sale-based products, credit risk would take the form of settlement/payment risk depending on whether the debt created is in the form of commodity/asset (e.g. in a *salam* or *istisna* contract) or money (e.g. in a *murabahah* or *bai-muajjal* contract). The non-performance can be due to external systematic sources. In the case of profit-sharing modes of financing (like *mudarabah* and *musharakah*) the credit risk will take place as counter-party risk and can occur with the non-payment of the due share of the bank by the entrepreneur.

Market risks can be systematic, arising from macro sources, or unsystematic, related to specific asset/commodity. Thus, whereas currency and stock market risks would fall under the systematic category, changes in the price of the commodity or asset the bank is dealing with will fall under specific market risk. Systematic risk also arises from changes in market interest rates as Islamic banks use a benchmark interest rate to price different financial products. Market risks arise from changes in the benchmark rate as the mark-up rates on fixed-income products cannot be adjusted accordingly.

In structuring products, all the risks affecting products need to be understood and mitigated. The bank can mitigate the risks and protect itself by imposing some covenants or restrictions on certain clients' activities that threaten the repayment of the bank's funds. A well-structured product will also include the course of action in cases where the debtor faces problems in payments. To understand the risks involved in Islamic financial products, the product is observed at three stages: beginning of transaction, transaction period and conclusion of transaction. The risks at different stages of transaction for some of the modes of financing are outlined below.

Murabahah

Murabahah is a sale contract that indicates the rate of profit or percentage mark-up. The financial institution buys the good and sells it simultaneously to the client at a mark-up. The financial institution must sign separate contracts with the supplier and buyer for the transaction to be valid. Furthermore, before entering the sale contract, the bank (seller) must own and possess the good. The profit rate (mark-up) along with other details like quantity and quality of the good, the terms of payments, and so on should be specified in the contract. The bills of trade resulting from a *murabahah* transaction cannot be traded at discount but transferred at face value. *Murabahah* are usually short-term instruments with tenor of one year or less. The various financial risks involved in different stages of the transaction in the case of a *murabahah* transaction are discussed below:

- *Beginning of transaction.* The Islamic bank buys the asset based on a promise from the buyer. If the promise is not binding, then the Islamic bank may get stuck with the asset and be exposed to market risk as the price of the good can change when disposing it off. Furthermore, any loss arising from damage of the good before its delivery to the buyer has to be borne by the bank. To eliminate the market risk, Islamic banks usually make the promise binding on the buyer.[24]
- *Transaction period.* Once the good is delivered to the buyer, the Islamic bank faces credit risk. To reduce this risk, the bank can ask for guarantees and collateral in case the debtor defaults on payments. In case of delinquency, the bank can foreclose on the collateral or go to court, but may not increase the outstanding debt.
- *Conclusion of transaction.* If the payment is made, the Islamic bank gets it due cash and there are no further risks.

Istisna

Istisna is a commissioned manufacture of a non-generic object. It takes the form of a pre-production sale contract used when an item/equipment/building/project needs to be constructed, manufactured or assembled according to specification. The bank makes the item available (by getting it manufactured/constructed/assembled) and sells it to the client by adding a profit margin. The quality and quantity of the good sold and its price should be known fully at the time of the contract. The price of the good can be paid at the time of the contract, at the time of delivery or any time afterwards by lump sum or instalments. The seller (i.e. the bank) of the good can either manufacture it or subcontract it to others. The latter would be in the form of a parallel *istisna*. The seller (bank) is liable if the goods delivered are not according to specifications or there are hidden defects. The contract may, however, specify that such claims may be made against the subcontractor, but the seller must remain guarantor in case the subcontractor does not conform. *Istisna* is usually a medium to long-term contract.

- *Beginning of transaction.* After the Islamic bank commits to the contract, it has to select sub-contractors who can construct/manufacture the asset/good.
- *Transaction period.* As *istisna* involves constructing/ manufacturing and payments made in instalments during the transaction period, the Islamic bank faces market risks and counter-party and/or credit risk. The former can arise if the cost of production increases and the latter if the buyer either declines to accept the asset/ good or defaults on payments.
- *Conclusion of transaction.* In cases where the asset/good is delivered and the payments received, there are no other risks.

The banks usually sub-contract the *istisna* transaction into a parallel *istisna*. This is done mainly because the Islamic bank is not in the business of manufacturing/building and to mitigate the market risk arising from higher costs of production. A parallel *istisna*, however, creates other risks if the supplier fails to deliver the asset or delivers one that is not according to specification. This increases the counter-party risk at the conclusion of the contract.

Ijarah

Ijarah (operating lease) constitutes the sale of the usufructs rights of durable goods/assets. The owner of the asset gets lease payment or rent periodically as long as the lessee can use the usufructs. An *ijarah* contract is similar to that of operating lease in which the ownership of the asset does not get transferred to the lessee. While the lease contract must specify who pays the maintenance costs, the costs arising from accidental damage or total loss of the asset are borne by the owner. The ownership of a leased asset can be sold to a third party, including the lessee. In case of the third party, the lease contract can also be transferred to the new owner. Unless the contract explicitly prohibits sub-leasing, the lessee can sub-lease the asset to a third party at a rental rate that may be higher/lower than rental paid by the lessee.

Ijarah wa Iqtina (hire-purchase) is a leasing contract in which the ownership of the asset is transferred to the lessee at the end of the contract. The instalments amortise rent and a part of the capital. At the end of the lease period, the lessee has an option of purchasing the asset at either the market price or a price specified in advance in the contract. Scholars (*fuqaha*) have objections to financial lease. They contend that the purchase contract cannot be binding, but optional, at the beginning of the sale contract. Furthermore, the price of the sale of the asset cannot be fixed in advance but should be market determined at the time of the sale as it will depend on the quality of the good which is unknown at the beginning of the lease contract. Islamic banks have resolved this issue either by giving away the asset at a nominal value or as a gift at the end of the lease period. One implication of a pure financial lease is that it is a sale contract with deferred payments. Thus the lease payments constitute debt payments, and can be sold or transferred at face value only. *Ijarah* contracts can have tenors of short, medium or long terms.

- *Beginning of transaction.* If the asset is not leased (in a non-binding contract) then the Islamic bank faces market risk in disposing of the asset. This will not be the so in the case of binding lease.
- *Transaction period.* There is a credit risk in terms of non-payment of rental instalments by the counter-party.
- *Conclusion of transaction* In case of *ijarah* (or operational lease), an Islamic bank has to deal with the market risk related to the residual value of the asset. No market risk exists with *ijarah wa iqtinah* as the asset is transferred to the lessee at the end of the contract period.

Mudarabah

Mudarabah is a form of partnership to which some of the partners only contribute capital (*rab-ul mal*) and the other partners (*mudarib*) provide labour. *Mudarabah* is a principal–agent relationship, the financier (*rab-ul-mal*) is a sleeping partner and does not interfere in the management of the firm. The *mudarib* or manager as an agent manages the project with the objective of earning profits. Profit is shared among the parties at an agreed-upon ratio and explicitly specified in the *mudarabah* agreement. A variable of escalating share of profit that is dependent on the level of profit achieved is permissible (ElGari 2002). The financier cannot ask for a guarantee of the capital nor claim a fixed amount of profit or percentage of capital. The financier, however, can ask for guarantees for losses arising from negligence and mismanagement of the project by the *mudarib*.

Mudarabah can be restricted or unrestricted (Chapra 2001). Under unrestricted *mudarabah*, the funds are provided to the *mudarib* without any conditions related to the type, place, timing or the people with whom the business will be undertaken. In restricted *mudarabah*, the *rab-ul-mal* has a right to specify the terms and conditions of the use of capital but cannot intervene in the management of the *mudarabah*. If the conditions of the *mudarabah* are violated, it will constitute a failing in the fiduciary duties and the manager will be responsible for any losses arising from it. *Mudarabah* contracts usually have short- to medium-term tenors.

- *Beginning of transaction.* Adverse selection problem and banks' existing competencies in project evaluation and related techniques are limited.
- *Transaction period.* The counter-party risk arising from an information asymmetry problem is expected to be high under this mode. The counter-party risk includes misreporting of profit by the manager.
- *Conclusion of transaction.* The counter-party risk of untruthful reporting of profit exists.

Musharakah

Musharakah is a partnership in which all partners contribute both capital and labour. The main difference with *mudarabah* is that in *musharakah* all the partners are entitled to participate in the management of the project. The profit share may be different for different partners depending on their involvement in the project and the capital contributed. Like the *mudarabah*, a variable profit share that depends on the level of profits is allowed. The tenor of *musharakah* is usually long term (three years or more).

- *Beginning of transaction* Adverse selection and the banks' existing competencies in project evaluation and related techniques are limited.
- *Transaction period.* The counter-party risk due to moral hazard and information asymmetry problems is expected to be high under this mode. The counter-party risk exists in the form of the manager not reporting the actual profit generated.
- *Conclusion of transaction.* Depending on the asset type, counter-party and market risk may exist. If the investment is in physical assets (e.g. *musharakah* with *ijarah* sub-contract or *musharakah* with *murabahah* sub-contract) then the bank will face asset-price risk and/or counter-party risks.

The products offered by different Islamic banks will depend on the legal and regulatory environment on the one hand and the organisational format and skills of different business units within an organisation on the other. Given the overall formal rules in the institutional environment and the organisational structures, development of new products will depend on how a bank's strategic goals relate to innovation and the availability of different resources including human capital to meet the goals. The details of product development processes in banks are detailed in the following chapters.

Notes

1. This definition conforms to the view of new institutional economics. See North (1991, 1994) and Williamson (2000) for a discussion on new institutional perspectives.

2. Note that with the exception of contract law, no exhaustive Islamic laws related to organisation, banking and taxation exist for contemporary times. While Islamic law has concepts of partnerships, these essentially fall under the ambit of contract law not organisational law. Islamic law has rules related to taxes and levies, but does not have detailed regulation related to corporate income, transactions, and goods and services.

3. While the personal law in most Muslim countries is still Islamic, the commercial laws are either common law or civil law based.

4. Note that International Accounting Standards require accounting to be reported in terms of economic substance and not the legal format (Sultan 2006: 24).

5. The interpretative letter by OCC for *ijarah* (leasing) is no. 806 issued in December 1997 and the one for *murabahah* is no. 867 issued in November 1999.

6. Malaysia has an Islamic money-market where the liquidity needs of Islamic banks can be met to some extent. But this model cannot be replicated in other jurisdictions due to *Shari'ah*-related issues.

7. Chapra and Ahmed (2002) report that a survey shows that 381 (or 81.4%) 468 depositors from Bahrain, Bangladesh and Sudan will move funds to other banks due to non-compliance of *Shari'ah* and a total of 328 (70%) would move funds if they learnt that the income of the banks came from interest earnings.

8. Issues related to *Shari'ah* governance are discussed in a later section.

9. For IFSB risk management and capital adequacy standards, see IFSB (2005a, 2005b).

10. For details of these risks, see Khan and Ahmed (2001).

11. A survey of depositors in Islamic banks confirms this. See Chapra and Ahmed (2002) for the survey.

12. I am grateful to Dr Abbas Mirakhor who provided me with the information on the system in Iran.

13. Note that even though an NSA may not exist, an Islamic bank may still have to get their new products approved by the regulatory authorities. The regulatory authorities check the risk features of the product before approving it and not the *Shari'ah*-related issues.

14. For details, see Rose (1999, ch. 12).

15. The first four elements of the business operating model are similar to the ones identified in WEF (2007).

16. The advantages of Islamic banking are discussed in Chapra (1985), Khan (1995) and Siddiqi (1981, 1983).

17. Gangopadhyay and Singh (2000) also conclude that linking the return on liabilities to return on assets brings stability and can avoid bank runs.

18. In a survey of 23 banks, Khalil *et al.* (2002) found that misreporting the outcome by the agent is the prime reason that prevents banks from adopting *mudarabah* financing contracts.

19. For a review of the current state of Islamic finance, see Siddiqi (2006b).

20. As pointed out in Chapter 2, *tawarruq* involves buying a commodity on the spot and selling it with a mark-up with payment due at a future date. The buyer in turn sells the commodity spot and gets cash.

21. Maslow's hierarchy of human needs is further classified into physiological, safety and security, love and belonging, esteem and self-actualisation (Oleson 2004).

22. For a discussion on business and financial risks see Jorion and Khoury (1996: 2) and Gleason (2000: 21).

23. See Koch (1995) and Heffernan (1996) for a discussion on the different types of risks that financial institutions face.

24. As discussed in Chapter 2, the Islamic *Fiqh* Academy (decision 2 and 3, fifth session, 1988) makes a promise legally binding on the promisor in a *murabahah* sale if the promisee incurs expenses as a result of the promise.

CHAPTER 4
INNOVATION AND PRODUCT DEVELOPMENT: STRATEGY, STRUCTURE AND PROCESS

Innovation can be viewed as firms' response and adaptation to the changing conditions of markets and the environment. In a marketplace that is constantly evolving, firms that do not innovate and come up with new products can eventually 'languish and die' (Fuller 2005: 1). Two broad categories of factors affecting financial product innovations can be identified. The first is the institutional environment under which financial firms operate. This would include international factors such as increased globalisation, risk and technological shocks, and national factors like the legal and regulatory regimes. Among the important determinants of innovation is the 'institutional architecture' that can include supportive public laws, regulations, and institutions that facilitate constructive product development (PD). The second broad category affecting innovation relates to organisational aspects. Some of the organisational factors relevant to innovation in financial institutions are examined next.

PD is driven by strategic directions, growth strategy, future business directions and market conditions. Given the legal and regulatory environment, growth potentials in markets and the orientation of banks towards innovation will determine their PD systems. Miles and Snow (2003) suggest that the way in which an organisation can cope with new situations depends on how three organisational problems are resolved: entrepreneurial, engineering and administrative. The entrepreneurial problem is to identify the product-market domain the organisation would participate in. The top management performs the entrepreneurial function by identifying the preferred markets the bank will operate in and the products it will offer. The engineering problem makes material the entrepreneurial problem by providing resources and suitable technology for developing and producing the product. The administrative problem is solved by creating processes and procedures to ensure efficient delivery of the product. While a major objective of the administrative problem is to reduce risks, it also entails processes allowing firms to adapt and evolve to meet challenges arising from changing environments.

The three problems identified above can be used to define the building blocks of a PD system within an organisation. Whereas the entrepreneurial problem relates to overall strategy and goals, the technological problem is associated with the structures in place that facilitate the development of products. The administrative problem deals with the PD processes and procedures. Developing successful products would require a strategic intent that is implemented by an enabling organisational structure, adequate resources and efficient processes. Different aspects of strategy, structure and processes related to developing new products are discussed below.

Strategy and plans

The importance of PD within a firm is reflected in its overall vision of how it wants to position itself in the future.

Firms that recognise the changing nature of the markets understand the need to adjust to be relevant in the future. These firms will have innovation as an integral component of their mission and strategic goals. After the strategic goals are set, they are implemented by using operational plans. Aspects of strategic intent and plans to implement them are discussed below.

Strategic positioning

The strategy of a bank provides the guiding framework of how its visions and mission can be achieved. Guided by the Board of Directors (BOD), the senior management of the bank anticipates future directions and prepares the overall business strategy. A bank's strategic focus and priorities related to innovation will depend on the markets it seeks to move into and its risk-return appetite. In larger firms, the PD system may be more formalised and these firms can participate in riskier ventures. Other banks may not want to go into new products as they entail risks and opt to be followers in the market.

Strategic positioning of organisations can be of various types. Ansoff (1965) provides four strategic choices that a firm can make in the product-market dimension. The first is a passive approach of *market penetration* whereby a larger volume of a current product is sold in the existing market to increase the market share. In the strategy of *product development* new products are introduced in the current markets to replace existing products. In the *market development* strategy, a firm seeks newer markets for existing products. Finally, in the strategy of *diversification* firms explore new markets for new products.

Miles and Snow (2003) provide another classification of strategic approaches that firms may adopt. They classify organisations as prospectors, analysers, defenders and reactors. Prospector organisations continuously explore new product and market opportunities. Analysers operate in two product-market domains, one stable and the other that evolves. While the products in the stable market segment do not change, new products are introduced in the evolving market mainly by following the prospectors. Defenders have niche product-market domains which they protect. As these firms have relatively stable markets they rarely change. Reactors are slow in responding to changing environments due to static strategic outlook and rigid organisational structures.

Strategy and operational plans

After innovation is incorporated as a part of the overall strategy, the bank has to identify the business opportunities it plans to exploit. From the corporate strategy, a PD strategy that aligns the portfolio of products with the company's strategic intent has to be developed. The PD strategy would determine the product portfolio needed to serve these segments. This will include identifying the types of products to be developed and general features of the products to be introduced. Specifically, under the broad classifications of banking practices of retail and corporate divisions, there will be further segmentations according to income/revenue of clients, industrial sectors, and so on.

Implementing the product strategy would require transformation of goals into operational plans. Once the appropriate market segments of the bank are successfully identified in the strategy, the specific products that meet the needs of these groups can then be detailed. The corporate plan will include a PD plan that outlines goals for the number and types of products to be developed. This plan will specify the budget and expected revenue targets for new products. New products should appear in annual

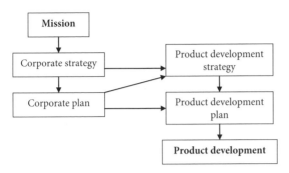

Figure 4.1 *Linking products to corporate mission and strategy*

operational plans of the PD unit/department and all relevant business units. The position of PD in the overall corporate and PD strategy and plans are shown in Figure 4.1.

The strategy of Islamic banks will be qualitatively different from conventional banks in one respect. In conventional banks the objective of PD is economic or profit maximisation (Reinertsen 1997: 10). While Islamic banks also have economic goals, these are achieved by offering products that are within the ambit of Islamic principles and values derived from the Islamic worldview. Ideally the products would not only comply with legal requirements, but also the ethical and social values of Islamic law. Sometimes *Shariʿah* requirements may be costlier and riskier and economic considerations may incline banks to move towards products that compromise on *Shariʿah* requirements. The banks have to decide at the level of overall mission and vision whether the products will strictly comply with *Shariʿah* requirements.

Structure and resources

PD is a multifaceted process involving input from various departments of an organisation. Completion of any PD project requires distribution of authority and responsibilities to various departments of the bank. As such, the efficiency with which a project can be completed will depend on the interactions, communication and coordination among the relevant departments. The structure of the organisation and the resources provided determine the speed and efficiency of developing new products. These aspects are discussed next.

Organisational structures

Organisational functions are distributed in different departments of a firm. Ulrich and Eppenger (2008) and Vermeulen and Raab (2007) discuss the implications of different types of organisational formats related to PD. The structure of an organisation can be based on function and/or project linkages. Function relates to knowledge and skills in some specific area, like marketing, accounting, research and development, and so on. Projects use different functions to achieve certain goals, which in the case of PD would be to introduce new products.

In a *functional* organisation, units are formed according to specific functions and members from these functional groups are assigned to different projects. Managers of functional units are responsible for their respective budget and employees. In developing products, the functional manager coordinates the process by getting the necessary input from other functional units. While functional structure introduces efficiency at the functional level, it can also introduce problems of cross-functional communication that can slow down the PD process (Reinertsen 1997). In a *project* organisation, experts with different functional skills work on a particular project. The people working on the project report to the project manager. A PD project would have members representing different functions and the manager drives the team to complete the product within the stipulated budget and timeframe. The problem with a project organisation is that personnel may be used below optimal levels during cycles of low activity on a project.

A *matrix* organisation combines elements of both functional and project organisations. However, depending on which factor dominates, there can be *heavyweight* and *lightweight* project organisations. While a heavyweight project organisation is dominated by project links, the lightweight one has stronger functional elements. In a heavyweight project structure, PD responsibilities are with the project manager who has authority over the functional managers. The project leader becomes the product champion and completes the development of products by getting the work done by different functional units. In the *lightweight* project organisation, the functional manager takes the responsibility for PD. Representatives from other functional groups assist in various stages of developing products and the project manager plays a facilitating role by communicating and coordinating activities across functional units.

Reinertsen (1997) and Vermeulen and Raab (2007) identify an *autonomous team* structure that brings people from different functional units to work on specific projects on a full-time basis. Under this structure, members from different functional departments are placed in one team under the control of a team leader. These teams, sometimes referred to as tiger teams, are given special privileges and can work under relaxed rules and procedures. The autonomous teams are more flexible and can reduce the problems of cross-functional communications that exist in functional organisations. Problems with autonomous structure include building lack of expertise along functional lines, not using all the skills of the organisation's resource pool and a narrow focus on individual projects without considering the broader organisational perspective.

The above discussion indicates that the department driving PD will depend on the organisational orientation of the banks. Whatever the structure, implementation of PD would require ownership of the process by some specific department/unit within the organisation. Owners of products are drivers of development in the pre-launch stage and ensure that the product is developed within time and budget, and ownership in the post-launch stage provides guarantee of its success. Identifying ownership of products within an organisation is an important determinant of whether products are successful (Watson 2005).

The size and location of the PD department/unit within the organisation will differ in different banks. In larger organisations a separate PD unit/department is likely to exist. While many banks have their PD unit located in the marketing department, some others report to the finance department, relevant business unit or are under the CEO. If a separate PD unit does not exist, the responsibility of developing products may be vested with some other relevant department in the organisation.

An important department/unit in Islamic banking is the *Shari'ah* organ. Depending on the size of the organisation, this may be in the form of a department or unit. Other than getting the products cleared by a *Shari'ah* board, the role of the *Shari'ah* organ is to assist in different stages of PD. Specifically, the *Shari'ah* organ would provide input in idea generation, developing products in the pre-launch stage and the *Shari'ah* audit in the post-launch phase of the product.

Resource availability and management

While PD implementation will depend on the type of organisational structure described above, it would require availability and efficient use of resources. It is expected that larger organisations will have relatively more resources for

PD and as such more projects can be undertaken simultaneously (de Brentani 1986). Resources needed for developing new products include financial, human and technological ones. While provision of financial and technological resources will depend on the strategic intent of the bank related to innovation and the funds provided by the management to back this desire, the human capital is more complex. Not only would the bank require people with the right skills, but also a structured administrative process that coordinates the implementation of various phases of PD.

PD involves input from various departments within an organisation at different steps of the process. This requires good communication and coordination of activities between various departments of the bank. Given the multi-functional nature of work required to develop products, there may be a need to have teams/committees to implement the projects. One way to resolve this problem is to have a cross-functional team with representatives from various functional units. The cross-functional team will be headed by a project or PD team leader. One key role of the team leader is to have an efficient communication between different relevant departments that provide input in developing products.

The efficiency of PD would depend on communication and coordination of the cross-functional team. This can be achieved by adopting and following a common code or procedures so that the tasks can be managed effectively in different steps. A detailed procedure would determine the time taken to do different tasks so that transparency and accountability of the tasks undertaken at different steps can ensure the completion of the development cycle on time. The roles, functions and decision-making authority of the members of PD teams or committees will determine the speed of the PD process.

Smith and Reinertsen (1998) suggest creating a core team that is responsible for developing the product. The advantages of a core team are that it does not engage members from other functional units with steps that are not relevant to their functions, thereby saving time and resources. The project leader works closely with the core team in developing the product and communicates and coordinates with other functional units when necessary. While the composition of the core team would depend on the product being developed, in the case of Islamic banks members can include representatives from PD, the relevant business unit, risk management department and the *Shari'ah* representative. It is assumed that a core team headed by a PD manager drives the different steps of the PD process described below.

Product development process

The PD process is the structured flow of activities and information required to accomplish the creation of new products (Ulrich and Eppinger 2008: 22). The process identifies the sequence of activities undertaken and the distribution of responsibilities among relevant personnel to develop new products. An important aspect of this process is to have a well-planned scheme that details the various phases and steps in each phase. This scheme acts as a roadmap to develop new products. Cooper (1994) identifies benefits of a well-planned process as introducing discipline, reducing technical risks and ensuring completion of tasks by a cross-functional team. Elements of the PD process determine the execution time and the performance of the product after launch. Edgett (1996) finds that financial institutions with rigorous PD process are more likely to produce successful products.

While there is no unique PD process that applies to all banks, many authors have suggested different elements of the process. Johne and Harborne (1985) identify three main phases of PD process: initiation, evaluation and implementation. Cooper (1994) identifies four stages: preliminary investigation, building business case, development, and test and validation. Others have pointed out more detailed steps involved in PD. Avlonitis *et al.* (2001) maintain that a PD process would involve five activities: idea generation and screening, business analysis and marketing strategy, technical development, testing, and commercialisation/launching. While Cooper and Edgett (1999) propose thirteen steps, Scheuing and Johnson (1989a, 1989b) detail fifteen different activities required for developing products in the service sector.

In a stage-gate process popularised by Cooper (1990, 1994), PD goes thorough different phases and checkpoints or gates.[1] At each gate, the product is assessed by a relevant authority and a decision of 'go/kill/hold/recycle' is made (Cooper 1994). The objective of having checkpoints after each development phase is to reduce the probability of failure. By screening good ideas and products, an organisation can reduce the costs of failed products.

Product development cycle

Given the unique nature of Islamic financial products, a PD cycle for the industry is outlined in this section. The PD cycle for Islamic banks has three broad phases: idea generation and acceptance, converting concept into product, and commercialisation. Each phase has six steps. The different steps in each of these phases of the PD cycle are shown in Figure 4.2 and discussed in detail below.

Idea generation and acceptance

The idea generation and acceptance phase is an important pre-development component of the development cycle as

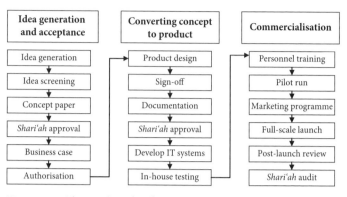

Figure 4.2 *The product development cycle*

it determines what new products will be introduced by the bank. Cooper and de Brentani (1991) show that the quality of execution of pre-development activities is a good indicator of successful products. An idea-search methodology with a formal process and system through which ideas can be stimulated, formulated and accepted is key to developing successful products (Kelly and Storey 2000). The different steps involved in identifying ideas for new products are discussed below.

A.1. Idea generation

The starting point of PD is idea generation. The search for ideas should not be ad hoc, but a continuous routine within an organisation (Bowers 1986). In firms that have instilled an innovative culture, ideas are generated continuously not just when they are needed. Sources of new ideas can be broadly classified as internal or external. Internally, ideas can be proposed by different departments. Kelly and Storey (2000) identify marketing, sales, operations, customer service, information technology, and research and development as key departments searching for new ideas. External input of ideas comes from regulatory changes, outside agencies (consultants), customers, competitors, suppliers and overseas markets.

Market research plays an important role in identifying the needs of different segments of customers, determining the potential market size and ascertaining the possible competition. For Islamic banks, competitors include both their Islamic counterparts and conventional financial institutions. Cooper *et al.* (1994) show that a market-driven PD process can come up with successful products. They find that at the idea-generation stage, this would require using sufficient resources for market research to identify the needs of the customers. Among other things, the market research identifies the segment of the market the product is targeted for and research is undertaken to test the response of customers at the product-concept stage. Another aspect that needs attention is to understand the strategy of competitors and to know what products already exist in the market.

A.2. Idea screening

The objective of screening ideas is to identify the ones that fulfil the strategic and financial goals of an organisation. While many firms may opt for informal idea screening procedures, a formal and systematic process can reduce risks and costs and enhance the success of new products (de Brentani 1986). Different quantitative and qualitative criteria can be used to screen ideas. These include fit to overall strategy, financial potential, corporate and technological/production synergy, product differential advantage, product life, and so on.

Kelly and Storey (2000) identify various idea-screening criteria used by the service sector. The highest-ranked category is financial implications of the new product. This may require examining the costs, potential turnover, likely profit, cost benefit analysis, and impact on revenue. The second group of factors relates to market considerations. Among others, market benefits, client needs, global market needs and matching competitors are important screening criteria under market considerations. To screen ideas input is also sought from various departments of the organisation, including the relevant user department, product manager and department heads. A fit with the overall corporate strategy and plan is also important. Finally, an important aspect of identifying ideas for further development would be to judge the product against the capabilities of the organisation. Capabilities for product development relate to both people and systems. The former would entail the availability of relevant personnel to develop and deliver the product and the latter would be the capacity of various systems in the organisation to convert the ideas into new products.

For Islamic products, an important aspect would be to identify the appropriate *Shari'ah*-compatible contracts that can be used for the product. To do this would require examining the pros/cons and risks/returns implications of using different contractual formats.

A.3. Development of concept paper

After an idea is selected, it is converted into a concept. The concept paper outlines the basic structure of the product, detailing the major elements, structure and processes. The objective of the concept paper is to enable the initial screening of the product concept by senior management and the *Shari'ah* board. Though presenting the *Shari'ah* structure and processes of the product is enough for the presentation to the *Shari'ah* board, the paper would include a preliminary market and business assessment, analyse the risks involved and also the feasibility of the product from a technical viewpoint. In the pre-product launch stage, the SSB can contribute to the development of new products by advising on the different *Shari'ah*-compliant structures for the product. This concept paper should be prepared by the core team, headed by the PD manager. The *Shari'ah* organ of the bank will have an important role to play in developing the concept paper.

A.4. Shari'ah *approval (concept)*

The concept paper has to be formally presented to the *Shari'ah* board for approval. The PD manager should present the paper along with the representative of the *Shari'ah* organ of the bank so that they are able to answer any queries that the members of the *Shari'ah* board may have. The SSB's role is to formally approve the product structure before it goes for full-scale development. The goal of getting the concept cleared by the *Shari'ah* board is to minimise the risks of *Shari'ah* incompatibility before developing the product.

A.5. *Business case*

Once the concept paper is approved by the SSB, a detailed business case for the product has to be prepared. The business case is the first comprehensive document that guides the development of the product in the later stages. Input from different relevant departments are sought to prepare the business case. The important issues that need examination relate to risks, legal, treasury, finance, compliance and IT.

While there can be different formats, a typical business case would start with the objective of the new product in terms of what the product is expected to achieve and highlight how it fulfils the overall strategic objectives of the bank. After describing the structure and features of the product, the business case is expected to address among others, the market and competition, resources required and expected return and profitability. The business case also would identify the target segment and customers and give reasons as to why this segment is chosen. If similar products exist in the market, the unique nature of the new product needs to be identified and reasons given as to why the product may be preferred by the clients over others. The document should also provide the basis of customers demand for the product vis-à-vis the competitors' products.

A detailed financial statement would estimate the total cost of developing and marketing the product along with the expected revenue streams. The expected number of customers, along with sales volume and expenses over the years need to be presented. To come up with the revenue stream, the pricing structure and the expected targets for sales need to be estimated for the coming periods. After the cost of the product (both development and delivery) is assessed, a break-even price/timeframe can be arrived at. Bowers (1986) identifies the three most common financial goals used by banks as profit contribution, return on investment and payback period. The business case should also have a SWOT (strengths, weaknesses, opportunities and threats) analysis, highlighting the risks and opportunities, strengths and weaknesses of the product. The expected price of the product also has to be identified keeping in mind the competition, risks and profit expectations.

The document should also outline the organisational issues related to the product. Not only should the business case provide the resource needs in terms of funds, people and technology to develop the product, it should also point out the fit or synergy of the product with the resource availability of the bank. Issues related to marketing, packaging and delivery of the product also need to be highlighted. The channels of delivery of the product and the training needed for personnel selling the product should be clearly specified. The technological requirements in terms of IT systems and processes needed to deliver the products should be pointed out.

Compliance with various internal and external rules, regulations and laws also needs to be specified. The accounting and reporting treatment of the product for regulatory purposes needs to be outlined. Similarly, the tax implications for the bank and clients, the capital adequacy requirement for the new product, has to be factored in. The business case paper will end with a budget for development and schedule for completion of the project with a date of product launch.

A.6. Authorisation

Before committing resources to develop the product, the senior management must study the business case and approve it. The management would examine, among others, the compatibility of the product with the corporate strategic goals and business plan. The head of the relevant business unit that will be responsible for selling the product should also endorse the proposed product.

Converting concept into product

Once the management authorises the development of a new product, the next phase will be to translate the concept into a product. This requires various steps that involve different departments of the bank. The specifications of the work required and the role of different departments are discussed below.

B.1. Product design and process flow

Before a product can be developed a product design with all the process flows needs to be prepared. Shostack (1984) lays out the basic framework of a product design. The first step is to prepare a blueprint for the product. To do so requires laying out the detailed steps and processes of the product.

For each step, the inputs required from different units of the bank need to be identified and the resulting output specified. Given its nature of intangibility and simultaneity, the blueprint for developing services must view a product's features from two perspectives (Lovelock 1984). It must see systems and procedures from the bank's viewpoint and also understand the service delivery system from the clients' perspectives.

The bank needs to develop detailed processes to ensure high quality delivery of the product (de Brentani 1993: 16). The time required to deliver a product is an important factor that determines the quality of a service. Thus, an important factor in designing products would be to determine the execution time required to deliver the product. To ascertain this, the approximate time for each step and process needs to be calculated to arrive at the total time required to provide the service. To minimise the operational risks associated with the product, it is important to identify the fail-points in the blueprint of the product (Shostack 1984). This would require going over each step and process trying to identify what can go wrong. After the fail-points are identified, sub-processes need to be developed to correct these. Furthermore, there has to be checks against fraud in particular products such as credit cards.

While process flows and procedures can be codified into written documents, the clients' interaction and experience with the product should not be ignored. While designing the product and building the steps and processes, it is important to examine it from the clients' perspectives. Note that the clients interact with only some of the steps/processes of the service and do not observe many steps that take place in the background. The steps not visible to the clients are, however, very important as these along with the ones that clients see together form and determine the quality of the product. An important aspect that may improve the perception of quality service is that of tangible evidence of providing the service (Shostack 1984).

B.2. Sign-off from various departments

After the product design and process flow of the product development is complete, the next step is to implement various aspects to make the product live. As mentioned, a financial product is a service that requires contact with the bank staff, but the dealings have implications for various departments of the bank. The role and implications of a new product on various departments are briefly outlined below.

2.1. *Finance.* Being responsible for the financial health of the organisation, the finance department would look into the costs and revenue from the new product (Fuller 2005: 203). Other than financial control, the finance department of a bank will also identify the financial accounting treatment of the new product. Among other things, new codes for balance sheet and general ledger entries for the new product need to be created. These will be later used by the IT department to execute the software necessary for the product.

2.2. *Treasury.* As the treasury department is responsible for the asset-liability management of the bank, it would examine the implications of the product in terms of it being a liability or an asset. While an asset will require resources for financing, a liability would generate funds that need to be placed appropriately. Considerations of the treasury department include the duration or length of the tenor and pricing of the product, the requirements for resources, implications for capital adequacy requirements, the cost of funds and the income stream of the bank.

2.3. *Risk management.* The RM department will study the various risks (credit, market, operational, liquidity, etc.) associated with the product and enquire how the risks are mitigated. The department will also examine the implications of the product on enterprise risks. If risks are identified that were not addressed by the PD team, they may ask them to come up with appropriate measures to mitigate the risks.

2.4 *Compliance.* The role of the compliance unit is to ensure that the new product fulfils all the internal rules and external regulations of the country. To guarantee that the product does not violate any laws of the country, regulatory rules or standards, the department may have to liaise with the relevant regulatory authorities and get the product cleared.

2.5. *Operations.* The operations department will be responsible for setting the necessary process flows within the organisation needed to implement the delivery of the product. The product design blueprint provides them with the guidelines of how to make the product live.

B.3. Documentation

An important component of a product's development is the preparation of various supporting documents. Two sets of documents are required: one set for use by in-house staff and the other set for the clients. These comprise the documents related to the product information, forms, terms and conditions and legal documents and contracts used by the clients, and a product description, product manual and communications related to the product for in-house use. The legal department will study the various contracts used in the transactions to ensure that these are consistent with the laws of the country. They will scrutinise the documents to ensure that the legal risks are mitigated.

For the personnel who will deal with different aspects of the product, a Product and Policy Manual that details all the issues related to the product and its operations needs to be prepared. This manual should include the policies, procedures, standards of performance, detailed process flow and operational aspects of the product (Bowers 1986). These documents can be prepared to cater to the needs of staff from different departments. For example, while a Credit Administration Manual would outline the operations and disbursement criteria a System User Guide will be used by the sales personnel at branch level.

Other important documents include Business Requirement Specifications prepared for the IT department specifying the required parameters, how to book a deal in the system, the expected output, accounting entries for the product, and so on. The document also identifies the essential and non-essential elements of the product; the former must be in place before the product launch, the latter are things that can be added later.

B.4. Shari'ah *approval (legal documents and process flow)*
After all the documents are prepared, these need to be presented to the *Shari'ah* board for review and approval. In particular, the contracts and processes through which a transaction would take place should be clearly pointed out for the board's consideration. The SSB would also review and approve the forms used in delivering the product.

B.5. *IT system development*
A major component of PD is the implementation of the associated supporting IT system. The IT system is developed according to the Business Requirement Specifications that includes requirements for both back-office support systems and the front-desk interface with clients. Furthermore, the

accounting rules and implications of the product on the balance sheet and general ledger in the bank's IT system have to be executed. The proposed remedies for dealing with different problem scenarios that can arise also need to be built into the system. For example, for a financing product, cases of default or late payment need to be built into the system.

Depending on the size, a bank may have different operating systems catering to the different needs. Usually there is a core banking system that is linked to other supporting systems such as the front-end branch system, risk management system, treasury operations, and so on. While a few IT systems are developed to handle Islamic contracts and transactions, most of these are built for conventional banking systems and adapted to Islamic finance. This anomaly can create problems for developing appropriate Islamic financial products.

B.6. In-house testing

When the systems and processes are in place there is a need to test the product in-house. Developing and testing services is more difficult than physical products. The system has to be tested to ensure that the operations follow the process flow. Before the IT department can clear the product it has to undertake Software Quality Assurance (SQA) by inviting relevant business nominees from different departments to perform the user acceptance test. Relevant business representatives should prepare test scenarios in coordination with the core team. Once the results from SQA are cleared by all business units, the IT department can sign-off the product.

Commercialisation

Once the in-house testing is done and no problem appears, the product is ready for launch. Before launching the product, the senior management should be informed and information about the product disseminated to all the relevant stakeholders. The various steps in launching the product are outlined below.

C.1. Personnel training

As the quality of the product depends on the personnel who are in direct contact with the clients, it is important to train these people to ensure the quality of product delivery. This requires training both the front-end and back-end staff. The relevant staff will include those from the branches and sales, call centres, credit administration, the legal department and *Shari'ah* department. The latter need training to conduct a *Shari'ah* audit of the product. Thus, before marketing the product to the clients, there may be a need to market the product to the front-line personnel (Bowers 1986). The product manual and other documents related to the product will be used to train the sales staff involved with the delivery of the product. Training will also include the appropriate use of the IT system for the product.

C.2. Pilot run – processes and systems

The system is tested with a few selected customers at selected branches. Real-life transactions are done with a sample of clients for a period of time to see if every thing is going as expected. The objective is to identify any problems that may arise. Once the system appears to be working without any difficulties, the pilot-run stage is complete.

C.3. Marketing programme

A marketing strategy and campaign to promote and advertise the product is an important step in developing successful products and in planning how to sell the product. The channels for product distribution have to be identified and targets set. The marketing will also involve publishing promotional materials and communications about the product for use by public relations. The brand name and features fulfilling customers' needs have to be highlighted. Depending on the budget and importance of the product, the bank may opt for a below-the-line or above-the-line option. In the former the bank will use internal channels such as brochures, banners, automated cash-machine screens, and so on. In the latter, various print and electronic media and news outlets, such as advertisements on television, newspapers and billboards, are used.

C.4. Full-scale launch

After the marketing campaign is complete and the senior management gives clearance, the product can be finally launched. While the product can be initiated by the bank quietly, a full-scale launch with fanfare is a good way to introduce new products. This can be done by having a formal launching of the product and announcing it in all types of media and through various channels to increase the awareness of the product among prospective clients.

C.5. Post-launch review

After the product has been live for a certain period, there is a need to review its different dimensions through feedback from staff, IT systems and customers. The performance of products can be assessed by both financial and non-financial criteria (Avlonitis *et al.* 2001). The performance of the product is compared with the projections made during the development phase. If any issues arise in the post-launch review, product features may have to be changed or fine-tuned to make it more suitable for the customers. Thereafter, an annual review of the product can be undertaken to assess its performance and accomplishments. Accordingly, product features can be changed if required. Changes in the over-all economic situation may require certain features of the product to be changed. For example, during economic downturns more stringent requirements, such as a higher down-payment, may be required for financing.

C.6. Shari'ah *audit*
After the product is launched in the market, the SSB through the *Shari'ah* department/unit has to ensure compliance with the approved procedures and processes. The in-house *Shari'ah* department/unit should also conduct internal *Shari'ah* auditing on the processes used in delivering products by the Islamic bank. Ideally, there should be an external *Shari'ah* auditor who would evaluate the in-house audit reports and make public the findings.

Though the actual management of the oversight of the *Shari'ah* requirements related to operational issues is done by the in-house *Shari'ah* department/unit, the SSB must be aware of the issues and correct them whenever required. As transactions can be void if they do not follow the prescribed processes, income generated from these cannot be included in the banks income. One of the roles of the *Shari'ah* audit is to ensure that the processes are followed according to approved schema. As mentioned above, the operational issues that need attention include the proper treatment of interest-based calculations, discounting, early and late payments, penalty income (in case of default), interest income (if any), the special charitable account, payment of *zakah* and ensuring the fulfillment of all contractual stipulations.

Risks and success factors in product development

As the PD system is complex involving many steps and departments of a bank, it entails various types of risks that can increase the probability of failure. While some of the risks inherent in products (such as credit and market risks in financing products) are mitigated during the PD process, other risks related to the PD system are addressed in this section. Reinertsen (1997) maintains that risks can be reduced in PD by gathering as much information as possible and having back-up plans in case an unfavourable event occurs. The objective of risk management would be to decrease the probability of the occurrence of different events that can have a negative impact on the performance of a product. This would require first identifying the risk factors and then planning and implementing tasks that decrease the probability of occurrence of these factors. Baxter (1995) proposes a risk management funnel to increase the probability of developing successful products.

Smith and Reinertsen (1998) identify the technical risk that arises from poor execution of the PD process, which can result in missing the targeted quality, schedule or costs. Costs are incurred while developing products and the risks include delay in development and the lack of expected sale and revenue from the product. A good PD system would enable the development of products efficiently and minimise the development risks.

Note that while some of the steps in the different phases outlined in the PD cycle above are essential, others are not. For example, whereas steps such as formal idea screening and development of concept paper are not essential in the sense that these will not stop the development of a new product, some other steps like preparation of documentation and development of the IT system cannot be evaded. Having a structured PD cycle and inclusion of different steps reduces the risks of failure. The factors that reduce the PD risks would require undertaking all the steps that can increase the probability of success. Several empirical studies show the factors that can improve the success rates of new products. These factors are discussed under the headings of strategy, structure and processes below.

Strategy and plans

Following a clear strategy and implementation plan can reduce the risks of failure of new products. Empirical findings indicate that the overall corporate environment towards innovation is an important determinant of PD culture in an organisation. A new product strategy will be successful if an innovative PD culture and a supportive environment are created (de Brentani 1993). To develop this culture, resolve must exist at the board of director's level and the management should play a supporting constructive role by communicating and involving the responsible employees for high quality implementation of the projects.

Other than a stagnant company culture affecting PD negatively, Kelley and Storey (2000) also find a lack of capacity to manage change, the attitude towards risks, lack of strategy and direction, poor business planning, and lack of entrepreneurial flare as key constraints to PD. Drew (1995) confirms that unfocused strategy and lack of management support are key barriers to innovation. He also finds excessive bureaucracy as an impediment to innovation.

Well-structured plans can reduce the costs (time and resources) and reduce risks of failure. De Brentani (1991) shows that organisations with detailed, formal and planned PD processes and procedures are more likely to come up with successful products. The findings of Cooper *et al.* (1994) confirm that a well-planned and well-executed PD process with sufficient resources is needed to develop successful products.

Structure and resources

Kelly and Storey (2000) and Drew (1995) find lack of resources in general as a barrier to new PD in the service sector. These resources include bank employees who understand the complexities of PD. In particular, a lack of people who have the knowledge, creativity and skills to understand and implement the various steps in the PD process is a key impediment. Lack of financial resources can also affect the quality and extend the time of PD.

Cooper *et al.* (1994) find managerial and financial expertise, resources and synergy necessary for successful products. Among others, they find that innovative technology used to enhance the quality of the product and improve the delivery and operating systems are important determinants of successful products. Cooper and Brentani (1991) show synergy in terms of compatibility of the product with the delivery system of the organisation, expertise and skills, existing production facilities, marketing potentials and sales personnel as important determinants of successful products. Edgett and Parkinson (1994) find organisational features for successful products to include good coordination among the various relevant departments involved in the development process, an awareness of the people involved of the reason for their engagement and of the importance of the product.

Product development process

Edgett (1996) finds that the management of a robust PD process increases the likelihood of successful products in commercial financial institutions. He asserts that success can be managed by ensuring the quality of execution of the process. While using a stage-gate process can reduce certain risks and provide a well-organised PD procedure, it can make the process slow if it becomes bureaucratic. Cooper (1994) provides four ways in which the PD process can be made more efficient. First, each stage can be made less rigid and adaptable. Second, instead of waiting for clearance at the end of each stage that can slow down the process, conditional decisions to go forward can be given. Third, products can be prioritised so that resources can be used on the best options. Finally, the stages themselves can be made flexible and different stage-gate processes can be introduced for different products.

Smith and Reinertsen (1998) also suggest a couple of ways in which the products can be developed quickly in the stage-gate set-up. One simple way to improve the speed is to remove some of the gates in the process. The second way is to use overlapping information during the process. As PD involves gradually building a body of knowledge from different sources, the stage-gate process may imply that the new set of information can only be acquired once the preceding stage is complete. However, in some cases information needed in different stages can be generated in parallel, thereby cutting the development time.

Idea generation

A study of Kelly and Storey (2000) identifies weak operational support capabilities, failure to screen new good ideas and identification of consumer needs as some of the constraints that can affect the new PD process negatively. Along with market research, Edgett and Parkinson (1994) identify market synergy as an important factor that can predict successful products developed by financial organisations. De Brentani (1991) identifies corporate synergy in which the product matches the resources and capabilities of the organisation as a key element of successful products. He also shows that products closely linked to existing ones are more likely to be successful. This is because completely new products entail more risks and are new to customers.

Good market surveys improve the probability of success of products. Smith and Reinertsen (1998) and Edgett and Parkinson (1994) also find market research factors for successful products include a clearly thought out and detailed market study using a relatively large sample. Smith and Reinertsen (1998) maintain that market risks arise when the product fails to meet the market requirements. This risk may arise due to not being able to assess the needs of the customers and overestimating the demand for a particular product. A way of reducing market risks is to have a better assessment of the customers' needs. Studies reveal that the majority (75%) of the products that fail do so due to miscalculating the market, and only a quarter due to technical reasons (Smith and Reinertsen 1998: 224).

The results from studies done by Cooper and de Brentani (1991) link synergy and product/market fit, product advantage, a unique superior product, market size and growth factors with successful products. The implication is that overestimation of market size, problems with product design, a product incorrectly positioned, priced or marketed (advertised) and high costs are causes of failure. Cooper *et al.* (1994) show that product responsiveness in terms of the new product being a significant improvement over existing products in the market, being flexible and adaptable to the individual customer's needs and with the ability to be updated to meet changing customer needs are indicators of success. Edgett's (1996) findings also show product advantage and the nature of the market place as important determinants of successful products.

Converting concept to product

The product design and its implementation determine whether the product entails operational risks after it is launched. Shostack (1982) identifies two states of a service such as a financial product. First is the potential which entails the capability or capacity to provide the service. This would be the ideal case when everything goes as planned. The second state is the actual one and is the realisation of the service when it is offered to the client. Note that the actual provision of the service may deviate from the potential and each client has a unique experience. As different people may deal with a client during the lifetime of the product, one problem is to provide standardised products (Lovelock 1984). In developing financial products care has to be taken to reduce the variability of the services provided. To minimise the deviations in service and have them within a tolerance level, there is a need to have a well-structured blueprint for the operating process.

Cooper *et al.* (1994) find proficient operating and delivery systems as main operational factors for successful products. Operational risks arise in the development phase due to improper oversight of various parts of the delivery system. Failure to acknowledge all factors that can go wrong can create problems in the post-launch stage. The delivery of the product will be affected if something new comes up that has no solution in the system or the personnel are not trained to handle it properly.

Risks can arise due to lack of proper implementation of the IT systems that can create glitches in the system. New products require improvement in operating systems/software for the product operation/delivery and upgrading the hardware for the new product's operation/delivery. Kelley and Storey (2000) identify IT as the main barrier in PD. They find inflexibility of the IT systems to accommodate new products, the system development speed, systems support, and IT development resources among barriers to developing new products.

Commercialisation

Cooper *et al.* (1994) indentify various issues related to launch preparation that can increase the probability of success. The factors include understanding and support of the product by all relevant staff, extensive knowledge of the customer-contact staff, extensive training for all customer-contact staff, marketing of the new product internally before launch, and extensive training of the operations and technical staff. They also find that customer services such as providing friendly, courteous, prompt and efficient service can make products successful.

Bowers (1986) identifies some specific issues related to selling banking services compared to manufacturing products. As banks deals with services that are sold from different outlets, maintaining the uniformity of the services provided from different branches of the bank become very important. Thus, it is very important to train the personnel to have uniformity in providing the service.

Edgett (1996) finds marketing support at the launch stage to be important for producing successful products. Cooper *et al.* (1994) identify various effective marketing communications factors that can make a product successful. The important factors include expertise and resources related to promotion and distribution/sales. Product performance is better if the customers are made aware of the benefits of the new product. This can be done with a more effective promotional campaign than competitive products, creating a 'brand' image for the product that is distinct for the targeted market.

Edgett and Parkinson (1994) observed that products with strong support after launch were seen as superior to the competitors' offerings. Along with quality of execution of launch and marketing activities, Cooper and de Brentani (1991) indentify execution of technical activities, service delivery and service expertise as additional success factors.

Note
1. See Cooper (1994) and Cooper and Edgett (1999).

CHAPTER 5
PRODUCT DEVELOPMENT PRACTICES IN ISLAMIC BANKS

As Chapter 4 demonstrates, product development (PD) is a complex process involving many steps and requiring input from different departments of a bank. While various studies examine PD systems in different industries, empirical works on the financial sector are relatively few. Being a relatively new industry, no detailed study on the PD system in Islamic banking exists. This chapter presents results on the practices of PD in Islamic banks gathered from a survey of Islamic financial institutions. The objective of the empirical work is to examine the status of the PD system and identify the constraints facing Islamic banks in developing new products.

The empirical assessment of PD in Islamic banks is based on two surveys. The first survey examines the status of PD in Islamic banks, based on the answers to questionnaires that were sent to Islamic banks globally. Data on the size of the bank (assets and number of staff), PD unit/department, and policy and procedures related to PD in the organisation were sought. The objective of this survey was to have an overview of the status of the PD systems in Islamic banks globally. Questionnaires were sent to 177 Islamic financial institutions in thirty-six countries of the world. A total of twenty independent Islamic banks from twelve countries responded to the questionnaire.[1] The sample includes seventeen commercial banks, two investment banks and one cooperative bank. Note that the numbers of banks in the sample is relatively small and the results may not be robust. The survey, however, provides some indication of the practice and processes of PD in Islamic banks.

The second empirical component comprises an in-depth appraisal survey of a few well-established Islamic banks in Malaysia and the UAE. The objective of the semi-structured interviews with PD personnel was to get an in-depth view of different practices of PD in these banks. Officials from four Islamic banks in Malaysia and four in the UAE were interviewed. In these interviews, detailed information on different stages of the PD process and the constraints arising in developing new products were sought. This chapter reports the results from the surveys and also then presents the barriers and risks that were identified in the questionnaires and interviews.

Product development system in Islamic banks

Some basic features of the banks in the sample are reported in Table 5.1. The table shows that size and age varies significantly among the Islamic banks. The average age of the banks in the sample is 13.2 years, with the oldest established in 1978 and the youngest in 2008.[2] Different measures of size indicate a wide disparity in the size of the banks as seen by the minimum, maximum and standard deviation figures of number of branches, staff size and total assets. While investment banks typically operate from a single office or headquarters, commercial banks have a large number of branches spread around the country. The largest commercial bank in the sample has 1,967 branches with staff numbering 20,648. The average capital of the banks in the sample is USD 462 million and the corresponding figure for

Table 5.1 *Size of Islamic banks in the sample*

	Age of banks (in years) (20)[a]	No. of branches (20)[a]	Staff size (20)[a]	Capital (Mil. USD) (19)[a]	Total assets (Mil. USD) (19)[a]
Average	13.2	171.8	2,665.2	462.0	4,649.8
Maximum	31.0	1,967.0	20,648.0	1,378.9	32,784.3
Minimum	1.0	1.0	35.0	33.9	121.1
Standard deviation	10.2	432.0	4,596.6	442.3	7,451.4

[a] The number indicates the number of banks in the sample.

assets is USD 4,649.9 million. Again the minimum, maximum and standard deviation figures indicate wide variation in the size of the banks. For example, the values of assets range from a minimum of USD 121.1 to a maximum of USD 32,784.3 million.

Information on various aspects of the PD system was sought following the structure discussed in Chapter 4. Accordingly, the results of the practices in Islamic banks are reported under the headings of strategy and plans, structure and resources, and PD process.

Strategy and plans

The banks in the sample were asked to identify their strategic positioning according to Ansoff's (1965) market-product classification outlined in Chapter 4. The responses from the banks are reported in Table 5.2. Note that many banks in the sample had indicated more than one strategic option. However, the dominant strategy appears to be *product development* with 80 per cent of the banks reporting that their approach is to introduce new products in existing

Table 5.2 *Strategic positioning of Islamic banks*

Strategic positioning type	Number of banks	Percentage of total
Diversification: Developing new products in new markets	3	15
Product development: Developing new products in existing markets	16	80
Market development: Marketing existing products in a new market	4	20
Market penetration: Expanding existing products in existing markets	8	40

markets. This is followed by *market penetration* (40%) whereby banks expand existing products in existing markets. Only a small number of banks have the strategic intent to expand into newer markets. Four banks report to have a *market development* strategy in which existing products are introduced to new markets. Only three banks have *diversification* as a strategy whereby new products are developed for new markets.

The specific questions related to banks' strategic perspectives towards innovation and PD are reported in Table 5.3. Innovation appears in the mission and vision statements of most (90%) of the Islamic banks. Only two banks report that their vision or mission statements do not include innovation or similar terms. Similarly, all Islamic banks except one have PD as one of the objectives in their overall strategy. All banks in the sample report that relevant business units encompass PD in their annual operating plans. The number of banks that have annual plans for the number of products to be developed is only fourteen (70%). The majority of the banks (55%), however, report that there is no separate budget set aside to develop new products.

Table 5.3 *Strategic outlook and plans for product development*

Question	YES (%)	NO (%)
Does the bank's mission or vision statement include 'innovation'?	18 (90)	2 (10)
Does the overall strategy of the bank include *product development* as one of the objectives?	19 (95)	1 (5)
Is PD built into the annual operating plans of relevant business units?	20 (100)	0 (0)
Is there an annual plan for the number of new products to be developed?	14 (70)	6 (30)
Is there an annual budget set aside for developing new products?	9 (45)	11 (55)

The results in Table 5.3 indicate that while the majority of Islamic banks have 'innovation' in their mission and/or vision statements and have PD in their strategies and annual operating plans, less than half of the banks in the sample report that specific budgetary support is available for PD. This may be an indication of a lack of resources available to back up the strategic intent and make the plans operational.

Structure and resources

Given the differences in the age and size of the Islamic banks, the structure and organisational format of PD within each organisation will differ widely. As discussed in Chapter 4, organisations can be structured based on function and/or project linkages. While it is expected that most Islamic banks would have a matrix organisational structure in which units combine various elements of functions and projects, a central PD unit indicates the *lightweight* form with dominant functional elements. Smaller banks are expected to have a central department or unit where PD needs would be carried out. As there will be a need to get the necessary input

Table 5.4 *Drivers and authorisation of product development*

	Drivers	**Authorisation**
Board of Directors	3 (15%)	2 (10%)
CEO/general manager	4 (20%)	11 (55%)
Marketing head	3 (15%)	
Relevant business department head	1 (5%)	2 (10%)
Strategy/planning head	2 (10%)	
Research/product/business development head	7 (35%)	
Committee (management, new product, etc.)		3 (15%)

from other functional units of the bank in this structure, the efficiency of PD will depend on the proficiency of cross-functional coordination. Fourteen (70%) Islamic banks in the sample report a central PD unit responsible for developing new products.

Whereas in larger banks there can be PD units attached to different business segments, in smaller banks one centralised unit performs the function. In some larger banks, the organisational format is heavyweight with stronger project links. These banks have different departments or divisions, such as retail, corporate, trade, and so on, and different functional units such as marketing and PD exist within each of these departments.

The main drivers of PD in Islamic banks vary, as shown in Table 5.4. In seven banks (35%), new products are directed by the Board of Directors (BOD) and senior management. In all other banks, PD is led by different departments. In the departments, the head of research/product/business development is driving PD in seven banks (35%), the marketing head in three banks (15%) and the strategy/planning head in two banks (10%). The authorisation of new products in

Table 5.5 *Department responsibilities for product development and maintenance*

Departments	Product development	Post-product-launch maintenance[a]
Research/product/business development	11 (55%)	9 (45%)
Relevant business department (retail, consumer, corporate, etc.)	4 (20%)	6 (30%)
Marketing	3 (15%)	4 (20%)
Strategy/planning	2 (10%)	
Operations		3 (15%)
Internal audit		1 (5%)

[a] In some banks, more than one department is responsible for product maintenance.

most banks (55%) is done by the CEO/general manager. The BOD authorises new products in two banks and in three banks a committee clears new products. In two banks the relevant business department head approves the products that need to be developed.

In many banks pre-launch development and post-launch maintenance of new products is done by different departments. While the product or business development department in eleven banks is responsible for PD, in the remaining banks PD takes place under some other department. Four banks have PD responsibilities with a relevant department (such as retail and corporate), three banks have it with the marketing department and the remaining two with the strategic planning department.

The departments responsible for maintenance of the product during the post-launch stage are shown in Table 5.5. Note that in some banks, more that one department

Table 5.6 *Core teams and cross-functional teams*

Banks with	Number	Percentage
Core teams	13	65
Cross-functional teams	16	80
Authority of cross-functional team members to take decisions	11	55

takes the role of maintenance. While the product/business development departments take the responsibility of overseeing the product after its launch in most banks (45%), the relevant business departments do this in the case of six banks. The marketing department maintains the product in four banks (20%), the operations department does so in three banks and the internal audit department also contributes in one bank.

Tables 5.6 to 5.8 show various aspects of the teams used to develop products. While sixteen banks report having cross-functional teams, thirteen report having an additional smaller core team responsible for PD (Table 5.6). In eleven banks, the members of the cross-functional team have the authority to make decisions about the product. In the remaining five, decisions are made by people who are not in the team. This arrangement can delay the PD process.

Table 5.7 shows how the formation of cross-functional teams is formalised in three banks in the sample whereby the teams are formed using permanent service level agreements (SLA). In four banks a different SLA is signed for each product and in eight banks (40%) nominations to the cross-functional teams are made on an ad-hoc basis without written agreements. While the permanent SLA provides the most stable team, an SLA for each product can be time consuming. Teams formed on an ad-hoc basis would be expected to have the least commitments from the members

Table 5.7 *Formation of cross-functional teams*

Banks with	Number	Percentage
Permanent SLA among relevant departments	3	15
Different SLA with departments for each product	4	20
Nominations made by departments on ad-hoc basis	8	40

Table 5.8 *Coordination quality of cross-functional teams*

Members of cross-functional team	Number	Percentage
Always perform their part without delays	7	35
Perform their part with some delays	8	40
Perform their part with significant delays	1	5

as their roles will not be clearly defined. Thus in a large number of banks in the sample, the PD cycle may be delayed due to coordination problems.

Table 5.8 indicates the quality of coordination among members of the cross-functional team in terms of time taken to perform various functions. Seven banks (35%) report no delays in the performance of the work of the cross-functional team. Interestingly, all banks using permanent SLA along with two banks in which an SLA is signed for each product (reported in Table 5.7) are included in this category. A large number of banks responding to the question (40%), however, indicate some delays and one bank reported significant delays in the performance of the team members.

The resources needed for PD can be broadly identified as financial, human and technological. The banks were asked

Table 5.9 *Resource availability for product development*

Resources	Average score[a]	Banks with scale 5 (resources sufficiently available)
Financial (funds)	3.55	6 (30%)
Human (people, knowledge, skills, etc.)	3.80	7 (35%)
Technology (appropriate hardware and software)	3.70	6 (30%)

[a] The number indicates the average in a Likert scale with 5 indicating sufficiently available and 1 indicating not available.

to rank the availability of these resources using a scale of 1 to 5, where 1 indicates non-availability and 5 indicates sufficiently available. The average scores for the banks in the sample are shown in Table 5.9. While all three types of resources have an average score of more than 3, implying a satisfactory level of resources, only about one third of the banks indicate sufficient resource availability for developing products. Of the resources, human capital appears to be most available and financial the least.

Table 5.10 shows the average number of members and staff in the *Shari'ah* boards and relevant departments of banks in the sample. As the number of staff members in different departments will be linked to the size of banks, the figures show a large disparity. The average number of SSB members is 4.3, with a maximum of 13 and minimum of 2. While the average size of the in-house *Shari'ah* unit or department is 4.4, the staff number varies from a maximum of 25 and a minimum of 1. Similarly, the average of full-time PD staff is 5.4 with a minimum of 1 and a maximum of 17.

Table 5.10 *Staff members in relevant departments/bodies*

	Shari'ah board members (19)[a]	In-house Shari'ah organ members (19)[a]	Full-time product development staff (19)[a]
Average	4.3	4.4	5.4
Maximum	13.0	25.0	17.0
Minimum	2.0	1.0	1.0
Standard deviation	2.4	5.4	4.1

[a] The number indicates the number of banks in the sample.

Table 5.11 *Role of in-house* Shari'ah *organ in product development*

Activity	Number of banks	Percentage of total
Idea generation	12	60
Product development	8	40
Shari'ah audit	14	70
Training	1	5

Table 5.11 shows the different activities the in-house *Shari'ah* unit or department is involved in at different stages of PD. In the pre-launch phase, the *Shari'ah* organs of twelve banks assist in idea generation and in eight banks they are associated with developing the product. It appears that in a large number of banks, the *Shari'ah* department provides input at the idea generation stage, but does not participate in the phase of converting the idea into a product. After the product is launched, the *Shari'ah* department performs an audit of the product in fourteen (70%) of the banks.

Product development process

Given the variety in the age and size of banks in the sample, the PD cycle is expected to differ widely across banks. Furthermore, given the different nature of products offered, PD will vary in commercial and investment banks. The legal and regulatory regime will also have an impact on the products developed and offered by Islamic banks.

A first indicator of a robust PD process is to have a formal framework under which it takes place. The framework for PD processes for the banks in the sample is shown in Table 5.12. A formal written process or manual for PD exists in twelve banks (60%). While some broad written outline for developing products is used in six banks (30%), in two banks (10%) PD takes place informally without any written guidelines.

Results for the three phases of the PD cycle outlined in Chapter 4 are shown for the Islamic banks surveyed. Note that banks may not follow the sequence of steps as outlined in Chapter 4. Banks have their own processes and development cycles that either add more steps or combine two or more steps in one. The results in the tables below report the answers in which the banks *always* perform the relevant step of the PD cycle, irrespective of the sequence. Banks that responded that they either do not or sometimes carry out a specific step are considered to not have the step in their structured PD cycle.

Table 5.13 shows the number of banks in the sample that

Table 5.12 *Product development process*

Banks with	Number	Percentage
Formal written process/manual	12	60
Some broad written guidelines	6	30
Informal (no written guidelines)	2	10

Table 5.13 *Status of idea generation and acceptance*

Steps	Always undertaken (no. of banks)	Percentage of total
A.1. Structured idea generation process	8	40
A.2. Formal idea screening process	8	40
A.3. Development of concept paper for new product	12	60
A.4. Approval of concept by *Shari'ah* board	16	80
A.5. Detailed business case	11	55
A.6. Authorisation to develop product by senior management	18	90
Average	*12.2*	*60.8*

always perform the different steps under the 'Idea generation and acceptance' phase. Only eight banks (or 40%) have structured idea generation and formal screening processes. These figures indicate that the majority of banks in the sample do not have any process to generate and screen ideas for new products. Twelve banks (60%) prepare a concept paper for the new product and sixteen banks always get the concept approved by the SSB. The implication is that four banks get the approval of the concept without preparing a formal concept paper. After the approval of the concept by the SSB a detailed business case is prepared by eleven banks (55%) in the sample. Senior management always authorises developing new products in eighteen banks (90%) before proceeding to the next phase of the development cycle. The average number of banks that undertake the steps in the 'Idea generation and acceptance' phase is 12.2 (or 60.8%). This average provides an indication of the prevalence of various steps undertaken in the idea generation and acceptance

Table 5.14 *Status of converting concept into product*

Steps	Always undertaken (no. of banks)	Percentage of total
B.1. Product design and process flow	15	75
B.2. Sign-off from various relevant departments	15	75
B.3. Preparation of documentations	18	90
B.4. *Shariʿah* approval (documents and process flow)	18	90
B.5. Development of IT system	17	85
B.6. In-house testing	18	90
Average	*16.8*	*84.2*

phase and shows the overall strength of this phase of the PD cycle among the banks in the sample.

The results for the second phase of 'Converting the concept into product' for the sample banks are shown in Table 5.14. Fifteen banks (75%) prepare a product design and process flow for the product. The same number of banks also report getting the product reviewed and signing off the product from the different relevant departments. A large number of banks (18; 90%) prepare the relevant documents related to the product. These include forms, contracts, the product manual, policy and procedures, and so on. In eighteen banks (90%), the documents and process flow are approved by the SSB. The implication is that in two banks the concept paper is approved by the SSB, but the documents related to the product are not. Only seventeen banks (75%) report that they always develop/alter the IT system for new products. This implies that for the remaining banks the IT system is either fully Islamic and does not require alternations for new products or products are developed in

Table 5.15 *Status of commercialisation*

Steps	Always undertaken (no. of banks)	Percentage of total
C.1. Training of personnel	16	80
C.2. Pilot-run of the product	15	75
C.3. Marketing programme	15	75
C.4. Full-scale launch	11	55
C.5. Post-launch review	12	60
C.6. *Shari'ah* audit of the product	12	60
Average	*13.5*	*67.5*

a way that may not always require changing IT specifications. In eighteen banks (90%), the new products undergo in-house testing. As investment banks have unique products, the need for in-house testing may be small. The average number of banks that always carry out all the steps in the 'Converting the concept into product' phase is 16.8 (84.2%).

The responses given by banks in the sample for different steps in the 'Commercialisation' phase are shown in Table 5.15. Sixteen banks (80%) report that they always train the personnel dealing with the new product. Investment bank products being different would not require the training of staff for each new product. A total of fifteen banks (75%) indicate they always have a pilot run and have a marketing programme for the product. Only eleven banks (55%) indicate they always have a full-scale launch for a new product. These results indicate that in many cases new products are introduced either gradually or without fanfare. After the product is launched, only twelve banks (60%) review the performance or do a *Shari'ah* audit of the product.[3] The average number for all the steps in the 'Commercialisation' phase is 13.5 (67.5%). This figure indicates that on average around fourteen banks always undertake the various steps in this phase of the PD cycle.

The averages of different phases in the PD cycle indicate the overall prevalence of different steps among the banks in the sample. When these averages are compared (see Tables 5.13 to 5.15), it is observed that the weakest phase is 'Idea generation and acceptance' with an average of 12.2 (60.8%) and the strongest is 'Conversion of concept to product' with an average of 16.8 (84.2%). The 'Commercialisation' phase is also on the weaker side, with an average of 13.5 (or 67.5%), but is better than the 'Idea generation' phase.

A couple of issues related to the idea generation phase of the PD cycle are further explored. The sources of ideas are important to identify the possible range of products that can be developed. Once the ideas are gathered, banks use different criteria or factors to identify the ones that will be developed into products. Issues related to sources of ideas and the criteria used to identify products that are developed are shown in Tables 5.16 and 5.17 respectively. The banks were asked to rank different sources/factors according to importance from first to fifth. The last column in both tables shows the weighted total score of each of the sources/factors for all banks in the sample across all rankings. To estimate the total weighted score the first rank is given a weight of 5, second rank 4, and so on with the fifth rank getting a weight of 1. The weighted total score is computed by adding the frequency of banks in different ranks multiplied by the weights. Thus, if all twenty banks in the sample choose a source/factor as the first option, its total weight would be 100 (20x5). Similarly if a factor is ranked fourth by five banks and fifth by six banks, its weighted average would be sixteen (5x2+6x1).

Table 5.16 indicates that the highest-ranked source of ideas according to the weighted total score is market

Table 5.16 *Sources of ideas for new products*

Sources	Ranks					Weighted total score
	1st	2nd	3rd	4th	5th	
Products of conventional banks	3	2	4	4	3	46
Products of Islamic banks	4	5	2	3	1	53
Outside agencies/ consultants	0	0	0	0	2	2
Customers	4	2	5	0	2	45
Market research	5	2	6	3	1	58
In-house R&D	1	5	0	3	6	37
Internal departments	2	2	0	5	2	30
Others	0	0	1	0	0	3

research (with a score of 58). This is followed by the products offered by other Islamic banks (score of 53). The third source of ideas for new products comes from conventional banks (score of 46), closely followed by feedback from customers. In-house research is ranked fifth as the source of ideas for new products with a score of 37.

Table 5.17 shows the criteria used to identify new products to be developed. The first ranking factor used to identify products according to the weighted total score is *Shariʻah* compliance (with a score of 71). The second ranking factor is financial considerations (with a score of 59) relating to expected revenue, costs, and profit and loss projections of the product. Market considerations such as competition and client needs rank third with a score of 53. The fourth factor used to identify products to develop is fit with corporate strategy and plan. With a total weighted score of 35, Islamic values such as equity, risk sharing, social factors, and so on rank fifth in indentifying products that are to be developed.

Table 5.17 *Criteria used to identify new products for development*

Factors	Ranks					Weighted total score
	1st	2nd	3rd	4th	5th	
Financial considerations	3	6	3	5	1	59
Market considerations	4	3	2	5	5	53
Fit with corporate strategy and plan	2	3	5	2	2	43
Resource availability	0	0	2	2	4	14
Shari'ah compliance	10	2	3	1	2	71
Islamic values	0	4	3	3	4	35

The results in Tables 5.16 and 5.17 allude to some interesting perspectives on PD in Islamic banks. First, ideas for a large number of products come from products offered by other banks (both Islamic and conventional). In-house research plays a small role in generating ideas for new products. Second, while Islamic banks pay attention to *Shari'ah* compliance in making decisions about new products, the Islamic values are not given priority. Furthermore, note that even though the score for *Shari'ah* compliance is the highest, the results in Table 5.17 show that half of the banks in the sample do not give *Shari'ah* compliance the top priority in identifying new products. These results provide some indications about the dominance of products focusing on the legalistic forms of *Shari'ah* compliance.

Key constraints in product development

Banks were asked to identify the key constraints and risks faced in PD. The survey results indicate that Islamic banks face certain barriers and risks constraining the development of new products. The constraints that limit the choice in PD can be broadly classified as external and internal. While

Table 5.18 *External barriers and risks to product development in Islamic banks*

External factors	Barriers		Risks	
	Freq.	Specific issues	Freq.	Specific issues
Institutional environment	11	Regulatory requirements; understanding of regulators; tax structures; capital requirements; accounting standards; inadequate legislation	2	Regulatory risks; legal risks
Market conditions	13	Limited market; strong competition from conventional and Islamic banks; information about clients; satisfying customer needs; customer acceptance	8	Market risk; product acceptance risk; geographic risk; competition

the external factors can be discussed under the institutional environment (the regulatory and legal regimes) and market conditions, the internal factors are identified as those related to strategy, structure, resources and process.

External constraints

The key external constraints in PD identified by Islamic banks are shown in Table 5.18. As mentioned, the external constraints and risks can be categorised according to the institutional environment and market conditions. Note that while some banks did not respond to these questions, others listed more than one constraint. The frequency shown in the table indicates the number of times specific issues appeared in the responses of different banks. The most frequently cited barrier is market conditions (thirteen cases) followed by institutional legal and regulatory regimes (eleven cases). Among risks, external market conditions also dominate over the institutional environment. While the frequency of risk for market conditions is eight, only two institutional risks in the form of regulatory and legal risks are identified.

Some Islamic banks identify the lack of an appropriate legal framework as creating uncertainty and risks. If Islamic banking laws do not exist, the products developed have to fit into the existing legal framework. Even if Islamic banking law exists, there are other laws that are relevant to Islamic banking practices. As products of Islamic banks require the buying and selling of assets, other laws have implications for them. For example, in the case of real-estate financing, the relevant laws are related to land, real estate and tax. In Malaysia, laws relevant to banking practices are the national land code, the Housing Development Act, Contract Act, BAFIA and the Islamic Banking Act. In other countries, sets of laws arise from different sources. For example, in a country with a federal set-up, there are national laws and local laws that need to be abided by. In the UAE, the banking and contract laws are enacted at the federal level and the land and real-estate laws are administered by individual emirates. Banks have to closely study the implications of these laws in developing products.

Some other legal issues arise from the nature of Islamic banks' operations. For example, if a bank is financing services using the *murabahah* mode, it has to typically sell these to the client. This can raise certain pre-sale and post-sale risks. Pre-sale risks arise as usually firms need a license to sell services such as education and medical services. Banks do not have such licenses and are legally not allowed to sell services. The second problem arises if there is a negative shock after the sale. For example, if some liability arises due to medical negligence, the bank, being the seller, can be sued for malpractice. Given these risks, Islamic banks may opt for other controversial options such as *tawarrruq* whereby they mitigate these risks.

New products have to get the approval of the regulatory authorities in many jurisdictions. The regulatory authorities examine risk features of the product along with issues related to capital requirements, balance sheet implications, fees charged, and so on. A product cannot be launched if the regulatory authorities do not clear it. For example, if the regulatory authority views a *wakalah*-based deposit as an agency contract similar to mutual funds, it may not allow it as an alternative to a conventional savings deposit unless certain conditions are met.

The international accounting standards adopted by most countries sometimes can raise *Shari'ah* compliance issues, for example, when they emphasise substance over form (Sultan 2006). As a result, an *ijarah* product may take the form of a financial lease in the accounting sense and will not be shown in the balance sheet of the bank. This can raise *Shari'ah* objections as under an *ijarah* contract the asset should be legally owned by the bank and as such shown on its balance sheet. These issues create tension between the regulatory regimes and *Shari'ah* principles and affect the types of products that will be developed.

As discussed in Chapter 3, some regulatory authorities will also require banks to follow *Shari'ah* governance mechanisms and guidelines. In some countries, a national *Shari'ah* body/authority examines new products to ascertain compliance with *Shari'ah* principles. In countries that do not have a National *Shari'ah* Authority, problems of standardisation and legal/*Shari'ah* risks arise. As Islamic banks can choose the *Shari'ah* scholars who can be in the SSB, the products of various banks within a country will be different. Problems arise when the SSB in some Islamic banks allow a certain product which is not allowed by the SSB of another bank. This not only creates confusion and legal risks, but also makes the playing field uneven. For example, it was reported that certain banks were using a *tawarruq*-based product to convert conventional loans into Islamic products. As the SSB of some other banks did not allow the use of *tawarruq*, these banks were in a disadvantageous position as they could not use this method to get new clients. This creates incentives for Islamic banks to do '*fatwa* shopping' whereby they seek scholars who can approve product without difficulties.

Other than the legal and regulatory environment, another significant external factor related to products is market conditions. Banks have to deal with competition from other banks, both Islamic and conventional. As a significant proportion of clients of Islamic banks use conventional banking services also, Islamic banks are under pressure to keep their products not only competitive but also similar to the ones offered by conventional banks.[4] Some banks also report lack of knowledge among clients about Islamic products. On the one hand the mind-set of many clients is still conventional and they compare and expect the features of products offered by Islamic banks to be similar or better than those of conventional banks. On the other hand, there appears to be a reputation risk as many Muslim clients question the authenticity of Islamic products. While Islamic banks try to find out the appetite of the customers for the new product by market research, the customer acceptance risk exists if the product has too many innovative features.

Table 5.19 *Internal barriers and risks to product development in Islamic banks*

Internal factors	Barriers		Risks	
	Freq.	Specific issues	Freq.	Specific issues
Strategy	–	–	4	Strategic risk; reputation risk
Structure and resources	7	Organisational issues; adequate resources; experienced/ knowledgeable staff; appropriate sales staff; absence of centralised PD unit	–	–
Process	25	Product complexity; *Shari'ah* compliance and restrictions; IT adaptations/MIS; long time to develop products; proper financial models; advertising and sales campaign; high costs	22	Credit risk; operational risk; *Shari'ah* compliance risk; technological/ IT risks; profitability of the product; marketing risks

Internal constraints

The internal constraints faced by banks in PD are reported in Table 5.19. The most frequently occurring barriers (twenty-five cases) reported relate to the PD process. While the banks identify seven barriers in structure and resources-related issues, no strategic barrier is recognised. Most cases of risks (twenty-two) identified by banks also fall under the PD process category. Four banks identified strategic risks that included reputation risk as a cause for concern. No risks related to structure and resources are cited.

The internal risks related to PD can be broadly classified as risks related to the product systems and risks related to product features. The constraints to PD systems are related to strategy, structure and the process. Strategic risk arises when there are no strategic guidelines provided by the senior management regarding PD directions. The responsibility of establishing a strategic framework and providing resources lies with the BOD. The BOD, together with senior management, is responsible for establishing an organisation that has a culture of innovation and dynamism to cater to the changing needs of the economy.

Most banks report that the IT system is one of the main constraints in developing new products. As many IT systems are conventional and not adapted for Islamic transactions, they cannot handle features of Islamic products. If the system is not flexible, the changes needed for handling new products can take a long time and also be costly. Sometimes the changes required are so fundamental that the vendors are called in to make the changes. A good product sometimes cannot be launched due to IT restrictions. Issues related to IT include accounting issues and also structural issues. If the bank is using a conventional banking system that cannot link the returns on assets to those on liabilities, then developing a profit-sharing investment account may be constrained by this technical barrier. One option is to key in the returns manually, but this can create operational risks in calculating the returns and also inputting the data on a regular (monthly) basis.

A main hurdle identified is the human capital required to back Islamic finance at different levels. There is a lack of knowledge of Islamic transactions among staff who deal with the different aspects of the transaction. The level of understanding for some staff in the banks is so low that for them Islamic banking means just changing the word 'interest' to 'profit'.[5] This is partly because many staff members are trained in conventional banks and have a conventional mind-set. The different concepts of Islamic banking products have implications for the back-office pre-launch development areas such as accounting, IT development, risks, and so on and also for post-launch staff such as the sales people, who are not aware of the different features of products they sell.

Shari'ah risks can arise in accounting, documentation and process flows. Some of the accounting issues have been identified above. A part of the accounting problem is related to the IT software used. If the IT software is conventional, all its underlying structure will be linked to interest-based calculations. For example, if there is default by a client, the system may start adding compound interest on the overdue payments. This can raise *Shari'ah* problems as excess over a debt is not permitted. Even if the bank charges a penalty, it cannot be added to the income of the banks and has to be diverted to a separate pool meant for charity.

If there is breach of Islamic contract guidelines or the process is not followed as required, then the income resulting from the transaction would not be legitimate and has to be cleansed. In some banks with large *Shari'ah* organs that have adequate resources for a *Shari'ah* audit, non-compliance can be detected. If the audit finds irregularities in the processes that make transactions void from *Shari'ah* perspectives, the income from the transactions has to be separated from the income of the bank and given to charity.

The key risk that concerns the PD system is the operational risk related to the development and delivery of the product. The PD manager and the core team have to monitor the operational aspects of the process so that there are no losses arising from poor execution. While the PD manager and core team has to ensure that the risks of product processes are mitigated, the risk management department will examine the risks related to the product features. As noted in Chapter 3, the specific risks will also depend on the type of mode used. The risks involved in Islamic financial products are complex and evolve at different stages of the transaction. The choice of an appropriate mode depends on the associated risk factors and how these are mitigated.

Product development in Islamic banks: an assessment

Products developed by financial institutions are bound by the external laws and regulations on the one hand, and internal policies, rules and requirements on the other. The results from the surveys provide some insight into the dilemmas that Islamic banks face. The information also reveals various issues that can explain why certain *Shari'ah* principles are being diluted.

One of the key objectives of the regulatory regimes is to maintain stability in the financial sector by overseeing the risk profiles of banks and their products. As Islamic banking practice is new, there is little understanding of risk features and reluctance to approve new unfamiliar products. Due to the lack of understanding, Islamic financial products may either be delayed or not approved by the regulators.

Another indirect affect of regulatory regime on products is the capital adequacy requirements. According to Basel II and IFSB capital adequacy standards, riskier products require higher capital charges. As such, products that are equity-based or require the bank to hold assets will carry higher capital charge due to market risks. As capital is expensive, the banks tend to develop products that have lower capital requirements. This may result in introducing products that are not the most preferred in terms of the goals of *Shari'ah*. For example, financing products such as *mudarabah* and *musharakah* have higher capital requirements than debt-based products such as *murabahah*. Given the competitive markets, banks are likely to opt for the latter mode as they will not be able to add the higher risk premium and capital charges on to the price of the product. Similarly, an *ijarah*-based product that takes the form of an operating lease will have higher capital requirements, as the bank owns the asset, compared to a product structured as a financial lease. Even though an operating lease is a more appropriate form of contract from an Islamic perspective, disparity in capital requirements creates incentives to develop products that are similar to financial leases, thereby compromising on principles of *Shari'ah*.

The survey results also reveal some organisational issues that can account for the absence of *Shari'ah*-based products. The results in Table 5.3 show that strategy and planning at the organisational level appears to be strong, but the number of banks with specific plans and budgetary support for PD appears to be weak in many banks. This may be an indication of lack of effort on behalf of some banks to translate the strategic intent into specific plans and budget to support new products.

The averages for different phases of the PD cycle show that the weakest phase is 'Idea generation and acceptance' with an average of 12.2 (60.8%) and strongest is 'Conversion of concept to product' with an average of 16.8 (84.2%; see Tables 5.13 to 5.15). Furthermore, the lack of using structured idea generation and screening steps within the 'Idea generation and acceptance' phase have important consequences for the types of products developed by Islamic banks. While most of the technical aspects of the PD process in Islamic banks will be similar to their conventional counterparts, the distinguishing feature of the former will be the use of *Shari'ah*-based contracts. In other words, the 'Idea generation' phase will determine the types and quality of products that Islamic banks develop. Ignoring the importance of this phase may well be one of the reasons why Islamic banks opt to mimic conventional products instead of coming up with *Shari'ah*-based products.

The results in Tables 5.16 and 5.17 show the importance given to different sources in generating ideas and the criteria used to identify the ideas that are converted to products. Ideas for a large number of products come from those offered by both Islamic and conventional banks. In-house research and development has a small role in generating ideas for new products. While *Shari'ah* compliance is given priority in deciding which new products to develop, the Islamic values are not given importance. The results in Table 5.17 also show that half of the banks in the sample do not give *Shari'ah* compliance the highest priority in identifying new products. These results have important implications for the lack of development of *Shari'ah*-based products.

As discussed in Chapter 3, *Shari'ah*-based products are developed by first identifying the target market segment and then examining the function or purpose of the product. Once these are done, a product is developed using a suitable mode of financing. Developing *Shari'ah*-based products appears to be more complex and demanding compared to *Shari'ah*-compliant ones which require engineering replications of conventional products. The approach taken by many Islamic banks is to take the latter approach and develop products that are either offered by other Islamic banks or conventional banks.

Developing *Shari'ah*-based products would require opting for the difficult and challenging approach of innovative engineering. Being the apex decision-making body of an organisation, the BOD is primarily responsible for the direction a bank takes and ensures this by providing the necessary support and resources. The goals set by the BOD will be reflected in strategies and plans and determine the nature of business and the types of products offered by a bank. If the BOD wants *Shari'ah*-based products, there are important issues that need to be resolved. The first relates to strengthening the organisational capacities to develop *Shari'ah*-based products. As these products are more demanding, they require more investment in appropriate resources. Specifically, the survey indicates that this can be achieved by streamlining the PD strategy and plans, providing more funds to research and development and strengthening the 'Idea generation' phase of the PD cycle.

Appendix

List of banks included in the survey with countries of origin:

Country	*Bank*
Bangladesh:	Islami Bank Bd. Ltd
Bosnia:	Bosna Bank International
Indonesia:	PT Bank Syariah Mandiri, PT Bank Muamalat
Iran:	Bank Tejarat of Iran
Jordan:	Jordan Islamic Bank
Kuwait:	The International Investor
Malaysia:	Asian Finance Bank, Kuwait Finance House, Bank Rakyat, Bank Islam Malaysia
Pakistan:	Dawoud Islamic Bank
Sudan:	Sudanese Islamic Bank, Omdurman National Bank
Turkey:	Turkiye Finans Katilim Bankasi, Asya Katilim Bankasi
UAE:	Sharjah Islamic Bank, Noor Islamic Bank, Al Hilal Bank
UK:	European Islamic Bank

Notes

1. The Islamic financial institutions that responded to the questionnaire are listed in the Appendix.

2. Note that two banks in the sample were conventional banks which converted to Islamic institutions later. For these banks the year in which they started providing Islamic products has been used as the year of establishment.

3. This result may appear to contradict the findings reported in Table 5.11 in which fourteen banks indicate that the *Shari'ah* organ is involved in a *Shari'ah* audit. If there are banks which undertake a *Shari'ah* audit occasionally, it will be reported in Table 5.11 but not in Table 5.15; in the latter table only the banks that *always* conduct a *Shari'ah* audit are included.

4. A survey of 485 clients of banks in Malaysia revealed that 34.6 per cent of the respondents use Islamic banking only and 24.5 per cent used both Islamic and conventional banks (Haque *et al.* 2009).

5. This comment was made by one of the product development interviewees in the survey.

CHAPTER 6
ISLAMIC FINANCIAL PRODUCTS: CATEGORIES AND CONTROVERSIES

This chapter draws on the concepts and results discussed in previous chapters to examine the properties of products provided by Islamic financial institutions. This is done by assessing the *Shari'ah* requirements. As discussed in Chapters 1 and 3, the *Shari'ah* requirements have both social and legal dimensions. These requirements are scrutinised in the light of the *Shari'ah* principles outlined in Chapter 2 and the product development system presented in Chapter 4. To assess products according to their social and legal dimensions, a scheme of classification is suggested. The scheme provides an objective criterion to classify Islamic financial products into three categories: *Shari'ah*-based, *Shari'ah*-compliant and pseudo-Islamic.

As discussed, the types of products offered by Islamic banks will depend on the institutional environment and the organisational strategies, preferences and constraints. To understand the internal and external constraints under which Islamic banks operate, two product sets are identified. First, a *potential* product space consists of all modes of financing that can possibly be used for a particular product. Second, a *feasible* product set is a sub-group of the potential space and includes products that can be developed under the legal/regulatory environment and organisational constraints. Using the product development system perspective, the chapter attempts to investigate the rationale of the choices made among various categories of products (i.e. *Shari'ah*-compliant, *Shari'ah*-based and pseudo-Islamic products) by Islamic banks.

Product categories: a scheme of classification

Whereas products in conventional finance are concerned with economic aspects (such as high return, low risks, efficiency, etc.), Islamic financial products have to consider additional *Shari'ah* requirements which entails compliance with the form and spirit of Islamic law. The *Shari'ah* requirements entail legal and social components. While the legal requirements would necessitate the contractual arrangements of transactions to be compliant with *Shari'ah*, the social requirements arise from the underlying philosophical basis of Islamic finance. As discussed in Chapter 2, the objective of Islamic finance is to promote welfare or benefit (*maslahah*). Thus, fulfilling the spirit of Islamic banking would require inclusion of social dimensions in the operations of normal banking practices and avoidance of activities that are exploitative and harmful to the society (Grais and Pellegrini 2006a).

To examine *Shari'ah* requirements at the product level, the role of relevant bodies within a bank in determining the legal and social aspects of a product has to be clearly defined and assessed. This can be done by examining some features of the product structure identified in Table 3.5 in Chapter 3. The features pertinent to assessing the social requirements are market segment and the purpose/needs served by a product. The legal requirements will be determined by examining the modes of financing used. The ways in which these product features are used to assess the role of the banks in fulfilling their social responsibility and compliance with the legal requirements are discussed next.

Social requirements: a framework for assessment
While Islamic economists and scholars assert the importance of inclusion of *maqasid* and social goals in the operations of Islamic financial institutions, there are no specific discussions on how this can be done at the operational level. From a product perspective, the social role will be determined by the market segments and the needs served by Islamic banks. In what follows, an objective way of identifying and assessing the social goals in these two product features is provided.

1. *Market segment.* The market segment served by an Islamic bank will determine its social orientation. As pointed out in Chapter 3, the segments can be classified according to customer type and class. Customer types can be generally distinguished as the household and the business sectors. Three categories of classes can be indentified in each sector. For the business sector, Islamic banking products will first screen out the prohibited industries such as casinos, breweries, and so on. Market segments in the business sector will be grouped according to size as large, medium and small/micro enterprises. In the household sector, the market segments can be classified according to income levels. Accordingly, the affluent, middle-income group and the poor can be identified. Fulfilling the social goals of *Shari'ah* would entail serving the financial needs of all market segments in general and the small/micro enterprises and the poor/middle-class groups in particular.

2. *Needs/purpose.* Fulfilling social responsibility by the financial sector can be ascertained by examining the extent to which the various financial needs of different groups in a society are satisfied. As discussed in Chapter 3, needs in classical Islamic jurisprudence are classified as necessities (*dururiyyat*), complementary (*hajiyyat*) and luxuries or embellishments (*tahsiniyat*). These classical needs can be adapted in the financial sector as those satisfying survival, security and growth. The survival needs are satisfied by products such as checking and savings deposits, mortgages and financing required for essential activities/items. The security products would satisfy cash reserve and risk management needs and include insurance, pension plans, endowments and time deposits. Finally, growth needs will be satisfied by providing products that help investment opportunities in stocks, mutual funds, tax-protected bonds and financing speculative real-estate purchases, foreign travel for leisure, conspicuous consumption, and so on. Note that the market segment being served will also determine the kind of needs being fulfilled. For example, whereas financing a car for a poor family which can be used as a taxi and income-generating source will fall under survival or the essential category, financing a second or third car for an affluent individual would be categorised as growth or a luxury item.

The social aspects of financing are summarised in Table 6.1. The table shows how the needs and market segments interact to produce a matrix that can identify the range of activities that can be considered social. Across needs, providing products that fulfil survival needs (A1, B1 and C1 in Table 6.1) would rank higher socially than serving the security needs (A2, B2 and C2 in Table 6.1), which in turn will rank higher that satisfying growth needs (A3, B3 and C3 in

Table 6.1 *Social requirements and needs/segments matrix*

Needs \ Segments	Poor/ Micro/ Small	Middle-class/ Medium	Affluent/ Large
Survival (necessities)	A1	B1	C1
Security (complementary)	A2	B2	C2
Growth (luxuries)	A3	B3	C3

Table 6.1). Similarly, the social role of an Islamic bank can be enhanced if the poor and micro-enterprises market segments can also be served along with middle-class and affluent clients. Note, however, that assessing the social role in light of the needs/segments matrix will be relative and can differ for different countries. For example, whereas fulfilling the survival and security financial needs of the poor and micro- and small enterprises (A1 and A2 in Table 6.1) may be considered fulfilling the social goals in some countries, in others the needs of the middle-class income group and the medium-size businesses (B1 and B2 in Table 6.1) can also be included in the social realm.

Legal requirements

Contracts used by Islamic banks for transactions should fulfil the form and substance of *Shari'ah*. The guiding principles of Islamic law related to economic transactions and relationships identified in Chapter 2 have to be fulfilled. While the form of the contract relates to the contractual terms and conditions, the substance of *Shari'ah* is satisfied by fulfilling the overall goals of Islamic law or *maqasid al-Shari'ah* at the contract level. Kahf (2006) indicates that fulfilling *maqasid* at the product level is satisfying the objectives, principles and values underscored in the Islamic laws of transactions. This would include linking returns to risks and bearing the risks of ownership by the owner of the asset. An important related principle is fulfilling the conditions of a sale which is realised by transferring the asset to the new owner. Similarly, conditions of trust and guarantee relationships in terms of liability of loss have to be implemented.

One implication of the form and substance issue in Islamic contractual arrangements relates to the outcome of the transaction. Using ruses or legal stratagems (*hila*) to produce outcomes that are unlawful in substance or distort the legal principles would be contrary to *maqasid al-Shari'ah* (Habil 2007). Products that combine different legal Islamic contracts and produce illegal outcomes in substance or violate the legal maxims will be contrary to the spirit of *Shari'ah* principles and can be identified as pseudo-Islamic products. Some *Shari'ah* scholars have identified some products that focus on the form only. For example, Usmani (2007) believes that the majority of the *sukuk* (Islamic bonds) in the market violate the principles and spirit of Islamic law. Similarly, DeLorenzo (2007) views the total return swap unacceptable, even though the form is *Shari'ah* compatible. As pointed out earlier, the Islamic *Fiqh* Academy has ruled that organised *tawwaruq* as practised by the Islamic financial industry is not permissible as it contains elements of *riba*.

There are several other factors related to the operations of Islamic banks that must be compliant with the principles of Islamic law. From a PD perspective, various operational issues would be important to accomplish some of the legal requirements. These include appropriate treatment of interest-based calculations, discounting, early and late payments, defaults, and so on. To maintain the Islamic nature of the organisation, separation of penalty income (in case of default) and interest income (if any) from the income of the bank needs to be ensured. The impure income has to be put in a special account and used for charitable purposes. Similarly, the payment of *zakah* as an institution (or on behalf of its clients if it is deemed so) should also be implemented. Furthermore, all contractual obligations must be fulfilled by the Islamic banks. For example, the fulfillment of the stipulations of the contract with depositors in terms of profit-sharing has to be ensured. The processes for different Islamic transactions have to follow a specific sequence to satisfy *Shari'ah* requirements. For instance, in a *murabahah* sale, the bank must own the product before selling it. As such, the sale contract to the ultimate client can only be signed after the product has been purchased by the bank.

Shari'ah *requirements and product categories*
Based on the product features described above, different types of products can be identified. As pointed out, the social aspects of the product can be recognised in the role played by the bank, in the market segment served and purpose/needs met. The legal mode can be deliberated in terms of form and substance. Accordingly, the following three types of products can be identified:

1. *Pseudo-Islamic product.* A pseudo-Islamic product conforms to the legal form only; it does not fulfil the substance of *Shari'ah* or serve the social needs. This will be the case when *hila* is used to develop products that fulfil the legal form of contracts, but in substance represents an illegal transaction. Note that in certain cases where there are no alternatives to serve a pressing need, the maxim of necessity can be invoked. Under such situations, the prohibitions can be relaxed and *hila* may be used to satisfy the dire need. However, once the need ceases to exist and/or alternatives are available the lawful ruling due to necessity becomes void. Using *hila* when

there are no dire needs or other alternative modes can be used would result in pseudo-Islamic products. The example of organised *tawarruq* (hereafter *tawarruq*) will be used in the remainder of this book as an example of pseudo-Islamic product as it is widely used in many contemporary transactions.

2. Shariʿah-*compliant products*. Shariʿah-complaint products would satisfy the form and substance of Islamic law, but fail to pay attention to the social goals. Fulfilling the legal requirements entails satisfying the contractual requirements and compliance of all necessary documents, processes and operations with the principles of Islamic law. A Shariʿah-compliant product, however, would not consider the legitimate needs of different segments of the population. Specifically, the products will not meet the survival and security financial needs of the poor and small/micro-enterprises adequately.

3. Shariʿah-*based products*. A Shariʿah-based product is a Shariʿah-compliant product that fulfils the legitimate needs of all market segments. While the contracts satisfy the form and substance of Islamic law, a Shariʿah-based product will also satisfy the survival and security needs of all sections of the population, including the poor and small/micro-entrepreneurs.

The features of different categories of products are summarised in Table 6.2. While pseudo-Islamic products satisfy the legalist forms of contracts, they do not fulfil the substance of Islamic law. An example of a pseudo-Islamic product is the use of *tawarruq* when Shariʿah-compliant alternatives are available. A Shariʿah-compliant product would fulfil the legal requirements, but not satisfy the social needs of the society. While providing mutual funds to the affluent only after setting very high minimum investment

Table 6.2 Shari'ah *requirements and product categories*

Product types	Legal		Social	
	Form	**Substance**	**Market segment**	**Needs**
Pseudo Islamic	✓	?	?	?
Shari'ah compliant	✓	✓	?	?
Shari'ah based	✓	✓	✓	✓

requirements would be *Shari'ah* compliant, it does not meet the social goals as it does not serve the middle-class and poorer sections of the population. A *Shari'ah*-based product is a *Shari'ah*-compliant one and fulfils the social goals. A home financing product that targets all segments of the population, including the poor, would be *Shari'ah* based.

Potential product space

The potential product space includes all possible modes that can be used to develop a product. Note that while different modes are used to identify alternatives in the potential product space, in reality Islamic financial products are more complex. Most products would entail one dominant contract and multiple supporting contracts. For instance, a simple *murabahah*-based financing transaction would involve a promise from the client to purchase the good, an agency contract whereby the bank appoints the client an agent to purchase the good from the vendor, a sale contract between the vendor and the bank, a sale contract between the bank and the client and a collateral or guarantee agreement to mitigate the credit risks.

A sample of potential product space for a selected number of products is presented in this section. The products presented as examples of the potential space represent the broad categories of liability, assets and off-balance-sheet items. On the liability side, an instrument for mobilising savings (investment account) is discussed and on the asset side, various financing instruments (financing durables and working capital, overdraft and credit cards) are presented. A forward contract is examined as an off-balance-sheet item. Note that by using legal/financial engineering, a pseudo-Islamic alternative for any product can be devised. As such, the potential product space for all products discussed below consists of at least one pseudo-Islamic alternative.

Investment deposits

Banks raise their funds by offering transaction (demand) and nontransaction (saving, fixed) deposits, and nondeposit investment products (mutual funds, stocks, pension fund reserves, etc.).[1] While demand deposits or checking/current accounts in Islamic banks take the nature of interest-free loans (*qard hasan*), saving and investment deposits can take various forms. The different modes that are used for investment deposits in Islamic banks are given below.

Mudarabah

Under a *mudarabah* arrangement, an investment deposit would represent a partnership agreement made between the capital providers (depositors) and the bank. The bank acts as an agent or manager to use the funds in productive profitable ventures. The profits are distributed based on a pre-agreed profit-sharing ratio between the bank and the depositors. In the case of losses, these are borne by the depositors according to their share in the assets financed.

Wakalah

Wakalah is an agency contract, whereby the client nominates the bank as an agent to invest funds on her behalf. The returns generated are paid to the client and the bank gets a nominal fee for its services. Returns paid to depositors may be capped (say at 3%) with the understanding that profit earned above this rate will be kept by the bank as incentive income.

Tawarruq

The client provides funds amounting to the intended deposit to the bank and nominates it as agent to buy/sell commodities on her behalf. As an agent, the bank buys the commodity from a broker with the cost equal to the deposit amount (say Saudi Riyals SAR 1,000) with immediate payment and spot delivery. The bank then purchases the commodity from the client at an agreed price of cost plus profit on a deferred payment and spot delivery basis. The profit determined depends on the rate of return and tenor of the deposits. Thus, for a one-year investment deposit of SAR 1,000 paying a return of 3 per cent per annum, the bank will buy the commodity at SAR 1,030. The bank sells back the commodity to another broker on spot and realises the funds equal to the deposit amount (i.e. SAR 1,000). The result of the organised *tawarruq* deal is that the bank has SAR 1,000 in hand and owes the client an amount of SAR 1,030 after a year.

Financing durables

Durables are goods/assets that are consumed over a period of time. The range of items under durables can include real estate, land, building material, machines, equipment, boats, vehicles, motor cycles, furniture, electronics, and so on. The various modes of financing that can be used for durables are given next.

Murabahah

Upon receiving a promise to purchase a durable good, the bank buys the good/asset from the vendor/supplier and then sells it to the client at a mark-up. The price of the good is fixed and the payments can be made in instalments over a period of time.

Ijarah wa iqtinah

The bank buys the durable good/asset and rents it to the client for a specific period of time. The rental payments include the rent of the asset and a part covering the amortisation of capital. After the conclusion of the term the bank gets its capital and return and the asset is transferred to the client as a gift or sold at a token price.

Diminishing *musharakah*

The bank and the client jointly own the durable good/asset that is divided into a number of units. As the client uses the asset, she pays rent on the bank's share. The periodic instalments also include an amount that is used to purchase units/shares of the asset from the bank. Note that the purchase of shares has to be in the form of a separate promise and cannot be stipulated or attached to the partnership contract. Over time the client becomes the owner of the asset by purchasing all units owned by the bank. As the bank owns part of the asset before the conclusion of the transaction, it retains partial obligations/responsibility of asset.

Tawarruq

By using *tawarruq*, the client can get cash which can be used to purchase the durable asset. After the financing is agreed upon, the bank buys a commodity (say at price SAR 1,000) and sells it to the client at a mark-up (at price SAR 1,050) payable sometime in the future, say after a year. The client appoints the bank as an agent to sell the commodity on her behalf to a broker/vendor. The sale proceeds (SAR 1,000) are deposited to the client's account. The debt of the bank

(SAR 1,050) is paid back by the client in instalments in the future.

Working capital financing

The need for working capital financing arises as the production process involves a lag between input use and final sale of output. Firms need funds to purchase the inputs needed in production. One of the options to resolve the working capital needs would be to provide the necessary inputs for production to the firm. The ways in which working capital can be financed using Islamic modes of financing are given below.

Murabahah

The bank buys the necessary inputs and then sells it to the client at a mark-up. Note that the bank provides the exact requirements of raw materials and other inputs used in production to the client. The price paid back is either in a lump-sum at the end of the contract period or in instalments.

Istisna

The bank engages in a pre-production sale contract and pays, in advance, the price of specific quantity of goods to be delivered at a future date. At the end of the contract period the client delivers the goods to the bank. The bank sells the goods and gets its capital and returns from financing.

Temporary *musharakah*

The bank enters into a temporary partnership with the client for a specific productive activity by providing cash to the firm for a limited period of time. The firm keeps an account of the profit/loss arising from the specific activity. At the end of the contract period, the profit-share (or loss) and capital of the bank is paid back to the bank.

Tawarruq

The bank buys a commodity and sells it to the client at a mark-up with deferred payments. The client appoints the bank as an agent to sell the commodity to a vendor. The sale proceeds are deposited in the client's account which is paid back in instalments. Note that in *tawarruq*, the client gets the cash which she can use as working capital.

Overdraft facility

Businesses and individuals sometimes need overdraft facilities to cater for emergency and short-term financing needs. The various structures of Islamic overdraft facilities are presented below.

Mudarabah

Under this partnership facility, the client provides a feasibility report of a *Shari'ah* compatible business activity stating the expected profit in light of past performance. The *mudarabah* contract is for a fixed period of time and establishes a profit-sharing ratio. At the conclusion of the contract period, the capital of the bank is returned back with its share of profits earned. The following features are added to ensure a fixed return to the bank.

1. An undertaking is given by the bank or *rab-ul mal* (provider of overdraft financing) to give a bonus to the *mudarib* (client) if the share of the *rab-ul mal* exceeds a threshold level.
2. The client promises to buy *mudarabah* assets for a specific price if the return on *mudarabah* is less than the projected profit in the feasibility report.

Ijarah

The client must have an asset (land/building) which is split into a certain number of units (say a building with 100,000 units for GBP 100 each). When in need of overdraft, the client sells units of the asset to the bank and gets the payments for price. After owning the units, the bank leases these units to the client for a specified rent. Once the contract period is over, the bank sells back the asset to the client.

Musharakah

A model similar to the *ijarah* is the diminishing *musharakah* model whereby the bank and client agree to a partnership in the ownership of an asset. Whenever the client withdraws funds, it is treated as payments for buying part of the asset and the client pays rent on it to the bank. At the end of the contract period the *musharakah* is dissolved.

Tawarruq with rebate

A debt is created using *tawarruq* for the client by the bank for the period for which the overdraft facility is provided. As a result, the client owes the bank the overdraft amount plus the rate of return which is to be paid in monthly instalments for the period of the overdraft. The client's funds resulting from the *tawarruq* are put aside in a special account and linked to her current account on which the overdraft facility is provided.[2] When the client overdraws on her current account, the funds from the special account are used. Every month the payment due on the debt created by *tawarruq* is compared with the overdraft amount used by the client. The balance of the unused amount is given to the client as rebate. If the client uses the full overdraft amount during a month, she does not receive any rebate.

A numerical example clarifies the *tawarruq*-based overdraft facility. With a simple rate of return rate of 6 per cent per annum for an overdraft facility of Bahraini Dinar BHD 10,000, a debt of BHD 10,600 will be created through *tawarruq*. The monthly profit repayment due on the *tawarruq* will on average be BHD 600/12=BHD 50. The amount of BHD 10,000 will be deposited in a special account linked to the current account. If in the first month the client uses BHD 4,000 from the overdraft facility, then the bank will charge the client 6 per cent on the amount used (BHD 20= 4,000x0.06/12). As the payment due from *tawarruq* is BHD 50 and the overdraft charges amount to BHD 20, a rebate of BHD 30 is given for the month. Note that a flexible rate can also be used in a *tawarruq* and rebate-based facility. Under the flexible-rate facility, the *tawarruq* rate is fixed for the period of the facility, usually at a high rate. The monthly rate used to determine the variable cost of funds is linked to a benchmark rate. The periodic rebate given is determined according to use of funds calculated by using the flexible benchmark rate.

Credit card

A credit card (CC) issued by a bank provides a facility to the client to purchase goods or withdraw cash. When a credit card is used it is checked and authorised through the network systems (such as Visa or Mastercard) and payments for the goods made upon approval. The merchant/retailer sends the information to its acquiring bank, which transfers the amount to the merchants/retailer's account. AAOIFI (2003) has the following rulings related to credit cards:

> Article 3/3. It is not permissible for an institution to issue credit cards that provide an interest bearing revolving credit facility, whereby the cardholder pays interest for being allowed to pay off the debt in installments. (p. 22)

Article 4/3. It is permissible for the institution issuing the card to charge the cardholder membership fees, renewal fees and replacement fees. (p. 22)

Article 4/5 (b). It is permissible for the institution issuing the card to charge a flat rate service fee for cash withdrawal, proportionate to the service offered, but not a fee that varies with the amount withdrawn. (p. 23)

The permissibility to charge the cardholder membership fees or renewal or replacement fees is given against the right given to the customer to carry the card and to benefit from its services. The different types of Islamic credit cards used are given below.

Fee- (*ujrah*-) based CC

The fee-based CC is one that charges an annual fee as a service charge (*ujrah*). The annual fee charged depends on the amount of credit authorised. The annual charges are paid by the client in monthly/quarterly instalments. A minimum repayment of a certain amount or a percentage of the outstanding balance must be repaid every month. For example, a card with a credit limit of Kuwaiti Dinar (KWD) 1,200 may carry an annual fee of KWD 80 and require a monthly payment of the minimum of KWD 50 or 10 per cent of the outstanding balance.

Fee- (*ujrah*-) and rebate-based CC

The fee- and rebate-based CC works in exactly the same way as the fee-based CC with an additional component of rebate added to it. The rebate is used to charge the client for the actual usage of the card facility. In these types of CC the fee charged will usually be higher. For example, for a CC with a credit line of Malaysian Ringgit (MYR) 10,000 with an implied rate of return of 18 per cent per annum, the corresponding fees will be MYR 1,800 implying a fee of MYR 150 per month. If in the first month the client uses MYR 3,000 on CC, then the bank will charge the client 18 per cent on the amount used (MYR 45= MYR 3,000x0.18/12). As the bank has already charged the client for the full amount as fees (i.e. MYR 150 per month), a rebate of MYR 105 (= MYR 150–45) will be given to the client for the month. The same process is repeated for each month.

Maintenance-fee CC

Along with charging an annual fee, some banks charge a service fee for maintaining the outstanding balance. For example, a card issued by an Islamic bank with a credit limit of Emirates Dirham (AED) 10,000 can carry an annual fee of AED 800, and requires a payment of a minimum of 5 per cent of the outstanding balance or AED 100. Outstanding funds are transferred to a no-interest non-profit service account linked to the CC. A fixed monthly maintenance fee (*ujrah*) of AED 100/month is charged to maintain the service account and give rights of use of the credit card. The service fee is not charged for the months when all the outstanding balance is paid off in full (i.e. when balance in the service account is zero).

Pre-transaction tawarruq CCs

The principle of the *tawarruq*-based credit card is similar to the *tawarruq* and rebate-based overdraft facility discussed above. For example, with a simple rate of return of 18 per cent per annum for the credit care of MYR 10,000 a debt of MYR 11,800 will be created through *tawarruq*.[3] An amount equal to the credit card limit of MYR 10,000 owned by the client will be deposited in a special account linked to her current account. If in the first month the client uses MYR 4,000 on the credit card, then the bank will charge the client 18 per cent on the amount used (MYR 60= MYR 4,000x0.18/12). As the bank has already charged the client for the full amount on the *tawarruq* (i.e. MYR 150 per month), a rebate of MYR 90 (= MYR 150–60) will be given to the client for that month. At the end of contract period, the remains of the credit held in the special account are transferred to the bank as a final payment for the *tawarruq* transaction. As in the overdraft facility, a built-in flexible rate can also be used with the *tawarruq*-based credit card facilities.

Post-transaction *tawarruq* CC

The post-transaction *tawarruq* CC starts out as a charge card and converts into a credit card if any outstanding balance remains at the end of the billing period. If the client pays the whole amount, there are no charges. If the client pays part of it, leaving an outstanding balance, the bank does a *tawwaruq* on behalf of the client.[4] As a result of the *tawarruq*, the new balance includes a return share for the bank. At each consecutive billing period, the unpaid principal amount is again used as basis for *tawarruq* whereby the return of the bank is added onto the principal amount, and the process continues until the whole amount is paid up. Note that some banks charge the client administrative fees for the *tawaruq* transactions making the Islamic CC more expensive than its conventional counterparts.

Islamic synthetic forward

As pointed out in Chapter 2, contemporary forwards, which postpone both the payment and delivery of a commodity, are not permitted. This is due to prohibition of sale of debt with debt (*bai al-kali bi al-kali*). Given the restrictions on using a conventional forward, the different versions of Islamic forwards are presented below.

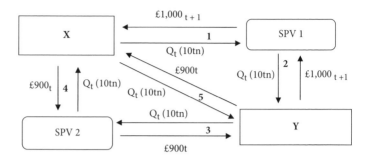

Figure 6.1 Murabahah- *and* salam-*based forward*

Murabahah- and *salam*-based forward

The structure of the *murabahah-* and *salam*-based synthetic forward discussed in ElGamal (2006) is shown in Figure 6.1. Two special purpose vehicles (SPVs) are involved and several transactions are needed to create a forward that produces a similar outcome to a conventional one. Assume the spot price of 10 tons of aluminium is £900. X and Y want to structure a forward contract whereby X would deliver 10 tons of aluminium after a year at a price of £1,000 to be paid at the time of delivery. To arrange this forward deal, X sells 10 tons of aluminium to SPV1 on credit (*murabahah*) for £1,000 payable in one year (shown by arrow-pair 1). SPV1 in turn sells 10 tons of aluminium to Y on a *murabahah* basis for £1,000 payable in one year (shown by arrow-pair 2). The two *murabahah* transactions create a debt of £1,000 that Y has to pay to X through SPV1. After receiving the aluminium, Y sells it to SPV2 for the standard spot sale price of £900 in cash (shown by arrow-pair 3). The SPV2 in turn sells 10 tons of aluminium to X at the spot sale price of £900 (shown by arrow-pair 4). The result of these transactions is that Y receives £900 today (through SPV2) from X and owes X £1,000 (through SPV1) payable after a year. The forward deal is completed with a *salam* contract between X and Y. After receiving the money, Y uses £900 to prepay X the price for 10 tons of aluminium to be delivered in a year's time (shown by arrow-pair 5). The final net result of all the transactions mimics a conventional forward contract: X will deliver 10 tons of aluminium to Y after a year in exchange for £1,000 to be paid by Y.

Tawarruq-based foreign currency forward

Assume that a client wants to buy USD 1,500 in three months at an exchange rate of GBP 1= USD 1.5 to hedge against currency risk. To structure a forward that is similar to a conventional one would require several transactions. The bank first buys copper at the price of GBP 1,000 and sells at GBP 1,000 to the client payable in three months. The client sells back the copper to a commodity broker (arranged by the bank) and gets GBP 1,000. The combination of these two transactions constitute a *tawarruq* deal leaving cash of GBP 1,000 with the client and creating a debt in favour of the bank of an amount of GBP 1,000 payable in three months The client uses her cash to buy aluminium at the price of GBP 1,000 and sells to the bank at USD 1,500 payable in three months. After receiving the aluminium, the bank sells it to a broker for a spot price of GBP 1,000. The result of these transactions is that the bank owes the client USD 1,500 payable in three months time. The net result of the two *tawarruq* transactions is that the bank will get GBP 1,000 from the client and pay USD 1,500 to her after three months. Note that the bank can charge a fee for offering a forward deal by adding this into the prices. For example, if the price of purchasing the forward is 2 per cent of the transaction, then GBP 20 can be added into the initial sale of copper to the client. Thus, the bank would sell copper worth GBP 1,000 to the client at GBP 1,020 and the difference would constitute the fee paid by the client for the forward arrangement.

Feasible product set

Other than fulfilling the *Shari'ah* requirements, products developed by Islamic banks must fulfil the legal and regulatory requirements on the one hand and the organisational constraints on the other. The feasible product set consists of the modes of financing that an Islamic bank can use under the institutional and organisational constraints. Whereas the potential product space includes the range of various modes of finance that can be used for a particular product, the feasible set constitutes the modes that an Islamic bank can actually develop and use. To comprehend how potential product space can result in a much smaller feasible set, the constraints faced by Islamic banks at institutional and organisational levels have to be understood. Note that while a bank can influence the organisational elements affecting product development, it does not have control over external factors such as the legal and regulatory environment. At the organisational level, the feasible product set can be understood in terms of the processes identified in the product development cycle. As a product must be cleared by different departments before it can be launched, it must fulfil the departmental requirements. Given the external and internal constraints, two feasible sets related to modes of financing used in developing products can arise. These are discussed below.

Feasible set with Shari'ah-*compliant products*
In the ideal situation, the feasible set will contain several *Shari'ah*-compliant options from which an Islamic bank can select to develop a product. Note that the pseudo-Islamic alternatives can always be added to the feasible set by using legal/financial engineering techniques. To choose an appropriate mode from the available *Shari'ah*-compliant

options, the PD cross-functional team will consider various risk-return features of different modes of financing. For example, to determine which mode to use for durable financing discussed in the potential product space, various associated risks will be considered. A *murabahah* contract is *Shari'ah* compliant if the sequence of transactions is done properly. From the client's point of view, there may be some delay in obtaining the product as there are certain steps that need to be followed. These include signing a promise to buy and agency contract, getting a quotation from the seller, buying the product on behalf of the bank and then finally signing a sale contract with the bank. From the bank's perspective, as the price is fixed, a rate of return risk will exist for contacts with longer tenors. Furthermore, as a debt is created, collateral of guarantee may be required to ensure repayment of dues.

The rate of return risk in financing durables with longer maturity periods can be minimised by using a floating-rate *ijarah* contract. The rate of return on *ijarah* contracts can be adjusted periodically to a benchmark rate. This mode is not controversial as long as the bank takes the obligations and responsibilities of ownership during the lease period, and the lease and sale contracts are separate. While the bank will not require any collateral, a potential risk arises if the client does not want to continue the lease contract, in which case the bank will have to dispose of the asset and face market risks. Diminishing *musharakah* is another acceptable *Shari'ah*-compliant mode which has some of the features of the *ijarah* contract. The rate of return risks can be avoided by having a floating rental rate on the bank's share of the asset. Furthermore, the asset acts as collateral as it is held in trust until the client pays it off fully.

If the benchmark rate does not change much and the tenor of the contract is relatively short, then the bank may opt for the *murabahah* mode. If the tenor of the contract is longer and the bank anticipates the benchmark rate to change, then either the diminishing *musharakah* or *ijarah* modes may be chosen. Under these modes, however, the bank has to bear the risks associated with the asset until the end of the contract. The choice of an appropriate mode will depend on which of these risks the bank has an appetite for and can mitigate efficiently.

Feasible set without Shari'ah-*compliant products*

Cases may arise when the feasible set does not contain any *Shari'ah*-compliant products due to constraints at the institutional and organisational levels. The externally induced institutional factors can limit the options available as the laws and regulations define to a large extent what Islamic banks can do. For example, consider the alternative modes presented in the potential product space for savings/investment deposits above. While the *mudarabah* is a preferable mode of generating deposits in Islamic banks due to its risk-sharing features, banks may not be able to use this mode due to a variety of reasons. At the institutional (legal/regulatory) level, a profit-loss sharing deposit may be restricted by the laws and regulations of a country. For example, in countries without Islamic banking laws, regulatory requirements may oblige banks to pay a fixed return on savings and term deposits. This is true in some jurisdictions such as the UK where deposits are legally characterised as fixed sums of funds that are returned to depositors in full, as long as the bank is solvent. This may make *mudarabah*- and *wakalah*-based deposits a regulatory compliance issue. Furthermore, the contractual nature of *wakalah* may not qualify it as a regular deposit product. Being an agency contract, *wakalah*-based deposits would be placed off the balance sheet and necessitate different regulatory treatment. Thus, in jurisdictions where *mudarabah-* and *wakalah*-based deposits cannot be provided due to legal and regulatory restrictions, the feasible set will contain *tawarruq*-based fixed returns deposits only.

There can be various constraints at the organisational level that limit the use of certain modes of financing. In countries where *mudarabah*-based deposits are allowed under the legal/regulatory regimes, it still may not be feasible to use this mode due to constraints at the organisational level. For example, if the core IT system of a bank uses a conventional banking framework, it will not be able to link the returns on liabilities of the balance sheet to the returns on assets as required in a *mudarabah* deposit contract. In this case, developing a *mudarabah*-based deposit will either be stalled in the development stage or an alternative has to be found in the IT system to cope with the problem. One option may be to install a new IT system that can link the returns on the asset side of the balance sheet to deposits. However, this may be too costly for the bank. Another option may be to calculate the returns on assets periodically and enter these figures on the liability side manually. This option, however, will be susceptible to errors and high operational risks.

Another limiting feature to the use of certain modes can arise from the nature of the transaction itself. As Islamic financing is either sale based or equity based, some modes may not be appropriate for certain market segments. For example, the potential product space for the overdraft facility presented above shows that the feasible set available for the household sector is limited. The first three modes identified in the potential product space (*mudarabah, ijarah* and *musharakah*) can be used mainly by the business sector. As these modes are attached to assets or commercial activities, they may not be feasible for providing overdraft facilities for the household sector. The only feasible option to provide overdraft facility to individuals appears to be *tawarruq*.

Shari'ah requirements and product categories: choices and concerns

As already stated, Islamic financial products can be categorised as *Shari'ah*-based, *Shari'ah*-compliant or pseudo-Islamic depending on how they address the social and legal *Shari'ah* requirements. The feasible sets limit the choices in product development and have implications for fulfilling *Shari'ah* requirements and the product categories offered by Islamic banks. When the feasible set does not have any *Shari'ah*-compliant products, the options available to a bank may be to provide a pseudo-Islamic product or no product at all. In such cases, the maxim of necessity can be invoked to come up with pseudo-Islamic products if the needs are dire. Even though the resulting product may fulfil only the form but not the substance, it will be a solution under the constraining circumstances.

A key question arising in situations in which the maxim of necessity is invoked is to ascertain what constitutes dire needs. One objective way to resolve the issue may be to examine the alternatives in Table 6.1. For example, a narrow view may consider survival needs across all market segments as dire needs. A more liberal interpretation can also include the security needs identified in Table 6.1 as dire needs. Note that use of ruses may be permissible only under the maxim of necessity when *Shari'ah*-compliant solutions are not available in the feasible set. Once *Shari'ah*-compliant alternatives are added to a feasible set or dire need ceases to exist, the maxim of necessity will not apply. In such cases, use of ruses to come up with pseudo-Islamic alternatives will not fulfil the *Shari'ah* requirements.

When the feasible set contains *Shari'ah*-compliant products, pseudo-Islamic products can be added to it by financial/legal engineering. For example, while *ijarah* may be a *Shari'ah*-compliant mode of financing, it can be used to come up with a product that dilutes the spirit of Islamic legal principles. Instead of using a *Shari'ah*-compliant mode of buying an asset and leasing it to a client, a bank may opt to buy an asset from a client (paying cash for it) and then leasing it back to the client. During the tenure period the client pays rent on the asset. After the end of the tenure, the asset is sold back to the client at the initial price. The sum of these transactions is a disguised loan with interest using the veil of an asset.

The specific products developed from the feasible set will depend on many factors. In this section the internal dynamics of decision making related to the social and legal requirements are presented. Using the PD system perspective, different domains of control and decision making regarding *Shari'ah* requirements are discussed. As PD is a complex process involving various actors and departments of a bank, frictions can arise in determining what mode of financing to use. Tensions can appear if there are trade-offs between economic factors and *Shari'ah* requirements. From a PD perspective, these conflicts will partly be resolved by the overall strategic goals that provide guidelines regarding treatment of competing interests. In developing products, the conflicts are settled by the relative weights given to economic and *Shari'ah* factors. The ways in which the social and legal *Shari'ah* requirements may be determined in a bank are discussed below.

Legal requirements: who decides?

The PD process shows that various departments of the bank are involved and provide input at different stages of the development cycle. The *Shari'ah* department and SSB play a vital role in ensuring the fulfillment of legal requirements. The SSB has direct responsibility to ascertain that the product complies with the principles and values of *Shari'ah* before it is launched in the market. The choice of the appropriate mode will depend on institutional and organisational constraints and the availability of alternatives in the feasible product set.

The objectives of banks, including Islamic ones, are to come up with products that are efficient and can generate high expected returns. An efficient product would imply lower risks and costs in terms of development and delivery. In many cases, however, the calculus of economic factors may conflict with the principles of *Shari'ah*. In these cases, the bank has to decide what the priorities are between expected return/profit and risks on the one hand and *Shari'ah* principles on the other. Too much emphasis given to economic factors can lead to choosing inferior modes of financing. This can happen if the SSB is lax and allows pseudo-Islamic alternatives even when the feasible set contains *Shari'ah*-compliant products.

An example of the trade-off between economic interests and *Shari'ah* principles can be seen in the case of a product for financing working capital discussed above. Assume that a product that provides cash as working capital has to be developed to help firms pay for operating costs such as salaries and utilities. The potential product space for working capital includes *Shari'ah*-compliant modes (*murabahah*, *musharakah* and *istisna*) and a *tawarruq*-based alternative. As *murabahah* supplies the client with the necessary inputs used in production, it will not be a feasible mode to provide cash. Temporary *musharakah* provides cash to the firm through equity participation. *Istisna* and *tawarruq* provide cash in debt-based modes, with in-kind debt created in the former and monetary debt in the latter. The risk with the *musharakah* mode is the loss that the bank may have to incur due to moral hazard problems and also from dishonesty in the reporting of accounts in the absence of monitoring. In *istisna* counter-party risk can arise due to delay or non-delivery of goods on time. In the absence of parallel *istisna*, the bank may face market risks when the goods are delivered. *Tawarruq* appears to be the least risky alternative as it entails credit risk only.

As mentioned above, all new products have to be cleared by various departments including risk management. When product proposals using *musharakah* and *istisna* modes are presented to the risk management department, they may not clear these options as they entail excessive market and counter-party risks. Though these products are *Shari'ah*-compliant as they satisfy both the form and substance of Islamic law, they may not be accepted due to high capital requirements or stringent credit risk guidelines meant to protect the returns. From a risk perspective, only *tawarruq* may be the acceptable mode as it carries the least risk. If the risk management department does not clear the *Shari'ah*-compliant modes, the choice available to the product development manager may be to develop a *tawarruq*-based product or no product at all.

Whether a bank will adopt the *tawarruq*-based pseudo-Islamic product or one of the *Shari'ah*-compliant alternatives for financing working capital will depend on the SSB. When *Shari'ah*-compliant products are available in the feasible set, the SSB should choose these over the pseudo-Islamic alternatives. However, as the product development manager faces objections from the risk management department, he may try to convince the SSB about the risks involved in the *Shari'ah*-compliant modes and request approval of *tawarruq*-based product. The decision of the

SSB in favour of the latter type of product should depend on whether it considers the risks involved in *Shari'ah*-compliant modes compelling enough to invoke the maxim of necessity. The case for using the maxim of necessity to simply avoid risks inherent in financial transactions is weak as the underlying principles of Islamic finance emphasise linking returns to risks. It has been noticed that when the SSB strictly adheres to *Shari'ah* principles, the banks produce *Shari'ah*-compliant alternatives. For example, as the SSB of the Dubai Islamic Bank and Emirates Islamic Bank in the UAE do not permit *tawarruq*, the bank has come up with many other *Shari'ah*-compliant products. Unlike the Dubai Islamic Bank there are other Islamic banks in the UAE that are using *tawarruq*-based products as their SSB appear to be permissive and have succumbed to the pressures of the bankers.

While the SSB has an important role in minimising the use of pseudo-Islamic products, tension between the *Shari'ah* requirements and economic interests can also be reduced significantly if there are clear directives from top management about *Shari'ah*-related issues vis-à-vis profitability. Ideally, in Islamic banks the norm should be that in situations where trade-offs between *Shari'ah* principles and economic factors arise, the former should prevail. However, too much emphasis given to profitability and economic factors by top management will create incentives to dilute the *Shari'ah* requirements.

Social requirements: who decides?

As pointed out, a bank's social performance can be established by identifying the market segments and needs that its products serve. As market/product decisions are made at strategic levels, social responsibility of the bank and its implications at product level will be established at the highest levels of organisational decision making. The banks have to decide at the level of overall mission and vision whether the products will be *Shari'ah* based or *Shari'ah* compliant. As producing *Shari'ah*-based products can be costlier and riskier, economic considerations may incline banks to move towards *Shari'ah*-compliant or pseudo-Islamic products. The BOD along with top management determine the overall strategy of the bank that will include a markets/products dimension. Once the BOD determines the social orientation of the organisation by identifying the market/product targets in the overall strategic goals, the senior management devises the PD strategy and plans for implementation. The feasible set for each product type determines the options available to Islamic banks to realise these plans.

Though the role of the Islamic financial industry in realising social goals is not uniform, many Islamic banks appear to be fulfilling the social aspects of business to varying degrees. This is made possible partly because many Islamic banks have social objectives in the articles of association and/or in their aims and mission statements. Grais and Pellegrini (2006b) report that in a sample of thirteen Islamic banks, all were involved in distributing *zakah*, the majority were providing interest-free loans to economically disadvantaged groups, and three were involved in charitable activities.

A related decision that the BOD has to make is to identify their preferences in the *Shari'ah* goals/profitability domain. As *Shari'ah*-based products may be developed and offered at some cost, there may appear to be some trade-off between economic and *Shari'ah* goals in certain cases. If profitability is the only concern, the banks may sacrifice certain *Shari'ah* requirements. For example, providing finance to the poor is socially desirable but may not make economic sense in terms of profitability. While the bank may opt out of financing this market segment by considering the economics of the financing, the *Shari'ah*-based approach would be to develop appropriate products that minimise the associated risks and provides the bank with a satisfactory rate of return. The BOD has to clearly demonstrate preference for *Shari'ah*-based products by accepting this approach and providing the resources to develop them.

Some contend that the SSB should be responsible for ensuring the social role of Islamic banks. For example, Siddiqi (2006a) asserts that the SSBs should be overseeing the fulfillment of the overall objectives of Islamic law (*maqasid al-Shari'ah*). Note that the role of the SSBs is to ensure that the spirit of Islamic law at the contract level is achieved by fulfilling the principles and values of *Shari'ah*. This would require approving *Shari'ah*-compliant products and avoiding pseudo-Islamic ones. As pointed out, control of the broader social character of banking operations in terms of product and market features lies in the hands of the BOD and senior management, not the SSB.

Shari'ah requirements, efficiency and equity

With the growth of Islamic finance, the main focus of the industry shifted to providing *Shari'ah*-compliant alternatives to conventional products. This approach led to replicating conventional products and sometimes in the process diluting the *Shari'ah* requirements. The potential spaces of different products presented above have cases that mimic the substance of conventional financial products. For example, all *tawarruq*-based products have features of a synthetic interest-based loan. Even when traditional *Shari'ah*-compliant modes are used, these are transformed to be similar in substance to conventional products by attaching additional conditions and contracts. For instance, whereas a *mudarabah* is a profit-loss sharing contract, the *mudarabah*-based overdraft facility has removed this feature by adding two conditions that provides the bank with a fixed return. Though these conditions ensure a fixed return to the bank, it dilutes *Shari'ah* principles by negating the basic risk-sharing feature of a *mudarabah* contract. Similarly, returns in some products are linked to time and amount of financing by using a rebate to produce the effect of an interest-based loan (as seen in the overdraft and credit card structures discussed above).

Other than compromising on the legal requirements, the approach of Islamising conventional products also raises questions related to efficiency. As has been discussed, developing pseudo-Islamic products that are similar to conventional ones in substance requires adding several conditions and contracts. For example, a synthetic forward that imitates a conventional forward is created by using multiple contracts to circumvent *Shari'ah* prohibition on these transactions. Specifically, the Islamic forward has five sale transactions (two *murabahah* sales with deferred payments, two spot sales and one *salam* contract). Similarly, the overdraft facility with *mudarabah* complicates the transaction by adding two additional conditions. While these Islamic structures are similar to the conventional products in substance, they are more costly and riskier, and hence inefficient compared to their conventional counterparts.

Another contentious issue of using Islamic financial products relates to equity. For example, among the credit card alternatives presented in the potential product space, the fee-based *Shari'ah*-compliant alternative fulfils the legal requirements. However, the card holder has to pay the fee irrespective of card usage. Compared to a conventional CC, a fee-based Islamic card will be costly for clients who use their cards rarely. This problem is resolved in the fee and rebate CC model, where the client is given back a rebate equal to the amount of finance charges for the unused credit periodically. While the fee- and rebate-based CC replicates a conventional CC in substance, it appears to be more equitable to clients than the fee-only alternative.

The issue of equity is revealed more explicitly when financing a durable asset with a long maturity date is considered. For instance, assume a client takes a home mortgage finance deal amounting to GBP 100,000 for 15 years using a *murabahah* contract. With a rate of return of 6 per cent per annum, the *murabahah* price paid for the tenor of financing is calculated to be around GBP 152,000. Assume that after a year, due to some reason, the client wants to settle early and pay-off all the financing dues owed to the bank. In a conventional bank, the client will pay the interest due for a year and an additional fine to break the contract. With one year's financing costs of GBP 6,000 and a fine of say GBP 4,000, the amount paid to the bank would be a total of GBP 110,000. In a *murabahah* contract, however, the agreed price of GBP 152,000 has to be paid in full by the client. This option appears to be less equitable than the conventional alternative. To remove the disparity, a solution is to structure the Islamic transaction similar to the conventional one by introducing a rebate. The rebate will be calculated as the difference between the *murabahah* price and finance charges for the year plus a fine (GBP 42,000= GBP 152,000-110,000).

The above examples indicate that Islamic contracts that do not include a rebate to compute the time value of money appear to be less equitable. While the product with the rebate is similar to the conventional one in substance, it is more equitable to the client in the case of early settlements. This is confirmed in a recent High Court decision in Malaysia, whereby the judge ruled that Islamic banks must grant a rebate in all *Bai bithaman ajil* (BBA) contracts (which is similar to a debt-based *murabahah* contract). The judge rationalised her decision by stating 'I must vehemently stress that the purpose of this proceeding is to deal with what would be considered *fair* and *equitable*. . .' (the emphasis is mine).[5]

ElGamal (2006) questions the use of inefficient Islamic replications of conventional practices and the lack of social orientation of Islamic finance. Pointing out the use of ruses that produce inefficient replications of conventional products, he asserts that Islamic finance should focus on the substance rather than the form. If Islamic and conventional products are similar in substance, there is no economic reason to use inefficient and costly Islamic alternatives. He argues that Islamic finance should be focusing on social aspects, such as microfinance targeted to the poor. In doing so, the form in which it is done should not matter as using inefficient Islamic finance increases the costs of financing. The implication appears to be that using efficient conventional microfinance would be fine as long as social objectives are being realised.

The above argument may be difficult to accept. While substance is important, goals cannot justify using means that are not considered legitimate. The appropriate response to the problem is to develop and use *Shari'ah*-based products that entail their own risk-return features. Many problems of Islamic finance arise because it is trying to fit Islamic legal principles into the conventional financial framework. This is causing tensions between the *Shari'ah* principles and economic factors and often diluting the former. Development of a *Shari'ah*-based Islamic finance would require abandoning the risk-return domain of conventional products and adopting a system based on its own paradigm founded on principles and goals of *Shari'ah*. Adopting the Islamic financial paradigm would imply acknowledging and managing inherent and risk-return features of *Shari'ah*-based products. For example, instead of using a product for financing durables using *murabahah* and rebate, the diminishing *musharakah* mode can be used. Implementation of an Islamic financial paradigm, however, has to be reinforced beyond the product level. The next chapter discusses some issues at the organisational and institutional levels that can facilitate adoption of this *Shari'ah*-based paradigm.

Notes

1. Note that some non-deposit investment products can be classified as off-balance-sheet items. For a discussion on the various sources of funds available to banks, see Rose (1999, ch. 12).
2. Note that the special account can be a short-term investment account that pays a rate of return on the funds deposited.
3. In Malaysia, *bai-al-inah* may be used instead of *tawarruq*.
4. This is done using the concept of *bai al-fadouli*, whereby the bank acts as an agent of the client and undertakes the transaction. Note that the client has the right to annul the transaction taken on her behalf, if desired.
5. See Grounds of Decision for the judgment in *Bank Islam Malaysia Bhd* v *Azhar Bin Osman* and three other cases by Dato Rohana Yusuf, 28 January 2010, paragraph 22.

CHAPTER 7
SHARI'AH-BASED ISLAMIC FINANCE: THE WAY FORWARD

This book opened with expressions of concern about the divergence of the practice of Islamic banking from its ideal model. Various chapters in the book attempt to examine the diverse issues related to Islamic financial products and their development processes. Chapter 3 discusses the institutional environment under which Islamic banks operate and Chapters 4 and 5 examine the organisational characteristics affecting product development. Discussions in Chapter 6 identify two scenarios under which *Shari'ah* principles can be compromised. First, internal and external constraints produce a feasible set that does not have any *Shari'ah*-compliant alternatives. This will be the case in countries that do not have Islamic banking laws and appropriate supporting regulatory regimes or face technological restrictions to the use of *Shari'ah*-compliant products. In these situations, the options available to Islamic banks may be to use pseudo-Islamic products or have no products at all.

The second situation in which *Shari'ah* requirements may be diluted is not due to constraints, but because banks choose to do so due to economic reasons. In these cases, the feasible set contains *Shari'ah*-compliant products. Islamic banks, however, choose to use products that compromise the *Shari'ah* requirements due to economic factors.

Specifically, when tensions between *Shari'ah* principles and economic factors arise, the latter governs choices and decisions. As pseudo-Islamic products can be developed using legal/financial engineering, these may be preferred to *Shari'ah*-compliant products due to their resemblance to risk-return features of conventional products. In choosing these types of product, principles of Islamic law are being compromised and Islamic finance is gradually losing its unique features.

The above discussion indicates that moving towards a *Shari'ah*-based Islamic financial system would require resolving problems at different levels. First, external and internal constraints inhibiting the development of *Shari'ah*-compliant products need to be alleviated. This can be done by providing an enabling institutional environment under which Islamic banks can operate and also using alternative organisational formats that enable the internal constraints of achieving *Shari'ah* requirements to be appropriately addressed. Second, to expand the alternatives of *Shari'ah*-compliant products from which Islamic banks can choose in the feasible set, there is a need to have a new approach to innovation and research and development. Finally, a mechanism has to be introduced that creates incentives for choosing the appropriate *Shari'ah*-based products from the feasible set. This would require a better *Shari'ah* governance regime. Some of these issues that can help introduce a *Shari'ah*-based Islamic financial industry are discussed below.

Strengthening the institutional framework

Chapter 3 presents different legal and regulatory frameworks under which Islamic banks operate. Of the three legal regimes identified in the chapter, the feasible set for Islamic products will be most restricted in countries that do not have Islamic banking laws and supporting regulations. In the absence of Islamic banking laws, there are constraints under which Islamic banks can operate. As discussed above, the conventional legal and regulatory frameworks make the use of *Shari'ah*-compliant products unfeasible in many jurisdictions. This may not be the case in countries with Islamic legal systems and ones with Western legal systems with Islamic banking laws; these legal regimes will be more accommodating to Islamic banking products. However, an Islamic legal system or banking laws themselves may not be sufficient for a supporting institutional environment. As Islamic banking involves sale-and-equity-based financing, tax laws may also have to be changed to reduce the tax burdens on Islamic financial transactions.

Another contentious issue is the status of privately created Islamic law by SSBs at the transaction level under national legal systems that may not be Islamic. The duality of private-public laws has direct relevance to dispute resolution and will affect the type of products developed by Islamic banks. Sometimes *Shari'ah* principles are compromised to accommodate contracts within national laws. An appropriate dispute resolution framework in terms of courts where disputes related to Islamic financial transactions can be adjudicated under *Shari'ah* principles will facilitate using *Shari'ah*-compliant products.

At the regulatory level, Chapter 3 identified one of the roles of the regulators as ensuring soundness of financial institutions. Among other things, to mitigate systemic risks the regulators require financial institutions to have robust risk management systems and avoid engaging in risky investments. One tool used by regulators to mitigate risks in banks is regulatory capital requirements. While profit-loss sharing modes such as *mudarabah* and *musharakah* are preferable modes from an Islamic perspective due to their risk-sharing features, these are considered risky. As such, these financing instruments will require a higher regulatory capital charge.[1] As capital is costly, higher capital requirements for certain modes of financing would discourage their use from a product development perspective.

The issue of the regulatory capital for financial products should not be considered in isolation from the overall Islamic banking model. If Islamic banks have profit-loss sharing investment accounts, then the depositors are expected to share the risks and this should be factored into the calculation of the capital requirements (IFSB 2005b). However, if the liability side of the Islamic bank has *tawarruq*-based investment accounts, then the argument of risk-sharing will not hold. In these cases, Islamic banks may opt for debt-based financing instruments on the asset side to minimise the risks and capital they have to hold.

The above discussion suggests that it may be difficult to use *Shari'ah*-compliant equity-based products under the current banking models and regulatory framework. One solution to this problem is to opt for other organisational formats that are not constrained by regulatory requirements. Not only will the nature of sources and uses of funds of these non-bank organisations have less stringent regulatory requirements, the formats may be more suitable to fulfil the *Shari'ah* requirements. Some organisational formats that can facilitate fulfillment of legal and social *Shari'ah* requirements are discussed next.

Organisational diversity

The problem of using Islamic replications of conventional financial products has its origins in the genesis of Islamic banking under the shadows of conventional finance. Islamic finance was affected by its conventional counterparts when it adopted their debt-based corporate banking model. Not only did Islamic banks assume the for-profit banking model, they also employed professionals from conventional institutions to manage the operations. As the organisational format adopted and the professionals employed by Islamic banks were capable of managing risks in debt-based instruments, the Islamic versions of these products were transplanted in these fledging institutions. The trend of aligning the industry to the conventional was entrenched by market forces, profitability and competition. Being debt-based financial organisations, the format of conventional banks did not appropriately reflect the transaction needs of Islamic finance.

The above discussion indicates that one way in which the *Shari'ah* requirements may be accomplished is to utilise other more appropriate organisational formats. As many non-bank financial institutions have less stringent regulations, these can be used to circumvent the legal and regulatory constraints limiting the use of *Shari'ah*-compliant products and serving social needs. For example, ElGamal (2007b) suggests an organisational format of mutuality may appropriately reflect Islamic values in financing. He suggests establishing not-for-profit financial institutions such as cooperatives, credit unions and mutual insurance companies as alternatives to Islamic banks. Given the non-profit nature of these organisations, they will be able to engage in non-commutative transactions and hence avoid *riba* and *gharar*. While non-profit mutuals suggested by ElGamal can provide *Shari'ah*-based financing by avoiding *riba* and *gharar*, other organisational models can also be used to provide Islamic financial services that satisfy the social and legal *Shari'ah* requirements. Some examples of the organisational formats that can provide financial services aligned with the principles and spirit of Islamic law are discussed next.

Venture capital and private equity funds

At the contract level, the proponents of Islamic finance envisaged that Islamic banking would predominantly use equity modes of financing. However, the operational structure of Islamic banks is not suitable for equity financing. Equity financing can be enhanced in an economy by establishing institutions that can manage the risks arising in using this mode of finance. The appropriate model for *Shari'ah*-based equity modes of financing in businesses would be organisations like venture capital and investment banks.[2] Ahmed (2005) shows that the nature of risks in equity financing are qualitatively different from that of debt financing and a different operational structure is required to deal with these risks. Financiers manage counter-party risks in equity-based financing by judicious structuring, strong monitoring and control of projects. They play an active role in advising and participating in the activities of the firms to ensure that value is added before exiting by selling off their shares. Management of risks in equity financing requires comprehensive skills that entail the understanding of both the financial and business risks.

Equity financing would require the use of *musharakah* as the instrument of financing. *Musharakah* contracts would allow financiers to monitor and actively participate in the activities of the project. Scarcity of professionals who can manage both business and financial risks will remain the main bottleneck in expanding the use of equity modes of financing in the format of Islamic venture capital and private-equity funds. The growth and success of these equity-based Islamic organisations will ultimately depend on the availability of professionals with the comprehensive skills needed to manage the inherent risks of equity financing.

Cooperatives

In countries that do not have the legal and regulatory framework for Islamic banking, an option would be to provide Islamic financial services through cooperatives. Nasim (2003) discusses the operations of the Islamic Cooperative Corporation Ltd (ICCL) in Canada. Given the regulatory framework in the country, ICCL was incorporated as a cooperative in December 1980 under the Cooperative Corporations Act. However, there are two taxes that were applicable to the scheme: income tax and the land transfer tax that is charged when people buy and sell houses. The challenge was to select language for the documents that would comply with three legal requirements: *Shari'ah*, the Cooperative Act and the tax laws. In order to be successful, the institution had to comply with both legislations and be tax efficient for clients/customers.

ICCL serves a large number of community members all over the country. The cooperative has two kinds of shares. Common shares are shares in the equity of the cooperative and preferred shares are attached to the houses of individual members. The price of both, common and preferred, is fixed at $100 each. Initially every member is an investor or common shareholder. Investments by the individual members, many of whom are prospective home buyers, and the institutional members are the main sources of funds for the Cooperative.

The diminishing *musharakah* mode is used to finance houses. At the time of the purchase of the house, members surrender their common shares and are issued preferred shares to reflect their total contribution in the purchase price of the property. A rental value for the house is determined and the member pays proportionate monthly rent on the Cooperative's share in the house. The members are free to buy any number of preferred shares at any time and the proportionate rent is adjusted accordingly in the following month. When a member completes a 100 per cent purchase of the required preferred shares, she surrenders these to ICCL and the legal title of the house is transferred to her. The Cooperative pays annual dividends to all common share-holders from the rental income in proportion to their owner-ship of shares. The preferred shareholders are not entitled to any dividend since they receive an implicit share of the rental income every month by using their portion of the house.

Islamic pawning: ArRahnu *programme of Bank Rakyat*[3]

Bank Rakyat (BR) was established in 1954 and is a coopera-tive bank in Malaysia. It has grown and has 124 branches in the country (in 2009). While the bank is owned by the members (depositors), the Board of Directors is appointed by the government. As it is a cooperative, it is registered with the Ministry of Cooperatives and being a deposit-taking institution, it is regulated by the central bank, Bank Negara Malaysia (BNM). Furthermore, as its activities involve foreign currency/transactions it also has to report to the Ministry of Finance. Other than providing deposit facilities, BR's activities include providing financing through personal loans, hire-purchase, and so on. BR started a conversion to Islamic finance in 1993. The bank offers Islamic pawning services under the *ArRahnu* programme through all of its branches. The operational details and contracts of the pro-gramme are cleared by the *Shari'ah* board of the bank and the compliance department ensures that all operations are undertaken according to the approved rules and guidelines.

To avail financing from the *ArRahnu* programme, clients

must use jewellery made of yellow gold for pawning. When a client brings the jewellery to a branch, it is checked for authenticity and its value is ascertained. For a first-time customer 65 per cent of the value is given as an interest-free loan (*qard hasan*) and 70 per cent given to existing customers. The loan is given for six months, but can be extended for another six months. The gold is kept in safes in the bank and safe-keeping or storage fees are charged. The storage fee is calculated based on the value of the gold and equals 65 cents per month for every MYR 100 value. This rate converts to about 13.8 per cent per annum which is lower than the charges of conventional pawn-brokers (which can go as high as 2 per cent per month).

The loans are taken mostly for consumption purposes, but include other uses that require lump-sum payments, such as paying fees for universities. About 80 per cent of the loans are of small amounts and are in the range of MYR 10,000 to 15,000. Loans greater than MYR 30,000 account for around 15 per cent of the disbursements and are mainly taken by businesses. Two weeks before the due date, a reminder is sent to the debtor about the repayment date of the outstanding dues. Another reminder is sent on the due date. A final reminder is given after two weeks of the due date. If the loan is not paid back, then the gold is auctioned off after waiting seven months and seven days from the beginning of the transaction date. The starting bid price is 90 per cent of the day's gold price. After deducting the loan amount and the storage charges, the remaining amount is returned to the client. The default rate on loans disbursed is relatively low and ranges from 2 to 5 per cent.

Microfinance

The social role of the Islamic financial sector can be best exemplified by providing finance to the poor so as to increase their income and wealth. While Islamic microfinance institutions exist, a couple of unique concepts are presented below.

Microfinance provided by Islamic banks

One way of manifesting the social role of Islamic banks is to provide finance to the poor to increase their income and wealth. Ahmed (2004a) shows that Islamic banks can provide microfinance to the poor more efficiently and effectively. The theoretical arguments are supported by empirical evidence from the Rural Development Scheme (RDS), a microfinance programme of Islami Bank Bangladesh Limited (IBBL). The RDS was initiated in 1995 and started operations in 1996 to cater to the investment needs of poor micro-entrepreneurs, particularly in rural areas. The RDS is funded from IBBLs general investment fund.

In line with the social dimension of its operations, the objective of the RDS is to eliminate rural poverty through a community development approach. The target group of the RDS is the rural poor, defined as the landless or those households having less than 0.5 acres of cultivable land. Other than providing finance for microenterprises to generate income, the RDS also focuses on health, sanitation and education of its beneficiaries. The dominant mode of financing used by the RDS is *murabahah* or deferred-price sale. The scheme uses the group-based format of the microfinance institutions (MFIs). Small amounts (ranging from BDT 3,000 to 25,000) are given to individuals and repaid back in small weekly instalments. No physical collateral is required for obtaining funds. Instead, social collateral is introduced by forming groups and centres. The clients save BDT 5 per week as personal savings and have to give BDT 1 per week for the centre fund.

As of July 2009, the RDS has provided microfinance services in 10,628 villages from 139 branches of IBBL. A total of BDT[4] 21.76 billion was disbursed to 319,230 clients (organised in 119,941 groups and 22,147 centres). The average financing size was BDT 15,369, provided at a 10 per cent rate of return with 2.5 per cent rebate given for timely payment. Note that this rate is much lower than what is charged by a typical MFI. The recovery rate of outstanding finance was 98.83 per cent. IBBL also manages the Islami Bank Foundation, a fund created from *zakah*, charity donations and income of the bank that cannot be included in the profit of the bank.

Waqf-based microfinance

Suggestions of establishing *waqf*-based financing institutions serving the poor have been made by various scholars. Cizakca (2004) suggests a model in which the concept of cash *waqf* can be used in contemporary times to serve social objectives in society. One use of cash *waqf* would be to provide microfinance to the poor. Similarly, ElGari (2004) proposes establishing a non-profit financial intermediary, the *qard hasan* bank that gives interest-free loans (*qard hasan*) to finance consumer lending for the poor. The capital of the bank would come from monetary (cash) *waqf* donated by wealthy Muslims. Kahf (2004a) proposes establishing microfinance institutions based on *zakah*, *awqaf* and *sadaqat*. He suggests that the returns from *awqaf* and funds from *sadaqat* can be used to finance productive microenterprises at subsidised rates. In addition, *zakah* can be given out to the poor for consumption purposes to avoid diversion of funds from productive heads.

Ahmed (2007) discusses the operational issues related to a *waqf*-based microfinance institution. On the liability side, cash *waqf* will constitute the capital of the MFI.

Along with the *waqf* endowment donated by the founders, additional *waqf* funds can be generated by issuing *waqf* certificates. Other than the savings of the beneficiaries, the MFI can also attract deposits from the public by providing opportunities of *Shari'ah*-compatible saving. These deposits will take the form of *mudarabah* or profit-sharing contracts.

The assets of a *waqf*-based Islamic MFI will comprise different types of non-interest-bearing financial instruments. To mitigate risks, a *waqf*-based Islamic MFI will hold a combination of low-risk fixed-income assets along with microfinancing activities.[5] A variety of *Shari'ah*-compliant modes can be used for microfinancing. The type of financing instrument used will depend on the type of activity. As the capital of the MFI will be *waqf*, it is important to keep the corpus of the capital intact. As a result, *waqf*-based MFIs have to create some special reserves to insure against the risks arising from negative shocks.

Approaches to innovation and product development

In a dynamic world and knowledge economies, the level of research and knowledge creation determines innovation and the competitiveness of organisations and nations. As innovation involves converting ideas into new products, it can transpire only if new knowledge that generates new ideas is created. Thus, innovation and product development would require investments in research and development (R&D) and creation of new knowledge. As Islamic finance involves using Islamic commercial law to finance something that usually operates in non-Islamic legal and regulatory environments, developing new products becomes more challenging and R&D becomes particularly important.

The discussion on innovation and R&D related to Islamic finance comprises two perspectives. The first aspect relates to approaches to innovation and product development in Islamic finance. The second perspective is associated with the creation of knowledge that can be the basis for *Shari'ah*-based products. For this to happen, there is a need for comprehensive foundational research that can be the source of innovation and product development. These two perspectives are discussed below.

Approaches to product innovation

Innovations can be incremental or radical. The former entails insignificant changes in existing products and the latter is characterised by significant divergence from the status quo (Popadiuk and Choo 2006). Accordingly, two innovative approaches can be identified in developing Islamic products. The first approach is 'reverse engineering' practised at bank level resulting from commercial R&D with inadequate input from basic and applied research. The result of this approach is basically to develop Islamic replications of conventional products (Iqbal and Mirakhor 2007). While the contractual stipulations are fulfilled in a legalistic manner, the legitimacy of outcomes and social welfare are not given priority. The second approach of 'innovative engineering' would produce unique Islamic products fulfilling both the form and spirit if Islamic law.[6] Innovative engineering would be a radical departure from the status quo and not be possible without sufficient basic and applied research to provide a strong knowledge base.

One way to move from reverse engineering is to use a functional approach, instead of products-focused methods. Ahmed (2006) and Al-Suwailem (2006) maintain that a functional approach to product development will facilitate development of *Shari'ah*-based alternatives. The functional approach would examine the needs that banks satisfy and then come up with Islamic alternatives that can meet these needs. For example, one function of the financial sector is to provide financing to enterprises. The most common way to meet this need in conventional finance is to provide interest-bearing loans. Under the product-based approach taken by Islamic banks, this would result in using a product like *tawarruq* that mimics the loan in substance. The functional approach, however, would assess the need of the entrepreneur. The need is not money itself but the necessity of the entrepreneur to buy certain input with it (Al-Suwailem 2006). The function/need-based approach to financing would require an understanding of the need of the enterprise and would then devise appropriate modes of financing (like *istisna*, *murabahah* and *ijarah*) that appropriately fulfil the needs.

Similarly, in hedging, the function that financial institutions perform is minimising the risks. In conventional finance, derivates are widely used as hedging instruments. If the product approach is taken in Islamic finance, then one would try to develop Islamic versions of forward, swap, and so on. As conventional derivatives do not comply with *Shariʻah* principles, this may involve using financial engineering and stratagem/ruses to circumvent the prohibitions. Under the functional approach, however, the need to minimise the risks can be done by using other means.

The difference between product replication and the function-based approach can be illustrated by using the example of a *tawarruq*-based forward structure for foreign currency presented in Chapter 6. Even though the rules of *sarf* assert that currency transactions must be carried out on the spot, the synthetic Islamic forward replicates a conventional forward in substance contravening this rule. A functions-based approach would move away from prod-uct replication and come up with a solution that serves the function. The function a forward performs is mitigating currency risks. Al-Suwailem (2006) suggests using a coop-erative technique of hedging currency risks that does not employ any derivatives.

An example of cooperative-based hedging shows a radi-cally different approach. Under this arrangement, a coop-erative fund (Co-op) is established as a non-profit entity that acts as an intermediary in managing risks. Assume two parties A and B want to protect themselves from currency fluctuations at the current exchange rate of £1= $1.5. Say A needs $1,500 after three months (costs £1,000 today) and B will need £1,000 after three months (costs $1,500 today). If after three months the exchange rate is £1= $1.4, then A has to pay £1,071.4 (= $1,500/1.4) for $1,500. Being a member of the Co-op A is paid an amount of £71.4 to compensate for the excess over the anticipated price. As B would be buying £1,000, she has to pay £1,000x1.4= $1,400. As B is paying $1,400, instead of $1,500, she pays the savings to the Co-op ($100= £71.4). Note that there are no net-obligations on the Co-op as the amount paid in by B (£71.4) is equal to the amount paid out to A. If the exchange rate after three months is £1= $1.6, then the reverse flow of funds will occur. With the new exchange rate, A will be able to buy $1,500 with £937.5 ($1,500/1.6= £937.5) and will pay the Co-op an amount of £62.50 (difference between £1,000 and £937.5). To purchase £1,000, B has to pay $1,600 (£1,000x1.6). The Co-op pays £62.50 to B to compensate for the excess of $100 paid for buying £1,000 at the new rate.

The practice of the Islamic finance industry of replicating conventional products indicates that the nature of innova-tion is incremental. To change the direction of the Islamic financial industry to one that is *Shari'ah*-based would require radical innovation based on an Islamic paradigm and model. This, however, cannot be brought about without investments in basic and applied research to create a body of knowledge that provides the ideas for innovation and development towards a *Shari'ah*-based financial system.

Foundational R&D and innovation

As ideas are generated through knowledge creation, innovation will not take place if no new knowledge is created. Mitri (2003: 15) identifies the characteristics of knowledge relevant to firms as 'facts, opinions, ideas, theories, principles, and models, experience, values, contextual information, expert insight and intuition'. Furthermore, knowledge can be explicit and tacit. While the former is knowledge that is communicated and articulated using verbal symbols and codes, the latter relates to, among others, 'mental models, maps, beliefs, paradigms, and viewpoints' (Popadiuk and Choo 2006: 306).

Different types of R&D affect the growth and stock of knowledge on which new products can be based. OECD (2002) identifies types of R&D as basic, applied and experimental. Kim and Oh (2002) provide a similar classification of basic, applied and commercial R&D. Basic research is 'experimental or theoretical work undertaken primarily to acquire new knowledge of the underlying foundations of phenomena and observable facts, without any particular application or use' (OECD 2002: 77). Basic research would involve theoretical and systematic pursuit of new knowledge for use in general applications. Applied research is 'original investigation undertaken in order to acquire new knowledge' and directed to meet a specific practical need or objective (OECD 2002: 78). Applied research can be patented and form the basis for developing some specific commercial products. Experimental or commercial R&D

is 'systematic work, drawing on knowledge gained from research and practical experience, that is directed to producing new materials, products and devices' (OECD 2002: 79). Commercial R&D would involve the application of existing knowledge systematically to produce or improve a product, service, system or process.

Development of Islamic finance according to the principles and goals of *Shari'ah* would require input from all three types of research. Basic research in Islamic finance would include theoretical work on fundamental concepts such as the overall goals of Islamic law (*maqasid al Shari'ah*), legal methodology (*usul al-fiqh*), jurisprudence (*Shari'ah* and *fiqh*) and their applications in economic transactions during contemporary times. For instance, the implications of *maqasid* at the product level are not well understood and still need extensive research.[7] An important aspect of basic research would be to explore the compatibility of Islamic commercial law with non-Islamic national legal systems on the one hand and meeting the financial needs and requirements of the various market segments on the other. The output of this research would provide the theoretical foundations for Islamic financial operations.

Applied research in Islamic finance has also not kept pace with the demands of the growing industry. This research should produce models of Islamic financial institutions and products and specific solutions for the numerous problems faced by the industry: appropriate organisational formats, *Shari'ah*-compliant products of financing, mechanisms to manage risks, and so on. Commercial R&D in Islamic finance is mainly carried out in Islamic financial institutions and consultancy firms. The focus of the commercial research is to develop Islamic financial products that satisfy various market needs. To produce *Shari'ah*-based products, commercial research has to be built on foundational work done in basic and applied research. However, while financial engineers who develop the products may be aware of the basic restrictions imposed by Islamic law, they may not have a full understanding of the principles and overall goals of *Shari'ah*.

Bankers dominate the commercial research in Islamic banks with some input from their *Shari'ah* advisor or unit/department. The survey results on Islamic banks in Chapter 5 indicate that a minority of the banks (40%) in the sample have structured idea generation and formal screening processes. As little is invested in idea generation and screening mechanisms, producing new innovative products reflecting the principles and spirit of *Shari'ah* becomes difficult. Furthermore, given the infancy of Islamic banking, most of the professionals working in the industry have training and experience in conventional finance. The tacit knowledge of these professionals in terms of the mental models, paradigms and viewpoints regarding finance is conventional.[8] As such, commercial research and product development in Islamic banks is influenced by their conventional background, skills and mental frameworks.

One principle reason of the lack of innovative products that reflect the spirit of Islamic law is the deficient foundational basic and applied knowledge to back up the commercial R&D. One reason for scant basic and applied research is the limited resources invested compared to the needs. As the social returns from basic research outweigh the private returns, it is usually not undertaken at the firm level (Rosenberg 1990). As such, the bulk of this research needs to be financed by public entities. At the moment, basic research in Islamic finance is undertaken in a few universities and by specialised organisations. Many universities are offering PhD programmes both in Muslim countries and the West. Furthermore, there are specialised institutions such as the Islamic Research and Training Institute of the Islamic Development Bank Group based in Jeddah, Saudi Arabia and International *Shari'ah* Research Academy (ISRA) in Malaysia that are contributing to the growth of the body of knowledge. However, these endeavours are relatively new and scant. It may take some time before the outputs from basic and applied research can have any significant impact on the direction of the Islamic finance industry.

Islamic commercial law and *Shari'ah* governance

At the heart of Islamic finance lies the fulfillment of the principles and goals of *Shari'ah* in its financial transactions. In practice, Islamic nature should be reflected in the operations of Islamic financial institutions and the contracts used in different transactions. As PD requires deriving new concepts and their approval by some *Shari'ah* body, two issues become relevant. First is the methodological approaches taken to derive *Shari'ah* rulings or judgments to back the new products. The second important factor relates to the *Shari'ah* governance process. The significance and concerns of these two issues relating to PD are discussed below.

Methodological approaches to contemporary Islamic commercial law

Saeed (1997) identifies approaches that are being used to derive Islamic law during contemporary times. The first is the text-based *ijtihad* that uses the traditional methods of *usul al-fiqh* to derive new laws. The second approach is the eclectic *ijtihad* in which scholars do not confine themselves to their respective schools. This method does not pay attention to the specific methods of *usul al-fiqh* and tends to be ad hoc and opportunistic. When faced with a problem, the scholar provides an opinion and justifies it by using any suitable source or school. Saeed (1997: 283) considers this method to be the 'most hazardous and problematic approach of all; hazardous, because it has no clear boundaries, signposts or methods that one can conceptualise and follow in arriving at a decision'.

The third approach identified by Saeed is context-based *ijtihad*. In this approach the scholar will be guided by *maslahah* (public interest or common good) and inclined to 'understand a problem in both its historical and modern contexts' (Saeed 1997: 284). While deducing rulings concern is less with the outer form of the problem and more with the underlying objectives of *Shari'ah* such as fairness, justice and equity. The scholar uses context analysis to arrive at decisions and is not particularly interested in the specific *usul* methods or previous *fiqh*.

Of the three approaches identified above, Islamic finance appears to be using eclectic *ijtihad*. As discussed in Chapter 2, Vogel and Hayes (1998) identify choice and selection (*iktiyar* and *takhayyur*), necessity (*darurah*), and ruses (*hila*) as the dominant methods used to derive rules in Islamic finance. As asserted by Siddiqi (2006a, 2006b), the *Shari'ah* scholars in the SSBs have often disregarded the overall *maqasid al-Shari'ah* and concentrated on the legalistic issues of individual transactions in a technical way. The focus of the SSBs on specific transactions makes it difficult to consider the broader consequences on the industry as a whole (DeLorenzo 2007). In so doing, the wide-ranging implications in the economy and broader objectives of *maqasid al-Shari'ah* may be difficult to perceive and are often ignored in their decision making.

The eclectic approach of *ijtihad* has failed to come up with new innovative solutions, but has been used successfully to modify existing conventional practices. To move towards a context-based methodological approach would require incorporating *maqasid*-related factors at the product level. Though significant work exists on classical Islamic law and doctrines, research on how Islamic commercial law can be derived using a *maqasid*-based approach and then be used for contemporary finance is scarce. While Chapter 6 gives some guidelines of how social aspects can be objectively ascertained at the product level, there is a need to undertake more in-depth basic and applied research on this critical topic.

Appropriate Shari'ah *governance model*

Chapter 3 discussed various existing *Shari'ah* governance models. Other than a legally constructed *Shari'ah* governance system in which the Islamic banking law determines the products that can be marketed, the remaining governance structures involve SSBs at different levels. While the robust *Shari'ah* governance regimes have a national *Shari'ah* body to oversee *Shari'ah*-related issues in the Islamic banking sector, the passive *Shari'ah* governance and market-driven frameworks depend on the SSBs at the organisational level. It is in these latter two *Shari'ah* governance systems where the *Shari'ah* requirements can be potentially diluted. There are a couple of areas of concern that need to be noted with *Shari'ah* governance models with SSBs based in organisations.

First, a critical issue in *Shari'ah* governance at the organisational level is the use of control and authority by the BOD and management to serve their needs. As *Shari'ah* governance and supervision is a sub-system of the overall governance system of a bank, it appears to have embraced the basic framework of serving the interests of the shareholders. In jurisdictions where there are no regulatory *Shari'ah* governance requirements, the structure and functions of SSBs are determined at the organisational level. Specifically, the role and functions of the different *Shari'ah* organs including the SSB are defined and limited by guidelines and/or terms of reference prepared by the shareholders (at General Assembly)/BOD or the articles of association of the Islamic financial institutions. The fact that the Islamic banks decide who can be in the SSB and also that the members are paid by the organisation can lead to situations where the independence of the SSB may be compromised. By selecting the SSB members that fulfil the financial objectives of the Islamic banks by what is referred to as '*fatwa* shopping', the objectivity and role of SSBs can be limited and compromised (Grais and Pellegrini 2006c).

Second, many Islamic products designed by financial/ legal engineers take conventional products as benchmarks to produce their replications. As discussed in Chapter 6, cases may arise where there may be trade-offs between the *Shari'ah* requirements and economic factors. If the SSB is permissive, pseudo-Islamic products may be chosen even when the feasible set contains *Shari'ah*-compliant alternatives due to pressures representing economic interests. This raises questions about the objectivity of the *Shari'ah* scholars in the SSBs; Kahf (2004b: 27) points out that 'many of them are now accused of being bankers' window dressing and of over-stretching the rules of *Shari'ah* to provide easy *fatwas* for the new breed of bankers'.

The above issues raise the question of conflict of interest of the SSB at the organisational level and may necessitate regulatory intervention. From a regulatory perspective, there are additional reasons to have a *Shari'ah* overview at the national level. Leaving *Shari'ah* governance at the bank level can generate different risks that can create systemic risks and adversely affect the stability and growth of the industry. The first is the reputational risk arising from the products marketed by Islamic banks. Qattan (2006) points out that *Shari'ah* non-compliance can be a reason for reputation risk that can trigger bank failure and cause systemic risk and instability. The same can happen if the perception of stakeholders about the Islamic products becomes negative causing a serious loss of trust and credibility.[9]

The second type of risk is the legal risk arising from the diversity of *fatwas* issued by various SSBs within the same country. As SSBs produce *fatwas* by interpreting different legal sources, the possibility of coming up with conflicting opinions exists. Weiss (1978: 207) maintains that if every man creates his own laws though his own *ijtihad*, then there would be 'no law in the ordinary sense: every man would be a law unto himself'. He further asserts that to avoid the dispersion of law, maintain social stability and the sanctity of law, certain prerequisites and qualities of people who issues edicts (*mujtahid*) must be maintained. With the expansion of the industry, the likelihood of conflicting *fatwas* will undermine customer confidence in the industry (Grais and Pellegrini 2006c). This calls for maintaining the credibility of the *fatwas* by harmonising the *Shari'ah* rulings at the national level.

The regulatory measures that can improve *Shari'ah* governance for the industry can be divided into two broad categories. The first relates to requirements that can strengthen the organisational *Shari'ah* governance structures and processes. This can be done by providing guidelines for the appropriate structure and processes to ensure *Shari'ah* compliance of the operations of Islamic banks. There will also be guidelines delineating the qualifications and requirements of scholars who can serve in the SSB at the bank level. Second, there is a need to establish a complementary *Shari'ah* supervision mechanism at the regulatory level to accomplish the broader *Shari'ah* requirements of the industry. Other than minimising the reputation and legal risks, establishing a National *Shari'ah* Authority (NSA) would provide an oversight of the *Shari'ah*-related aspects of the Islamic financial sector in general and the products in particular. As the members of the NSA do not operate in an organisational environment, they are expected to be free of conflicting interests. While scrutinising and approving the products, the NSA will be able to integrate the *maqasid al-Shari'ah* in Islamic finance and promote products that ensure the stability of the sector.

The ideal regulatory environment related to *Shari'ah* governance would be one that would balance *Shari'ah* risk mitigation and demands for innovation. Good examples of the proposed *Shari'ah* regulatory regime are Indonesia and Malaysia. As indicated in Chapter 3, in Indonesia the National *Shari'ah* Board (*Dewan Sharia Nasional* or DSN) must approve all new products coming to the market. For example, recently (in 2005) one bank wanted to introduce a *tawarruq*-based product in Indonesia. The DSN gave approval to the product with fourteen conditions attached. The conditions are stringent and essentially convert the product into a *murabahah*-type product. As a result, the bank decided to delay the introduction of *tawarruq*-based products. Similarly, Malaysia has a national *Shari'ah* Advisory Council housed at the central bank that, amongst other things, reviews and approves new products introduced to the market.[10] The country is in the forefront of Islamic finance pioneering many new products under a robust *Shari'ah* regulatory regime that provides check and balance to the industry.

Notes

1. The Capital Adequacy Standards of the Islamic Financial Services Board (IFSB) indicate that the capital charge for

mudarabah- and *musharakah*-based products can go up to 400 per cent. See IFSB (2005b) for a discussion.

2. For a discussion of the different risks in equity and debt financing and implications for organisational formats, see Ahmed (2005).

3. The information on the *ArRahnu* Programme of Raykat Bank was gathered from an interview with the officials of the bank.

4. BDT is the currency of Bangladesh (USD 1= BDT 69.55 on 6 July 2010).

5. There are two types of placements for low-risk and risk-free assets: in savings accounts in Islamic banks or in fixed-income *murabahah* mutual funds.

6. The term 'innovative engineering' has been used by Iqbal and Mirakhor (2007) to define what can be considered *Shari'ah*-based products outlined in this book.

7. See discussion on methodological approaches to Islamic commercial law in the next section.

8. The conventional mindset of one of the professionals in an Islamic bank I interviewed was apparent as the person used the words 'interest paid' on a product repeatedly instead of 'profit' or 'return'.

9. Chapra and Ahmed (2002) report a survey that shows that 381 (or 81.4%) of a total number of 468 depositors from Bahrain, Bangladesh and Sudan will move funds to other banks due to non-compliance with *Shari'ah* and a total of 328 (70%) would move funds if they learnt that the income of the banks comes from interest earnings.

10. Chapter 3 provides a brief discussion on the *Shari'ah* governance system in Malaysia.

CHAPTER 8
CONCLUSION

From a bare handful of financial institutions set up in the 1970s to provide services compatible with *Shari'ah*, the Islamic financial sector has witnessed extraordinary growth and has now become a significant global phenomenon. While the growth of the industry in a short span of time is commendable, concerns about its uniqueness and the direction it has taken are being raised. The inclination of the industry to use Islamic versions of conventional banking products has been accentuated by market-driven and competitive forces whereby economic factors overshadow the *Shari'ah* principles. The use of pseudo-Islamic products and those replicating conventional products by the Islamic financial industry raises serious questions about the essence and future of Islamic finance.

Siddiqi (2004) asserts that the ingenuity of the Islamic financial sector would be to integrate the vision of a moral society and socially responsible finance into functioning institutions. ElGari (2004) concurs that were the Islamic civilisation thriving, it would be capable of creating a vibrant society with institutions and organisations manifesting the core values of Islam. In this system, organisations including banks would be based on Islamic roots and reflect the features of justice, equity and social welfare. This book suggests that realisation of *Shari'ah*-based Islamic finance would require changes that go beyond the level of products. Among others, an Islamic financial system should have diverse organisations serving various financial needs of all in the society. In this regard, there is a need to reposition Islamic finance away from current banking models towards ones with social inclinations as exemplified by the original Islamic finance experiment in Mit Ghamar in the 1960s. This change of course would require expanding Islamic finance to other innovative forms of organisation and practice.

A successful Islamic banking product would be one that not only complies with the legal principles and social objectives of *Shari'ah*, but also fulfils the internal organisational requirements and external laws and regulations. The discussions indicate that, in certain cases, circumstances arise when pseudo-Islamic products have to be used out of necessity. However, in many other situations the *Shari'ah* requirements are diluted even when the feasible set entails *Shari'ah*-compliant products. In these cases, the excuse of using the pseudo-*Shari'ah* products for economic reasons, such as avoiding risks, defeats the whole purpose of Islamic finance. Islamic finance has different risk-return features and these have to be accepted as an inherent component of the system.

A key factor that will determine the future development of the Islamic financial industry is its ability to come up with new products that will satisfy the needs of various segments of society on the one hand and the *Shari'ah* requirements on the other. However, the lack of an appropriate Islamic knowledge base, the tacit conventional banking skills of the majority of Islamic bankers and the use of eclectic *ijtihad* are reinforcing the replication of existing conventional products. To come up with *Shari'ah*-based products would require investment in basic, applied and commercial

R&D and the production of an appropriate Islamic knowledge base. One way for products to satisfy both form and substance of Islamic law is to shift from the product-centred approach of product development to the functional approach of innovating new Islamic banking products.

The types of products offered by Islamic banks will shape the perceptions of customers and the community and determine the level of trust and credibility that stakeholders have for the sector in the long run. Critical factors that will determine the nature of products and the future direction of the industry are the *Shari'ah* governance framework and the quality of *Shari'ah* supervision. As the quote in the opening sentence of this book indicates, there is serious concern about the perception of the industry among the most important stakeholder of the industry – the Muslim clients. When Islamic banks are dealing with other peoples' money and the credibility of the industry is at stake, the direction of the industry cannot be left in the hands of a few individuals sitting in SSBs at the organisational levels. A coherent *Shari'ah* governance regime needs to be instituted by establishing independent *Shari'ah* authority at the national level. By protecting the *Shari'ah* requirements in banking operations, the independent national *Shari'ah* body will be able to instill trust and enhance the credibility of the Islamic financial industry. More importantly, by scrutinising the *Shari'ah* requirements of products coming to the market, from both the legal and social perspectives, the independent *Shari'ah* authority will be able to guide the future direction of the industry towards one reflecting the form and spirit of Islamic law.

GLOSSARY AND ABBREVIATIONS

Glossary

ahadith	plural of *hadith* (for meaning, see below)
ahkam	*Shari'ah* rulings having general applicability (plural of *hukm*)
akhlaq	ethics and morality
al-ghurm bil ghunm	entitled to a gain only if one agrees to bear the responsibility for the loss
al-kharaj bil daman	entitlement to return or yield (*al-kharaj*) for the one who bears the liability (*daman*) for something, say an asset
al-quwaid al-fiqh	legal maxims of Islamic jurisprudence (see also *quwaid al-fiqh*)
amanah	trust
amin	trustee
'aqd	contract
aqidah	faith and belief
arboon	advance payment for a purchase
ariyah	loan of an asset for use of usufruct by the loanee
asl	original case
awqaf	plural of *waqf* (for meaning, see below)
ayn	specific or existent object

batil	invalid
bay'	sale
bay' al-dayn	sale of debt
bay' al faduli	sale undertaken by an un-commissioned agent
bay' al-'inah	sale and buy-back of something in order to create a monetary debt; selling something to someone at a given price on credit and then buying it back at the same time at a lower price in cash
bay' al-kali bil kali	sale of debt for debt or a sale in which both the delivery of the object of sale and the payment of its price are postponed to a future date
bay' al mu'ajjal	sale on credit, i.e. a sale in which goods are delivered immediately but payment is deferred
bay' al wafa	a sale contract whereby an asset is sold with a condition it will be returned back when the seller returns its price to the buyer
bay bi thaman al-ajil	a price-deferred sale in which the good is delivered spot and the payment is deferred to a future date
daf al darar	prevention of harm
daman	guarantee, security
damin	guarantor
darar	damage, harm, injury
darurah	necessity
dayn	debt or obligation
dururiyyat	essentials (plural of *dururah*)
fasid	defective or voidable
fiqh	Islamic jurisprudence based

	primarily on interpretations of the Quran and the *Sunnah*
fiqh al muamalat	jurisprudence related to commerce and transactions
fuqaha'	plural of *faqih* meaning jurist
gharar	ambiguity and excessive risk. Uncertainty about the price, the quality and the quantity of the counter-value, the date of delivery, the ability of either the buyer or the seller to fulfil his commitment, or ambiguity in the terms of the deal; thereby exposing either of the two parties to unnecessary risks
hadith	sayings of Prophet Muhammad
hajiyyat	complementary requirements
hajj	annual pilgrimage
halal	permitted by the *Shari'ah*
Hanafi	a school of Islamic jurisprudence named after Abu Hanifa Numan ibn Thabit (703–67CE)
Hanbali	a school of Islamic jurisprudence named after Imam Ahmad ibn Hanbal Ash Shaybani (778–855CE).
haram	Things or activities prohibited by the *Shari'ah*
hawalah	an arrangement whereby a debtor transfers the responsibility of payment of a debt to a third party
hibah	gift
hila	legal stratagem or device
hiyal	plural of *hila*
'ibadat	duties of man due to God or worship

ibahah	principle of permissibility stating that everything is permissible unless explicitly forbidden by *Shari'ah*
ibra'	surrendering right to a claim on debt either partially of fully. Used as rebate by Islamic banks for early settlement of debt
ijab	offer or proposal
ijarah	leasing or hire contract
ijarah muntahiyyah bil-tamlik	lease ending in ownership
ijarah wa iqtina	lease ending in ownership
ijma'	consensus. One of the sources of Islamic law
ijtihad	endeavour of a jurist to derive a ruling or judgment based on evidence found in *Shari'ah*
iktiyar	choice (choosing from a variety of sources)
'illah	effective cause
istihsan	juristic preference of a ruling in favour of another ruling
istishab	presumption of continuity
istislah	use of public interest to derive Islamic law
istisna	a sale contract that requires manufacturing/constructing of non-generic object/asset according to certain specifications. The object/asset is delivered upon completion by the seller and payments can be made in either advance or instalments in the future.

jahala	ignorance, lack of knowledge
ju'alah	performing a task against a fee
kafalah	guarantee or taking responsibility for a liability of another person
kafil	guarantor
khalifah	vicegerent
khiyar	option
mafasid	plural of *mafsadah*
mafsadah	harm
makarij	plural of *makraj*
makraj	exit or a way out
makruh	abominable or reprehensible acts
mal	asset or property
Maliki	a school of Islamic jurisprudence named after Imam Malik ibn Anas al Asbahi (717–801CE)
mandub	recommended acts
manfa'ah	usufruct
maqasid	basic goals (see also *maqasid al-Shari'ah*)
maqasid al-Shari'ah	basic goals of the *Shari'ah*
maslahah	benefit or social welfare
masalih	benefit or social welfare (plural of *maslahah*)
masalih mursalah	unrestricted interests or benefits
maysir	gambling or any game of chance
milk	ownership (of property)
mithliyyat	fungibles
mu'amalat	transactions/contracts among human beings
mubah	permissible acts
mudarabah	a sleeping partnership contract between capital owner(s) or

	financiers (*rab al-mal*) and an investment manager (*mudarib*)
mudarib	an investment manager in a *mudarabah* contract
mujtahid	a religious scholar qualified to pronounce *Shari'ah* rulings
murabahah	a sale with specified profit margin
musharakah	a partnership contract in which partners participate in the provision of capital and the management
nas	text from Quran or *Sunnah*
qabd	possession
qabul	acceptance (of a contract)
qadi	judge
qard or *Qard al-hasan*	a loan extended without interest or any other compensation from the borrower
qimiyyat	non-fungibles
qiyas	analogy. Use of analogical reasoning to derive new rule/law from *Shari'ah*
Quran	the Holy Book of Muslims consisting of revelations of God to the Prophet Muhammad
quwaid	legal maxims (see *quwaid al-fiqh*)
quwaid al-fiqh	legal maxims of Islamic jurisprudence
rab al-mal	capital owner (financier) in a *mudarabah* contract
raf al-haraj	removal of hardship
rahn	pledge or mortgage
riba	increase or growth. Excess in an unequal exchange and also interest on loans

riba al-fadl	*riba* of excess arising in trade contracts. It generally refers to spot exchange of different quantities of the same commodity
riba al-jahiliyyah	pre-Islamic *riba*. It refers to increase in the amount of debt with postponement of repayment time
riba al-nasiah	*riba* of delay pertaining to exchange over time, arising when exchanging different quantities of an item over time. Generally, it is *riba* linked to loan contracts
ribawi	items on which the rules of *riba* apply
rukhsah	concession
sadaqah	charity
sadd al-dhara'i	blocking the means (of a prohibited deed)
sahih	valid
salam	an object-deferred sale in which the buyer pays spot for a good that is delivered at a future date by the seller
sarf	currency exchange
Shafi'i	a school of Islamic jurisprudence named after Imam Muhammad ibn Idris al-Shafi'i (769–820CE)
Shari'ah	refers to the corpus of Islamic law based on Divine guidance as given by the Quran and the *Sunnah*
sukuk	certificates of ownership or rights in tangible assets, usufructs and services, or equity

Sunnah	traditions and deeds of the Prophet
ta'awun	cooperation (for good)
tahsiniyat	beatifications or embellishments
takaful	Islamic alternative for the contemporary insurance contract. A group of persons agree to collectively share a certain risk by each contributing a specified sum. A loss to any one of the group is met from the collected funds
takhayyur	selection of views from varied sources
talfiq	amalgamation and patching
tawarruq	monetisation of asset. In Islamic banking this takes the form of buying a commodity and selling it to get cash
tawhid	Unity of God
ulamah	scholars
Ummah	the Muslim nation
urf	custom or tradition
usul	principles or fundamentals
usul al-fiqh	methodology of Islamic jurisprudence or Islamic legal theory
wa'd	unilateral promise
wadi'ah	A contract of safekeeping
wajib	obligatory
wakalah	contract of agency. In this contract, one person appoints someone else to perform a certain task on his behalf, usually against a fixed fee

waqf	endowment established for family, social or religious purposes
zakah	obligatory alms that must be paid by Muslims owning more than a threshold amount of wealth

Abbreviations

AAOIFI	Accounting and Auditing Organization for Islamic Financial Institutions
AED	United Arab Emirates dirham
BAFIA	Banking and Financial Institutions Act (Malaysia)
BDT	Bangladeshi taka
BHD	Bahraini dinar
BIS	Bank of International Settlements
BNM	Bank Negara Malaysia
BOD	Board of Directors
BR	Bank Rakyat (Malaysia)
CBB	Central Bank of Bahrain
CC	credit card
CEO	Chief Executive Officer
CIBAFI	General Council for Islamic Banks and Financial Institutions
DSN	*Dewan Shari'ah Nasional* (Indonesia)
GBP	British pound
GCC	Gulf Cooperation Council
IBA	Islamic Banking Act (Malaysia)
IBBL	Islami Bank Bangladesh Ltd
ICCL	Islamic Cooperative Corporation Ltd (Canada)
IDB	Islamic Development Bank (Jeddah, Saudi Arabia)

IFA	Islamic *Fiqh* Academy (Jeddah, Saudi Arabia)
IFSB	Islamic Financial Services Board (Kuala Lumpur, Malaysia)
IRR	investment risk reserves
IRTI	Islamic Research and Training Institute (Jeddah, Saudi Arabia)
IT	information technology
KWD	Kuwaiti dinar
MFI	microfinance institutions
MYR	Malaysian ringgit
NSA	National *Shari'ah* Authority
OCC	Office of the Comptroller of the Currency
OECD	Organization for Economic Cooperation and Development
PD	product development
PER	Profit Equalising Reserves
PSIA	profit-sharing investment accounts
RDS	Rural Development Scheme (Bangladesh)
R&D	research and development
SAC	*Shari'ah* Advisory Council (Malaysia)
SAR	Saudi riyal
SB	*Shari'ah* Board (Pakistan)
SBP	State Bank of Pakistan
SLA	service level agreement
SPV	special purpose vehicle
SQA	software quality assurance
SSB	*Shari'ah* Supervisory Board
SWOT	strengths, weaknesses, opportunities and threats
UAE	United Arab Emirates
US	United States
USD	American dollar
WEF	World Economic Forum

BIBLIOGRAPHY

AAOIFI (1999), *Statement on the Purpose and Calculation of the Capital Adequacy Ratio for Islamic Banks*, Bahrain: AAOIFI.

AAOIFI (2003), *Shari'a Standards*, Bahrain: AAOIFI.

Ahmed, Habib (2002), *A Microeconomic Model of an Islamic Bank*, Research Paper no. 59, Jeddah: Islamic Research and Training Institute.

Ahmed, Habib (2004a), 'Frontiers of Islamic banking: a synthesis of social role and microfinance', *European Journal of Management and Public Policy*, 3(1).

Ahmed, Habib (2004b), *Role of Zakat and Awqaf in Poverty Alleviation*, Occasional Paper no. 8, Jeddah: Islamic Research and Training Institute.

Ahmed, Habib (2005), *Operational Format for Islamic Equity Finance: Lessons from Venture Capital*, Research Paper no. 69, Jeddah: Islamic Research and Training Institute.

Ahmed, Habib (2006), 'Islamic law, adaptability, and financial development', *Islamic Economic Studies*, 13(2), 79–101.

Ahmed, Habib (2007), '*Waqf*-based microfinance: realizing the social role of Islamic finance', paper presented at the International Conference on Integrating Awqaf into the Islamic Financial Sector, Singapore, 6–7 March 2007.

Ahmed, Habib and Tariqullah Khan (2007), 'Risk management in Islamic banking', in M. Kabir Hassan and Mervyn K. Lewis (eds), *Handbook of Islamic Banking*, Cheltenham: Edward Elgar.

Ainley, Michael, Ali Mashayekhi, Robert Hicks, Arshadur

Rahman and Ali Ravalia (2007), *Islamic Finance Regulation in the UK: Regulation and Challenges*, London: Financial Services Authority.

Al-Alwani, Taha Jabir (1990), *Usul Al Fiqh Al Islam, Source Methodology in Islamic Jurisprudence*, Research Monographs no. 1, Herndon, VA: International Institute of Islamic Thought.

Al-Dhareer, S. M. Al-Ameen (1997), *Al-Gharar in Contracts and its Effect on Contemporary Transactions*, Eminent Scholars Lecture Series no. 16, Jeddah: Islamic Research and Training Institute.

Al-Masri, Rafic Yunus (2002), 'The binding unilateral promise (*wa'd*) in Islamic banking operations: is it permissible for a unilateral promise (*wa'd*) to be binding as an alternative to a proscribed contract?', *Journal of King Abdulaziz University: Islamic Economics*, 15, 29–33.

Al-Suwailem, Sami (2006), *Hedging in Islamic Finance*, Occasional Paper no. 10, Jeddah: Islamic Research and Training Institute.

Al-Zuhayli, Wahbah (2003a), *Financial Transactions in Islamic Jurisprudence*, , trans. Mahmoud A. ElGamal, Beirut: Dar al-Fikr al-Mouaser, vol. 1.

Al-Zuhayli, Wahbah (2003b), *Financial Transactions in Islamic Jurisprudence*, trans. Mahmoud A. ElGamal, Beirut: Dar al-Fikr al-Mouaser, vol. 2.

Ali, Engku Rabiah Adawiah Engku (2003), 'Re-defining property and property rights in Islamic Law of Contract', *Jurnal Syariah*, 11(2), 47–60.

Allen, Franklin and Anthony M. Santomero (1997), 'The Theory of Financial Intermediation', *Journal of Banking and Finance*, 21, 1461–85.

Ansoff, H. Igor (1965), *Corporate Strategy: An Analytic Approach to Business Policy for Growth and Expansion*, New York, NY: McGraw-Hill.

Arbouna, Mohammad Burhan (2006), 'Combining contracts in *Shari'ah*: a potential mechanism for product development', in Tariqullah Khan and Dadang Muljawan (eds), *Islamic Financial Architecture: Risk Management and Financial Stability*, Seminar Proceedings no. 46, Jeddah: Islamic Research and Training Institute.

Avlonitis, George J., Paulina G. Papastathopoulou and Spiros P. Gounaris (2001), 'An empirically-based typology of product innovations for new financial services: success and failure scenarios', *Journal of Product Innovation Management*, 18, 324–42.

Ayub, Muhammad (2007), *Understanding Islamic Finance*, Chichester: John Wiley and Sons.

Baxter, Mike (1995), *Product Design: A Practical Guide to Systematic Methods of New Product Development*, Boca Raton, FL: CRS Press.

Beerens, Joris, Alexander van Boetzelaer, Georg List, Peter Mensing and Steven Veldhoen (2004), *The Road Towards More Effective Product/Service Development*, Booz Allen Hamilton Publications, http://www.boozallen.com.

BIS (1986), *Recent Innovations in International Banking*, Basel: Bank for International Settlements, http://www.bis.org/publ/ecsc01a.pdf.

Bowers, Michael R. (1986), 'The new product development process: a suggested model for banks', *Journal of Retail Banking*, 8(1), 19–24.

Chapra, M. Umer (1985), *Towards a Just Monetary System*, Leicester: The Islamic Foundation.

Chapra, M. Umer (1992), *Islam and the Economic Challenge*, Islamic Economics Series no. 17, Leicester: The Islamic Foundation, and Herndon, VA: International Institute of Economic Thought.

Chapra, M. Umer (2000), *The Future of Economics: An Islamic Perspective*, Leicester: The Islamic Foundation.

Chapra, M. Umer (2001), 'The major modes of Islamic finance', paper presented at the course on Islamic Economics, Banking and Finance, held at the Islamic Foundation, Leicester, 26–30 September 2001.

Chapra, M. Umer (2008a), *The Islamic Vision of Development in Light of Maqasid al Shariʻah*, Occasional Paper Series no. 15, London: International Institute of Islamic Thought.

Chapra, M. Umer (2008b), 'The global financial crisis and the Islamic financial system', paper presented at the Forum on the Global Financial Crisis, held at the Islamic Development Bank, Jeddah, 25 October 2008.

Chapra, M. Umer and Habib Ahmed (2002), *Corporate Governance in Islamic Financial Institutions*, Occasional Paper no. 6, Jeddah, Islamic Research and Training Institute.

Chapra, M. Umer and Tariqullah Kahn (2000), *Regulation and Supervision of Islamic Banks*, Jeddah: Islamic Research and Training Institute.

Cizakca, Murat (2004), 'Cash waqf as alternative to NBFIs bank', paper presented at the International Seminar on Nonbank Financial Institutions: Islamic Alternatives, Kuala Lumpur, 1–3 March 2004.

Cooper, Robert G. (1990), 'Stage-gate systems: a new tool for managing new products', *Business Horizons*, May–June 1990, 44–53.

Cooper, Robert G. (1994), 'Perspective: third generation new product development process', *Journal of Product Innovation Management*, 11, 3–14.

Cooper, Robert G. and Ulricke de Brentani (1991), 'New industrial financial services: what distinguishes the winners', *Journal of Product Innovation Management*, 8, 75–90.

Cooper, Robert G. and Scott J. Edgett (1999), *Product Development for the Service Sector: Lessons from Market Leaders*, New York, NY: Basic Books.

Cooper, Robert G., Christopher J. Easingwood, Scott Edgett,

Elko J. Klienschmidt and Chris Story (1994), 'What distinguishes the top performing new products in financial services', *Journal of Product Innovation Management*, 11, 281–99.

Dallah Albaraka (1994), *Fatawa: Shari'ah Rulings on Economics*, Jeddah: Dallah Albaraka Group.

Dar, Humayon (2007), 'A matter of principle: BMB Islamic structuring Shariah solutions', *Business Islamica*, 31 October 2007.

Davies, Howard (2002), 'Islamic finance and the FSA', *Review of Islamic Economics*, 12, 101–8.

de Brentani, Ulricke (1986), 'Do firms need a custom-designed new product screening model?', *Journal of Product Innovation Management*, 3, 108–19.

de Brentani, Ulricke (1991), 'Success factors in developing new business services', *European Journal of Marketing*, 25(2), 33–59.

de Brentani, Ulricke (1993), 'The new product process in financial services: strategy for success', *International Journal of Bank Marketing*, 11(3), 15–22.

Delcambre, A. M. (1993), '*Milk*', in C. E. Bosworth, E. Van Donzel, W. P. Heinrichs and C. Pellet (eds), *The Encyclopaedia of Islam*, Leiden: E. J. Brill, vol. VII.

DeLorenzo, Yusuf Talal (2007), 'The total returns swap and the "Shari'ah conversion technology" strategem', Availableat:http://www.failaka.com/downloads/DeLorenzo_TotalReturnsSwap.pdf.

Dien, Mawil Izzi (2004), *Islamic Law: From Foundations to Contemporary Practice*, Notre Dame, IN: University of Notre Dame Press.

Djojosugito, Reza Adirahman (2003), 'Relative stability of civil and common law regimes for Islamic banking', paper presented at International Conference on Islamic Banking: Risk Management, Regulation, and Supervision, Jakarta, 30 September–2 October 2003.

Dow Jones Indexes (2004), *Guide to the Dow Jones Islamic Market Index*, December 2004, http://www.djindexes.com/mdsidx/downloads/imi_rulebook.pdf.

Drew, Stephen A. W. (1995), 'Strategic benchmarking: innovation practices in financial institutions', *International Journal of Bank Marketing*, 13, 4–16.

Dusuki, Asyraf Wajdi (2008), 'Understanding the objectives of Islamic banking: a survey of stakeholders' perspectives', *International Journal of Islamic and Middle Eastern Finance and Management*, 1(2), 132–48.

Dusuki, Asyraf Wajdi and Shabnam Mokhtar (2010), *Critical Appraisal of Shari'ah Issues on Ownership in Asset-based Sukuk as Implemented in the Islamic Debt Market*, Research Paper no. 8/2010, Kuala Lumpur: ISRA.

Easingwood, Christopher J. (1986), 'New product development for service companies', *Journal of Product Innovation Management*, 4, 264–75.

Easingwood, Christopher J. and Vijay Mahajan (1989), 'Positioning of financial services for competitive advantage', *Journal of Product Innovation Management*, 6, 207–19.

Edgett, Scott J. (1996), 'The new product development process for commercial financial services', *Industrial Marketing Management*, 25, 507–15.

Edgett, Scott J. and Steven Parkinson (1994), 'The development of new financial services: identifying determinants of success and failure', *International Journal of Service Industry Management*, 5(4), 24–38.

ElGamal, Mahmoud (2001), 'An economic explication of the prohibition of gharar in classical Islamic jurisprudence', *Islamic Economic Studies*, 8(2), 29–58.

ElGamal, Mahmoud A. (2006), *Islamic Finance: Law, Economics and Practice*, New York: Cambridge University Press.

ElGamal, Mahmoud (2007a), 'Mutuality as an antidote to

rent-seeking, Shari'a arbitrage in Islamic finance', *Thunderbird International Business Review*, 49(2), 187–202.

ElGamal, Mahmoud A. (2007b), 'A simple *fiqh*-and-economic rationale for mutualization in islamic financial intermediation', in Nazim Ali (ed.), *Integrating Islamic Finance into the Mainstream*, Cambridge, MA: Harvard Law School.

ElGamal, Mahmoud (2008), 'Incoherence of contract-based Islamic financial jurisprudence in the age of financial engineering', *Wisconsin International Law Journal*, 25(4),

ElGari, Mohamed Ali (1993), 'Towards an Islamic stock market', *Islamic Economic Studies*, 1, 1–20.

ElGari, Mohammad Ali (2002), 'Essential requirements for major Islamic contracts', paper presented at Documentation of Islamic Banking Products, Conference and Workshop, London, 17–18 July 2002.

ElGari, Mohamed A. (2004), 'The *Qard Hassan* Bank', paper presented at the International Seminar on Nonbank Financial Institutions: Islamic Alternatives, Kuala Lumpur, 1–3 March 2004.

Fadel, Mohammad H. (2008), 'Riba, efficiency, and prudential regulation: preliminary thoughts', *Wisconsin International Law Journal*, 25(4), 655–702.

Freixas, Xavier and Jean-Charles Rochet (1999), *Microeconomics of Banking*, Cambridge, MA: MIT Press.

Fuller, Gordon W. (2005), *New Food Product Development: From Concept to Marketplace*, 2nd edn, Boca Raton, FL: CRC Press LLC.

Gangopadhyay, Shubhashis and Gurbachan Singh (2000), 'Avoiding bank runs in transition economies: the role of risk neutral capital', *Journal of Banking and Finance*, 24, 625–42.

Gleason, James T. (2000), *Risk: The New Management Imperative in Finance,* Princeton, NJ: Bloomberg Press.

Grais, Wafik and Matteo Pellegrini (2006a), 'Corporate

governance in institutions offering Islamic financial services: issues and options', World Bank Policy Research Working Paper 4052, available at: http://ssrn.com/abstract=940709.

Grais, Wafik and Matteo Pellegrini (2006b), 'Corporate governance and stakeholders' financial interests in in institutions offering Islamic financial services', World Bank Policy Research Working Paper 4053, available at: http://ssrn.com/abstract=940710.

Grais, Wafik and Matteo Pellegrini (2006c), 'Corporate governance and Shariah compliance in institutions offering Islamic financial services', World Bank Policy Research Working Paper 4054, available at: http://ssrn.com/abstract=940711.

Gulaid, Mahmoud A. (2001), *Land Ownership in Islam: A Survey*, Jeddah: Islamic Research and Training Institute.

Habil, Abdurrahman (2007), 'the tension between legal values and formalism in contemporary Islamic finance', in Nazim Ali (ed.), *Integrating Islamic Finance into the Mainstream*, Cambridge, MA: Harvard Law School.

Hallaq, Wael B. (2004), *A History of Islamic Legal Theories: An Introduction to Sunni Usul al-Fiqh*, Cambridge: Cambridge University Press.

Hamid, Mohamed El Fatih (1998), 'Facing the challenges to Islamic banking: an overview of issues', in Christian von Bar (ed.), *Islamic Law and its Reception by the Courts in the West*, Koln: Carl Heymanns Verlag KG.

Hamoudi, Haider Ala (2007), 'Jurisprudential schizophrenia: on form and function in Islamic finance', *Chicago Journal of International Law*, 7(2), 605–22.

Haneef, Mohamed Aslam Mohamed (1997), 'Islam, the Islamic worldview, and Islamic economics', *IIUM Journal of Economics and Management*, 5, 39–65.

Haque, Ahasanul, Jamil Osman and Ahmad Zaki Hj. Ismail (2009), 'Factor influences selection of Islamic banking:

a study on Malaysian customer preferences', *American Journal of Applied Sciences*, 6(5), 922–8.

Harrison, Tina S. (1994), 'mapping customer segments for personal financial services', *International Journal of Bank Marketing*, 12(8), 17–25.

Hassan, Hussain Hamid (1992), 'The jurisprudence of financial transactions (fiqh al muamlat)', in Ausaf Ahmad and Kazim Raza Awan (eds), *Lectures on Islamic Economics*, Jeddah: Islamic Research and Training Institute.

Heffernan, Shelagh (1996), *Modern Banking in Theory and Practice*, Chichester: John Wiley and Sons.

Hegazy, Walid S. (2007), 'Contemporary Islamic finance: from socioeconomic idealism to pure legalism', *Chicago Journal of International Law*, 7(2), 581–603.

Holden, Kelly (2007), 'Islamic finance: "legal hypocrisy" moot point, problematic future bigger concern', *Boston University International Law Journal*, 25, 341–68.

Horii, Satoe (2002), 'Reconsideration of legal devices (hiyal) in Islamic jurisprudence: the Hanafis and their "exists" (makharij)', *Islamic Law and Society*, 9(3), 312–57.

IFSB (2005a), *Guiding Principles of Risk Management for Institutions (Other Than Insurance Institutions) Offering Only Islamic Financial Services*, Islamic Financial Services Board, http://www.ifsb.org/standard/ifsb1.pdf.

IFSB (2005b), *Capital Adequacy Standard for Institutions (Other Than Insurance Institutions) Offering Only Islamic Financial Services*, Islamic Financial Services Board, http://www.ifsb.org/standard/ifsb2.pdf.

IFSB (2008), *Exposure Draft Guiding Principles on Shari'ah Governance System*, Kuala Lumpur: Islamic Financial Services Board.

Iqbal, Zamir and Abbas Mirakhor (2007), *An Introduction to Islamic Finance: Theory and Practice*, Singapore: John Wiley and Sons.

Iqbal, Munawar, Ausaf Ahmad and Tariqullah Khan (1998), *Challenges facing Islamic Banking*, Occasional Paper no. 1, Jeddah: Islamic Research and Training Institute.

IRTI and IFA (2000), *Resolutions and Recommendations of the Council of the Islamic Fiqh Academy*, Jeddah: Islamic Research and Training Institute.

Johne, F. Axel (1993), 'Insurance product development', *International Journal of Bank Marketing*, 11(3), 5–14.

Johne, F. Axel and P. Harborne (1985), 'How large commercial banks manage product innovation', *International Journal of Bank Marketing*, 3, 54–71.

Jorion, Phillippe and Sarkis J. Khoury (1996*), Financial Risk Management: Domestic and International Dimensions*, Cambridge, MA: Blackwell Publishers.

Kahf, Monzer (1998), 'The concept of ownership in Islam', in Monzer Kahf (ed.), *Lessons in Islamic Economics*, Jeddah: Islamic Research and Training Institute, part II, pp. 241–56.

Kahf, Monzer (2004a), '*Shari'ah* and historical aspects of *zakah* and *awqaf*', background paper prepared for Islamic Research and Training Institute, Islamic Development Bank, Jeddah.

Kahf, Monzer (2004b), 'Islamic banks: the rise of a new power alliance of wealth and Shari'ah scholarship', in Clement M. Henry and Rodney Wilson (eds), *The Politics of Islamic Finance*, Edinburgh: Edinburgh University Press.

Kahf, Monzer (2006), 'Maqasid al Shariah in the prohibition of riba and their implications for modern Islamic finance', paper presented at IIUM International Conference on Maqasid al Shari'ah, Malaysia, 8–10 August 2006.

Kahf, Monzer and Tariqullah Khan (1988), *Principles of Islamic Financing: A Survey*, Jeddah: Islamic Research and Training Institute.

Kamakura, Wagner A., Sridhar N. Ramaswami and Rajendra K. Srivastava (1991), 'Applying latent trait analysis in the evaluation of prospects for cross-selling of financial serv- ices', *International Journal of Research in Marketing*, 8, 329–49.

Kamali, Mohammad Hashim (1993), 'Fundamental rights of the individual: an analysis of haqq (right) in Islamic law', *American Journal of Islamic Social Sciences*, 10(3), 341–66.

Kamali, Mohammad Hashim (2000), *Isalmic Commercial Law: An Introduction*, Oxford: Oneworld Publications.

Kamali, Mohammad Hashim (2003), *Principles of Islamic Jurisprudence*, Cambridge: Islamic Texts Society.

Kamali, Mohammad Hashim (2006), 'Legal maxims and other genres of literature in Islamic jurisprudence', *Arab Law Quarterly*, 20(1), 77–101.

Kamali, Mohammad Hashim (2008), *Shari'ah Law: An Introduction*, Oxford: Oneworld Publications.

Kelly, David and Chris Storey (2000), 'New service develop- ment: initiation strategies', *International Journal of Service Industry Management*, 11(1), 45–62.

Khalil, Abdel-Fattah A. A., Colin Rickwood and Victor Murinde (2002), 'Evidence on agency-contractual prob- lems in mudarabah financing operations by Islamic banks', in Munawar Iqbal and David T. Llewellyn (eds), *Islamic Banking and Finance: New Perspectives on Profit-Sharing and Risk*, Cheltenham: Edward Elgar.

Khan, Mohsin S. (1987), 'Islamic interest-free banking: a theoretical analysis', in Mohsin S. Khan and Abbas Mirakhor (eds), *Theoretical Studies in Islamic Banking and Finance*, Houston, TX: Institute for Research and Islamic Studies.

Khan, M. Fahim (1995), *Essays in Islamic Economics*, Leicester: The Islamic Foundation.

Khan, Tariqullah (1999/2000), 'Islamic quasi equity (debt) instruments and the challenges of balance sheet hedging: an exploratory analysis', *Islamic Economic Studies*, 7, 1–32.

Khan, Tariqullah and Habib Ahmed (2001), *Risk Management: An Analysis of Issues in Islamic Financial Industry*, Occasional Paper no. 5, Jeddah: Islamic Research and Training Institute.

Kharoufa, Ala' Eddine (2000a), *Transactions in Islamic Law*, Kuala Lumpur: A. S. Noordeeen.

Kharoufa, Ala' Eddine (2000b), *Philosophy of Islamic Shari'ah and its Contribution to the Science of Contemporary Law*, Eminent Scholars' Lecture Series 19, Jeddah: Islamic Research and Training Institute.

Kim, Bowon and Heungshik Oh (2002), 'Economic compensation compositions preferred by R&D personnel of different R&D types and intrinsic values', *R&D Management*, 32(1), 47–59.

Koch, Timothy (1995), *Bank Management*, Orlando, FL: The Dryden Press.

La Porta, Rafael, Florencio Lopez-de-Silanes, Andrie Shleifer and Robert Vishny (1999), 'Investor protection: origin, consequences, reform', Financial Sector Discussion Paper no. 1, Washington, DC: The World Bank.

Larson, Erik W. and David H. Gobeli (1988), 'Organizing for product development projects', *Journal of Product Innovation Management*, 5, 180–90.

Levine, Ross (1997), 'Financial development and economic growth: views and agenda', *Journal of Economic Literature*, 35, 688–726.

Llewellyn, David (1999), *The Economic Rationale for Financial Regulation*, Occasional Paper Series 1, London: Financial Services Board.

Lovelock, Christopher H. (1984), 'Developing and implementing new services', in William R. George and Claudia E. Marshall (eds), *Developing New Services*, Chicago, IL: American Marketing Association.

Macey, Jonathan R. (1995–1996), 'Derivative instruments:

lessons for the regulatory state', *Journal of Corporation Law*, 21, 69–93.

Machauer, Achim and Sebastian Morgner (2001), 'Segmentation of bank customers by expected benefits and attitudes', *International Journal of Bank Marketing*, 19(1), 6–17.

Mahmasani, Subhi (1955), 'Transactions in the Shari'a', in Majid Khadduri and Herbert J. Liebesny (eds), *Law in the Middle East. Vol. 1 Origin and Development of Islamic Law*, Washington, DC: Middle East Institute.

Majallah (2001), *The Majelle: Being an English Translation of Majallah el-Ahkam-i-Adliya and a Complete Code of Islamic Civil Law*, Kuala Lumpur: The Other Press.

Maslow, Abraham H. (1954), *Motivation and Personality*, New York, NY: Harper & Row Publishers Inc.

Masud, Muhammad Khalid (1995), *Shatibi's Philosophy of Islamic Law*, Islamabad: Islamic Research Institute.

Messick, Brinkley (2003), 'Property and the private in a Sharia system', *Social Research*, 70(3), 711–34.

Merton, Robert C. (1992), 'Financial innovation and economic performance', *Journal of Applied Corporate Finance*, 4(4), 12–22.

Merton, Robert C. and Zvi Bodie (1995), 'A conceptual framework for analyzing the financial environment', in D. B. Crane *et al.* (eds) *The Global Financial System: A Functional Perspective*, Boston, MA: Harvard Business School Press.

Miles, Raymond E. and Charles C. Snow (2003), *Organizational Strategy, Structure, and Process*, Stanford, CA: Stanford University Press.

Miller, Merton H. (1992), 'Financial innovation: achievements and prospects', *Journal of Applied Corporate Finance*, 4(4), 4–11.

Mitri, Michel (2003), 'A knowledge management framework for curriculum assessment', *Journal of Computer Information Systems*, 43(4), 15–24.

Muslim (Imam Abul Hussain Muslim bin al Hajjaj) (2007), *English Translation of Sahih Muslim, Volume 4*, trans. Nasiruddin al-Khattab, Riyadh: Maktaba Darussalam.

Nasim, Pervez (2003), 'Islamic Cooperative Housing Corporation Ltd.', paper presented at an International Research Seminar on Non-Bank Financial Institutions: Islamic Alternatives, Kuala Lumpur, Malaysia, 7–9 April 2003.

North, Douglass C. (1991), 'Institutions', *Journal of Economic Perspectives*, 5, 97–112.

North, Douglass C. (1994), 'Economic performance through time', *American Economic Review*, 84, 359–68.

Noyer, Christian (2008), 'A new regulatory framework for a new financial system', BIS Review 161/2008.

Obaidullah, Mohammed (1999), 'Financial options in Islamic contracts: potential tools for risk management', *Journal of King Abdulaziz University: Islamic Economics*, 11, 3–26.

Obaidullah, Mohammed (2010), 'Court stays Islamic banking plans for India' comment on IBFNet 6 January 2010. http://finance.groups.yahoo.com/group/ibfnet/message/ 11648.

OECD (2002), *Frascati Manual 2002, Proposed Standard Practice for Surveys on Research and Experimental Development*, Paris: Organisation of Economic Co-operation and Development.

Oleson, Mark (2004), 'Exploring the relationship between money attitudes and Maslow's hierarchy', *International Journal of Consumer Studies*, 28(1), 83–92.

O'Riordan, Sheila (2008), *Research and Development in Financial Services and the Role of Innovation*, Cork: Financial Services Innovation Centre of University College Cork.

Owsia, Parviz (1994), *Formation of Contract: A Comparative Study under English, French, Islamic and Iranian Law*, London: Graham & Trotman.

Phillips, Abu Ameenah Bilal (2006), *The Evolution of Fiqh*

(Islamic Law and the Madh-habs), Riyadh: International Islamic Publishing House.

Pistor, Katharina and Chenggeng Xu (2003), 'Incomplete law – a conceptual and analytical framework and its application to the evolution of financial market regulation', *Journal of International Law and Politics*, 35(4), 931–1013.

Popadiuk, Silvio and Chun Wei Choo (2006), 'Innovation and knowledge creation: how are these concepts related?', *International Journal of Information Management*, 26, 302–12.

Qattan, Muhammad A. (2006), 'Shari'ah supervision: the unique building block of Islamic financial architecture', in Tariqullah Khan and Dadang Muljawan (eds), *Islamic Financial Architecture: Risk Management and Financial Stability*, Jeddah: Islamic Research and Training Institute, pp. 273–87.

Rahim, Abdur (1911), *The Principles of Muhammadan Jurisprudence: According to the Hanafi, Maliki, Shafi'i and Hanbanli Schools*, Madras: SPCK Press.

Rayner, S. E. (1991), *The Theory of Contracts in Islamic Law*, London: Graham and Trotman.

Reinertsen, Donald G. (1997), *Managing the Design Factory: A Product Developer's Toolkit*, New York, NY: The Free Press.

Rose, Peter S. (1999), *Commercial Bank Management*, Singapore: Irwin McGraw Hill.

Rosenberg, Nathan (1990), 'Why do firms do basic research (with their own money)?', *Research Policy*, 19, 165–74.

Saeed, Abdullah (1997), 'Ijtihad and innovation in neo-modernist Islamic thought in Indonesia', *Islam and Christian-Muslim Relations*, 8(3), 279–95.

Saleem, Muhammad (2006a), *Islamic Banking – A $300 Billion Deception*, Bloomington, IN: Xlibris Corporation.

Saleem, Muhammad (2006b), *Islamic Banking: A Charade:*

Call for Enlightenment, North Charleston, SC: BookSurge Publishing.

Saleem, Muhammad Yusuf (2008), 'Methods and methodologies in fiqh and Islamic economics', paper presented at the 7th International Conference on Islamic Economics, King Abdulaziz University, Jeddah, 1–3 April 2008.

Saleh, Nabil A. (1992), *Unlawful Gain and Legitimate Profit in Islamic Law: Riba, Gharar, and Islamic Banking*, London: Graham & Trotman.

Scheuing, Eberhard and Eugene M. Johnson (1989a), 'New product development and management in financial institutions', *International Journal of Bank Marketing*, 7, 17–21.

Scheuing, Eberhard and Eugene M. Johnson (1989b), 'A proposed model for new service development', *Journal of Services Marketing*, 3, 25–34.

Scholtens, Bert and Dick van Wensveen (2000), 'A critique on the theory of financial intermediation', *Journal of Banking and Finance*, 24, 1243–51.

Seniawski, Barbara L. (2001), 'Riba today: social equity, the economy and doing business under Islamic law', *Columbia Journal of Transnational Law*, 39, 700–28.

Shostack, G. Lynn (1982), 'How to design a service', *European Journal of Marketing*, 16(1), 19–63.

Shostack, G. Lynn (1984), 'Designing services that deliver', *Harvard Business Review*, 62(1), 133–9.

Siddiqi, M. Nejatuallah (1981), *Banking without Interest*, Lahore: Islamic Publications Ltd.

Siddiqi, M. Nejatuallah (1983), *Issues in Islamic Banking*, Leicester: The Islamic Foundation.

Siddidi, M. Nejatullah (2004), *Riba, Bank Interest and the Rationale of its Prohibition*, Visiting Scholars' Research Series no.2, Jeddah: Islamic Research and Training Institute.

Siddiqi, M. Nejatullah (2006a), '*Shari'ah*, economics, and the progress of Islamic finance: the role of *Shari'ah* experts',

Concept Paper presented at Pre-Forum Workshop on Select Ethical and Methodological Issues in *Shari'a*-Compliant Finance, Cambridge, MA, 21 April 2006.

Siddiqi, M. Nejatuallah (2006b), 'Islamic banking and finance in theory and practice: a survey of state of art', *Islamic Economic Studies*, 13(2), 1–48.

Smith, Presten G. and Donald G. Reinertsen (1998), *Developing Products in Half the Time: New Rules, New Tools*, 2nd edn, New York, NY: John Wiley and Sons.

Sultan, Syed Alwi Mohamed (2006), *A Mini Guide to Accounting for Islamic Financial Products – A Primer*, Kuala Lumpur: CERT Publications.

Tufano, Peter (1995), 'Securities innovations: a historical and functional perspective', *Journal of Applied Corporate Finance*, 7(4), 90–104.

Tufano, Peter (2003), 'Financial innovation', in George Constantinides, Milt Harris and Rene Stulz (eds), *The Handbook of the Economics of Finance*, Amsterdam: North Holland.

Ulrich, Karl T. and Steven D. Eppinger (2008), *Product Development and Design*, New York, NY: McGraw-Hill.

Usmani, Taqi (2007), *Sukuk and their Contemporary Applications*, available at: http://www.failaka.com/downloads/Usmani_SukukApplications.pdf.

Van Greuning, H. and S. B. Bratanovic (1999), *Analyzing Banking Risk*, Washington, DC: The World Bank .

Vermeulen, Patrick and Jorg Raab (2007), *Innovations and Institutions, an Institutional Perspective on the Innovative Efforts of Banks and Insurance Companies*, Abingdon: Routledge.

Vogel, Frank E. and Sauel L. Hayes (1998), *Islamic Law and Finance: Religion, Risk, and Return*, The Hague: Kluwer Law International.

Watson, W. M. (2005), 'Process ownership', in Kenneth B. Kahn (ed.), *PDMA Handbook of New Product Development*, 2nd Edn, Somerset, NJ: John Wiley and Sons.

WEF (2007), *Technology and Innovation in Financial Services: Scenarios to 2020*, Geneva: World Economic Forum, http://www.weforum.org/pdf/scenarios/Innovation_in_FS_section1_2.pdf.

Weiss, Bernard (1978), 'Interpretation in Islamic law: the theory of *ijtihad*', *American Journal of Comparative Law*, 26, 199–212.

Williamson, Oliver E. (2000), 'The new institutional economics: taking stock, looking ahead', *Journal of Economic Literature*, 38, 595–613.

Wills, Gordon (1985), 'Putting product development in its place', *International Journal of Bank Marketing*, 3, 47–59.

Xiao, Jing J. and Joan Gray Anderson (1997), 'Hierarchical financial needs reflected by household financial asset shares', *Journal of Family and Economic Issues*, 18(4), 333–55.

Y-Sing, Liau and Frederik Richter (2010), 'Islamic finance may "return to roots"', Reuters UK, 9 February 2010, http://uk.reuters.com/article/idUKLNE61801O20100209?pageNumber=3&virtualBrandChannel=0&sp=true.

Zarqa, Anas (2002), 'Comments', in Munawar Iqbal (ed.), *Islamic Economic Institutions and the Elimination of Poverty*, Leicester: The Islamic Foundation, pp. 259–62.

INDEX

Bold denotes entry in a table

accessory contract(s), 27–8
actual/constructive possession, 42–3
advance payment, 48–9
agency, 27–8
Ahmed, H., 48, 207–8, 209
Al-Suwailem, S, 35, 40, 209
analogy, 21
Anderson, J. G., 83
Ansoff, H. I., 99
Arbouna, M. B., 43
ArRahnu programme, 204–5
assignment, 28
Avlonitis, G. J., 12, 107

Bahrain, 57
Bai bithaman ajil (BBA) contracts, 194–5
Bangladesh, 56–7, 206
Bank of International Settlements (BIS),
    8, 12
Bank Rakyat (BR), 204–5
banks
    definition, 70
    objectives, 70–1
    see also Islamic banks
BBA (*Bai bithaman ajil*) contracts, 194–5
BIS (Bank of International Settlements),
    8, 12
blocking the means, 22
Bodie, Z., 8
Bowers, M. R., 112, 128
BR (Bank Rakyat), 204–5
Brentani, U. de, 76, 78, 108, 123–6, 128–9
Bretton Woods, 7
Business Requirement Specifications, 117

Canada, 58, 203
Chapra, M. U., 5, 62–3
Cizakca, M., 207
commercial law *see* Islamic commercial
    law
commercialisation, 118–21, 128–9
    Islamic banks, 145–6, **145**, 157
concept(s)
    conversion into product, 144–5, **144**,
        157, 158–9

implementation, 126–7
    on paper, 110–11
concession, 40
conflict resolution *see* dispute settlement/
    conflict resolution
consensus, 21
consumer protection, 62–3
continuity presumption, 23
contract(s), 24–9
    accessory, 27–8
    combination of, 43–4
    competence, 25
    conditions, 25–6
    consent, 25
    contemporary finance and, 38–46
    definition, 24
    disputes *see* dispute settlement/conflict
        resolution
    essence of, 35–6
    exchange, 26–7
    gharar in, 35–8
    gratuitious, 28–9
    guarantee, 29, 42
    hire, 27
    legal competence, 25
    major nominate, 26–9
    object *see* object of contract
    purpose/consideration, 25–30
    sale, 26–7
    stipulations, 45–6
    subject matter, 25
    substance and form, 39–40
    trust, 42
    validity, 26
    work done for reward, 27
    see also sale(s)
Cooper, R. G., 12, 76, 78, 107–9, 123–9
cooperatives, 203–4
    and hedging, 211
Credit Administration Manual, 117
credit cards, 176–9
    basic principles, 176–7
    fee-based, 177; and rebate-based,
        177–8
    maintenance-fee, 178

credit cards (*cont.*)
  tawarruq, post-transaction, 179;
    pre-transaction, 178–9
custom, 22

Davies, H., 62
de Brentani, U., 76, 78, 108, 123–6, 128–9
DeLorenzo, Y. T., 3, 166
deposit, 29
dispute settlement/conflict resolution,
  67–70
  civil law system, 68–9
  English law, 69–70
  Islamic law, 67–8
diversification strategy, 99, 134
Drew, S. A. W., 124
Dubai Islamic Bank, 5, 190
Dusuki, A. W., 2

Easingwood, C. J., 76, 79
Edgett, S. J., 107, 124–6, 128
ElGamal, M., 2–3, 195
ElGari, M. A., 49, 207, 223
Emirates Islamic Bank, 190
Eppinger, S. D., 11, 102
equity funds, 202–3
essence of contract, 35–6
exits, 40–1

finance *see* Islamic finance
financial durables
  murabahah, 171–2
  musharakah, 172
financial products
  contractual approaches, 48–50;
    multiple traditional contracts,
    49–50; reverse/innovative
    engineering, 48; traditional
    contracts, 48–9
  conventional, adaptation, 49
  legal methodology, 46–8; choice/
    selection, 47; *itjihad*, 46–7; legal
    artifice, 47–8; necessity, 40, 47
  see also Islamic financial products;
    products
financing durables, 171–3
  ijarah wa iqtinah, 172
  tawarruq, 172–3
fiqh, 17–18, 19, 20, 43, 44
foreign currency forward, 181
fungibles, 23

gharar, 33–8
  conditions, 34
  definition, 33–4
  in essence of contract, 35–6
  interpretations, 34–5
  in object of contract, 36–8

gift, 29
Grais, W., 53
gratuitious contract, 28–9
guarantee, 29, 42
Gulaid, M. A., 24

hadith, 19, 20
Hamoudi, H. A., 2
Harrison, T. S., 83
Hayes, S. L., 46, 216
hedging, 210–11
  cooperative, 211
  tawarruq-based, 210–11
Hijaz region, 19–20
hire contract, 27
Holden, K., 2

IBBL (Islami Bank Bangladesh Limited),
  206–7
Ibn Taymiyyah, 35
ICCL (Islamic Cooperative Corporation),
  203
ideas
  generation/acceptance, 107–9, 125–6;
    Islamic banks, 142–4, 146–7, **156**, 157–8
  screening criteria, 109–10
  Shari'ah role, 110
IFSB (Islamic Financial Services Board),
  61, 63–4
ijarah
  overdraft facility, 175
  product, 90–1
  risks, 91
  wa iqtinah, 91, 172
income separation, 166–7
Indonesia, 57, 65, 220
information technology *see* IT
innovation, 7–10
  basic factors, 7
  functional factors, 8–9
  institutional factors, 7–8
  in Islamic finance, 9–10, 208–15
  product development and, 97–8, 99,
    209–12
institutional environment, 54–70
  categories, 54–5
  regulation *see* regulatory regimes
  systems *see* legal systems
International *Shari'ah* Research Academy
  (ISRA), 215
investment deposits, 170–1
  mudarabah, 170
  tawarruq, 171
  wakalah, 170–1
investor protection, 62–3
Iqbal, Z., 48
Islami Bank Bangladesh Limited (IBBL),
  206–7

Islamic banks
  banking models, 71, 73–6; balance
    sheet options, 73, **74**, **75**, **76**;
    murabahah concept, 50, 73–4, 75–6;
    tawarruq system, 50, 75
  commercial research, 214
  commercialisation, 145–6, **145**, 157
  diversity of financing, 75–6, **77**
  ideas *see* ideas, generation/acceptance
  microfinance, 206–7
  non-Muslim use, 1
  product development; authorisation,
    136–7; basic features, 132–3,
    133; budget support, 135;
    commercialisation *see*
    commercialisation; concept *see*
    concept(s); conclusions, 156–9;
    constraints, 148–56; core teams/
    cross-functional teams, 138–9;
    department responsibilities, 137–8;
    drivers, 136–7; external constraints,
    149–52; ideas *see* ideas; internal
    constraints, 153–6; new product
    criteria, 147–8; process *see under*
    process; resources, 139–41; service
    level agreements, 138–9; *Shari'ah*
    units, 140–1, 143–4, 155–6; strategy,
    101, 133–5, **134**, **135**, 157; structure,
    135–9; surveys, 131–2, 159–60; *see
    also* product development
  risk *see* risks
  see also banks
Islamic commercial law, 18
  basic categories, 30
  permissibility, 30
  prohibitions *see gharar*; *riba*
  and *Shari'ah* governance, 215–20;
    appropriate model, 217–20, 225;
    methodological approaches, 215–17
Islamic Cooperative Corporation (ICCL),
    203
Islamic Development Bank, 4–5
Islamic finance
  applied research, 213–14
  contemporary finance and, 38–46
  contractual approaches, 48–50
  criticisms of, 3–4
  initiation, 4–5
  innovation, 9–10, 208–12; functional
    approach, 209–12, 224–5
  institutional framework, 198–200
  organisational diversity, 200–8, 223–4
  Shar'iah-based constraints, 197–8
  social objectives, 1–2
  see also cooperatives; private equity
    funds; venture capital
Islamic financial products
  choices, 186–7

classification of requirements, 162–9
efficiency/equity products, 192–6
feasible set, 182–6; basic principles,
  182; non-*Shari'ah*-compliant, 184–6;
  Shari'ah-compliant, 182–4
legal requirements, 165–9; choices,
  187–90
market segments, 163
needs/purpose, 164–5, **165**, 186
operational factors, 166–7
potential products, 169–70; *see also*
  credit cards; financing durables;
  investment deposits; Islamic
  synthetic forwards; overdraft
  facility; working capital financing
pseudo-Islamic products, 167–9, 223–4
Shari'ah issues, 161–2, 186–7
Shari'ah-compliant/*Shari'ah*-based
  products, 5–7, 72–3, 167–9, 182–4
social requirements, 163–5, 190–2
see also financial products; financing
  durables; investment deposits;
  overdraft facility; products; working
  capital financing
Islamic Financial Services Board (IFSB),
  61, 63–4
Islamic *Fiqh* Academy, 43, 44
Islamic law
  aims, 1, 2–3, 17–18
  fundamental matters, 20
  legal maxims (*quwaid*), 20–1
  methodology, 21–3
  sources, 19–21
  see also Shari'ah
Islamic pawning, 204–5
Islamic Research and Training Institute,
  215
Islamic synthetic forwards, 179–81
  basic principles, 179
  murabahah/salam-based, 180–1
  tawarruq-based foreign currency
    forward, 181
ISRA (International *Shari'ah* Research
  Academy), 215
istisna
  product, 88–90, 188–9
  risks, 89–90
  working capital financing, 173
IT (information technology), 154–5
  system development, 117–18
itjihad, 46–7, 215–16

juristic preference, 21–2

Kahf, M., 24, 39, 165, 207, 218
Kamakura, W. A., 83
Kamali, M. H., 39, 46
Kelly, D., 12, 109, 123–5, 127

Khan, T., 46, 62–3
Kim, H., 212
Kuwait, 57

law *see* Islamic law
legal artifice/stratagems, 47–8, 166; *see also* ruses
legal maxims, 20–1
legal systems, 55–9, 150–1
    constraints, 198–9
    Islamic, 56
    variants, 55–6
    Western, with Islamic banking law, 56; without Islamic banking law, 56–8
Levine, R., 8, 9
Llewellyn, D., 59
loan, 29
Lootah, Saeed Ahmed, 5
Lovelock, C. H., 12

Macey, J. R., 8
Mahajan, V., 79
Malaysia, 56, 65–6, 194–5, 220
market
    conditions, 152
    Islamic financial products, 163
    penetration, 99
maslahah, 18
matrix organisation, 103
Merton, R. C., 7
microfinance, 205–8
    Islamic banks, 206–7
    waaf-based, 207–8
Miles, R. E., 99
Miller, M. H., 7
Mirakhor, A., 48
Mit Ghamar, 4
Mitri, M., 212, 224
Mokhtar, S., 2
monetary exchange, 33
mortgage, 28
mudarabah
    concept, 91–2
    investment deposits, 170
    overdraft facility, 174
    products, 184–5, 192–3
    regulatory constraints, 199–200
    risks, 92, 156–7
murabahah
    concept, 50, 73–4
    financial durables, 171–2
    murabahah/salam-based, Islamic synthetic forwards, 180–1
    products, 87–8, 183–4, 188–9, 193–4, 196
    risks, 88, 150–1
    working capital financing, 173

musharakah
    cooperatives, 203–4
    equity funds, 202–3
    financial durables, 172
    overdraft facility, 175
    products, 92–3, 183, 185, 188–9, 196
    regulatory constraints, 199–200
    risks, 93, 156–7
    working capital financing, 173

Nasim, P., 203
National *Shari'ah* Authority (NSA), 64, 65, 66
necessity, 40, 47
non-fungibles, 23
NSA (National *Shari'ah* Authority), 64, 65, 66

Obaidullah, M., 3
object of contract, 36–8
    ability to deliver, 37–8
    attributes/quantity, 37
    price and delivery time, 38
obligation, 23
Oh, H., 212
operational plans, 100–1
organisational design, 70–6
    basic issues, 70–1, 157
    operating model, 71–3
    see also Islamic banks, banking models
organisational structures, 102–4
    functional structure, 102–3
    matrix organisation, 103
    size/location, 104
overdraft facility, 174–6
    ijarah, 175, 185
    mudarabah, 174
    musharakah, 175
    tawarruq, 175–6
ownership, 23–4

Pakistan, 56, 65–6
Parkinson, S., 124–6, 128
partnerships, 28
pawning, 204–5
Pellegrini, M., 53
penalty/interest income separation, 166–7
permissibility, 39
personal security, 29
personnel training, 119
Pilgrims' Management and Fund Board, 4
Pistor, K., 54
pledge, 28
possession, actual/constructive, 42–3
presumption of continuity, 23
private equity funds, 202–3

process
  Islamic banks, 142–8, **142**, 157
  principles, 12–13, 106–7, 113–15, 124–5
product development
  authorisation, 113
  basic issues, 10
  business case, 111–13
  commercialisation *see*
    commercialisation
  compliance, 116
  concept *see* concept(s)
  corporate position, **101**
  cycle, 107, **108**
  definitions, 11
  departmental sign-off, 115–16
  documentation, 116–17
  financial/treasury responsibility, 115
  ideas *see* ideas
  implementation plan, 123
  in-house testing, 118
  innovation and, 97–8, 99
  intangibility, 11–12
  IT system development, 117–18, 127
  launch, 120–1
  marketing programme, 119–20
  operational plans, 100–1, 116
  organisation *see* organisational
    structures
  personnel training, 119
  pilot run, 119
  process *see* process
  reason for, 10–11
  resources, 101–2, 104–6, 124
  risk management, 116, 121–3
  scope, 12, 121
  Shari'ah approval, 104, 106, 111, 117, 119
  strategy *see* strategy
  structure, 101–2
  target market segment, 82–3
  see also Islamic banks, product
    development
products, 76–85
  assets/liabilities/off-balance sheet
    items, 80
  basic features, 76–9
  business departments, 84–5
  features, 79–83
  functions, 80, 82
  heterogeneity, 78–9
  hierarchy of needs, 83–5; Islamic, 83–4
  initiation, 79–80, **81**
  intangibility, 78
  levels, 80–3, **82**
  new product criteria, 147–8, **148**
  perishability, 79
  simultaneity, 78
  see also financial products; Islamic
    financial products

profit-sharing investment accounts
    (PSAI), 63
promise, unilateral, 44–5
property
  definition/categories, 23
  rights, 24
pseudo-Islamic products, 167–9, 223–4

Qattan, M. A., 60, 218–19
Quran, 19, 21
quwaid, 20–1

Raab, J., 76, 102, 103
Rakyat Bank (BR), 204–5
rebate, 45
regulatory regimes, 59–63, 151–2
  basic issues, 59
  consumer/investor protection, 62–3
  disputes *see* dispute settlement/conflict
    resolution
  Shari'ah effects/constraints, 156–7,
    199–200
  Shari'ah governance *see under Shari'ah*
  soundness of institutions, 61–2
  systemic stability, 59–60
Reinertsen, D. G., 11, 103, 106, 122, 125–6
research and development (R&D), 208–9
  foundational, 212–15
  resources, 214–15
  reverse engineering, 209
resources
  product development, 101–2, 104–6,
    124
  R&D, 214–15
returns, 41–2
reverse engineering, 209
reward, work done for, 27
riba, 30–3
  definition, 30–1
  delay, 31, 32
  ex-anti, 31–2
  ex-post, 31
  sale of debt, 33
ribawi goods, 31, 32
risks, 41–2, 85–93
  classification, 85
  external, **149**, 150–1
  in financial products, 86–7
  ijarah, 91
  internal, 153–4
  in Islamic banks, 85–6
  istisna, 90
  mudarabah, 92
  murabahah, 88
  musharakah, 93
  product development and, 116
ruses, 40–1, 166; *see also* legal artifice/
    stratagems

Saeed, A., 215–16
sale(s)
    actual/constructive possession, 42–3
    contract, 26–7
    future, 36
    pebbles, touch and toss, 36
    suspended, 36
    two sales in one, 36
sarf, 33
Saudi Arabia, 56
Scott, S., 78
Seniawski, B. L., 2
service level agreements, 138–9
Shari'ah
    advisory committees/boards *see*
        Shari'ah Supervisory Boards
        (SSBs)
    banking requirements, 53–4
    compliance with regulatory
        authorities, 151–2
    governance regimes, 63–7; active
        system, 65–6; basic functions,
        63–4; framework criteria, 64–5; legal
        construction, 65; market-driven
        practice, 67; model, 217–20; passive
        system, 66–7
    International *Shari'ah* Research
        Academy (ISRA), 215
    maqasid (objectives), 18, 38–9, 53
    National *Shari'ah* Authority (NSA), 64,
        65, 66
    non-compliance, 60
    quwaid (maxims), 20–1
    regulatory regimes, 156–7, 199–200
    role of ideas *see* ideas
    Supervisory Boards (SSBs), 46,
        54, 63, 64–5, 143–4, 151–2; legal
        requirements role, 187–90;
        privately created laws, 199;
        product development, 104, 106, 111,
        117, 119; social requirements role,
        190–2
    see also Islamic law
Shostack, G. L., 78, 113, 126–7
Siddiqi, M. N., 5, 39, 216, 223
Smith, P. G., 11, 106, 122, 125–6
Snow, C. C., 99
Software Quality Assurance, 118
Storey, D., 12, 109, 123–5, 127
strategic positioning, 99–100

strategy
    banks *see under* Islamic banks
    basic elements, 98–9
    diversification, 99, 134
    operational plans, 100–1
    strategic positioning, 99–100
substance and form, 39–40
Sudan, 56
Sunnah, 19, 21
Sunni tradition, 20
SWOT analysis, 112
synthetic forward *see* Islamic synthetic
    forwards

tawarruq, 50, 75, 151, 152, 168
    credit cards *see under* credit cards
    financing durables, 172–3
    and hedging, 210–11
    investment deposits, 171
    overdraft facility, 175–6
    products, 188–90, 192
    tawarruq-based foreign currency
        forward, 181
    working capital financing, 174
tawhid, 17
trust, 42
Tufano, P., 8

Ulrich, K. T., 11, 102
unilateral promise, 44–5
United Kingdom, 58
United States, 58–9
unrestricted interests, 22
Usmani, T., 3
usul, 20

venture capital, 202–3
Vermeulen, P., 76, 102, 103
Vogel, F. E., 46, 216

waaf-based microfinance, 207–8
wakalah
    investment deposits, 170–1
    products, 184–5
working capital financing, 173–4
    istisna/murabahah/musharakah, 173
    tawarruq, 174

Xiao, J. J., 83
Xu, C., 54